# Joyce and Company

CONTINUUM LITERARY STUDIES SERIES

Also available in the series:
*Character and Satire in Postwar Fiction* by Ian Gregson
*Fictions of Globalization* by James Annesley
*Masculinity in Fiction and Film* by Brian Baker
*Women's Fiction 1945–2000* by Deborah Philips

Forthcoming titles:
*Beckett's Books* by Matthew Feldman
*English Fiction in the 1930s* by Chris Hopkins
*Novels of the Contemporary Extreme* edited by Alain-Phillipe Durand and Naomi Mandel
*Re-writing London* by Lawrence Phillips

# Joyce and Company

David Pierce

continuum
LONDON • NEW YORK

Continuum
The Tower Building, 11 York Road, London SE1 7NX
80 Maiden Lane, Suite 704, New York, NY 10038

www.continuumbooks.com

**British Library Cataloguing-in-Publication Data**
A catalogue record for this book is available from the British Library.

ISBN: 0–8264–9089–1 (hardback)

**Library of Congress Cataloging-in-Publication Data**
A catalog record for this book is available from the Library of Congress.

Typeset by Fakenham Photosetting Limited, Fakenham, Norfolk
Printed and bound in Great Britain by MPG Books Ltd, Bodmin, Cornwall

# Contents

# Acknowledgements

I would like to thank the James Joyce reading group at the University of Leeds for their unwitting help with several lines of argument in this book. This is also the place to record a special debt of gratitude to Alistair Stead and John Smurthwaite for their careful reading of several chapters. Ursula Zeller and Ruth Frehner at the James Joyce Foundation in Zurich also kindly commented on Chapter 6, and Peter de Voogd, Katie Wales and Wolfgang Wight did the same for Chapters 1, 5 and 7 respectively. Rosa González helped me out with some of the Spanish translations. My chief debt as ever is to my partner Mary Eagleton, who ensured that every sentence counted. This is also the place to thank Anna Sandeman and her team at Continuum for their courtesy, care and attention. It's been a pleasure working with them all.

Various chapters in this book arose from invitations to conferences and special issues of journals and I would like to thank the conference organizers, editors and publishers for permission to make use of the same here. In particular, Franca Ruggieri should be thanked for Chapter 2 which appeared as 'Joyce, Erudition and Thomas Arnold's *A Manual of English Literature*' in *Joyce Studies in Italy 8: Joyce and the Nineteenth Century* (ed. Franca Ruggieri) (Roma: Bulzoni, 2005). A version of this chapter was read at the University of Rome in May 2005 in honour of Giorgio Melchiori. Chapter 3 'Reading Dublin 1904' is an extensively revised essay which began as 'Wandering Rocks' in *James Joyce's 'Wandering Rocks'* (eds Steven Morrison and Andrew Gibson) (Amsterdam: Rodopi, 2002). I gave a version of Chapter 5 'The Issue of Translation' as a paper at the James Joyce International Conference held at Tulsa, Oklahoma in June 2003, which was subsequently published in the fortieth anniversary issue of the *James Joyce Quarterly* (2005). A version of Chapter 6 appeared as 'On Local Disturbances: Reflections on Joyce's Use of Language in "Sirens"' in *ABEI: The Brazilian Journal of Irish Studies No 7* (2005). Chapter 7 is an extensive revision of an essay written in 1996 entitled 'Lektüre des *Ulysses* nach dem Fall der Berliner Mauere' (trans Jörg Rademacher) in Jörg Rademacher (ed.), *Was Nun, Herr Bloom? Ulysses zum 75. Geburtstag Ein Almanach* (Münster: Daedalus, 1996).

# Abbreviations

D     James Joyce, *'Dubliners': Text, Criticism, and Notes,* (eds Robert Scholes and A. Walton Litz) (New York: Viking, 1979).

FW    James Joyce, *Finnegans Wake* (London: Faber and Faber, 1964). Page number is given first, followed by line number.

P     James Joyce, *'A Portrait of the Artist as a Young Man': Text, Criticism, and Notes* (ed. Chester Anderson) (New York: Viking, 1968).

U     James Joyce, *Ulysses: The Corrected Text* (ed. Hans Walter Gabler with Wolfhard Steppe and Claus Melchior) (London: The Bodley Head, 1986). Chapter number is followed by line number.

# Introduction

## The Company of Joyce

First encounters with the work of James Joyce rarely issue in wild enthusiasm. In fiction surveys, *Ulysses* invariably comes in the top ten of great English novels. He is on everyone's list of 'must read', but then comes a slight doubt, for his books are often picked up and as quickly put down again. The pages of the early editions of *Ulysses*, published by Shakespeare and Company in Paris in the 1920s, had to be cut before they could be read. Although he was an early champion of the novel, W.B. Yeats's copy remained uncut after page 433, a sign of an initial interest waning. I first came across Joyce as a teenager at a Roman Catholic seminary when what he had to say in *A Portrait of the Artist as a Young Man* was just a little close for comfort. Like Joyce, I too inscribed A.M.D.G. (*Ad Majorem Dei Gloriam*, for the greater glory of God) at the top of every assignment. The *magnum silentium*, the great silence between night prayers and morning Mass, ended and began each day, as it did for Joyce at his Jesuit boarding school at Clongowes Wood in County Kildare. The Four Last Things (death, judgement, hell and heaven) dominated our three-day annual retreat. The retreats tended to be given by suitably austere English Jesuits, who would regale us with dramatic stories about when they were padres to the forces in the Second World War and how they would hear what transpired were last confessions of Battle of Britain pilots. Duty, silence, obedience and behind it all fear and contact with powerful personalities and the eternal verities. A country apart, I grew up effectively in the same world as Joyce had done in Victorian Ireland, and, like Joyce, I was a model pupil, devout and devoted, scholarly, with a strong interest in sport.

It was an education away from others in the peace of the Sussex weald. Like the neophytes we were – and I still find it hard not to write 'we', although I have lost touch with all my contemporaries – we learnt the Church's music under the guidance of a spluttering Irish priest Fr Desmond Coffey, who, we had no reason to doubt, was the leading international expert on Gregorian plainchant after the Benedictine monks at Solesmes Abbey in France and Quarr Abbey on the Isle of Wight. We attended no meetings of the Sodality of the Blessed Virgin Mary, as Joyce did on Saturday mornings, but every evening amid the Chapel's dying light, we quietly sang the sweetest of all hymns to the Mother of mercy:

*Salve Regina, Mater misericordiae,*
*Vita dulcedo et spes nostra salve.*
*Ad te clamamus exsules filii Hevae.*
*Ad te suspiramus gementes et flentes,*
*in hac lacrimarum valle.*

(Hail holy Queen, Mother of mercy,
Hail our life, our sweetness and our hope.
To you do we cry poor banished children of Eve.
To you do we send up our sighs, mourning and weeping in this valley of
tears.)

Like Joyce, I too accepted I did not belong to this world, banished like all the other children of Eve, in exile from our true home. We looked forward to a world without end, filled our minds with the medieval devotional manual *The Imitation of Christ*, spoke in awe of the nineteenth-century French ascetic priest Jean Vianney, the Curé of Ars, and never stopped examining our conscience and reciting the rosary. We wondered who was the greatest intellect the world had ever produced, which of our teachers was the holiest, or, more irreverently, why an Arsenal supporter had been appointed Rector, and whether Scottish whisky or Irish whiskey was the cause of the Bishop of Southwark's shortness of breath. Unlike Joyce, throughout my teenage years I was never home to enjoy Christmas dinner with my family, but we made up for it with a twelve-course, three-hour meal – *a la Romana* as we thought. Every year, the Rector, lumbering into the Oratory with his squeaky new shoes and an air of distraction, would take care to insist that our real family was the College, a remark guaranteed to set us thinking about natural justice and the limits of the Church's authority. As Joyce discovered, periods of dryness followed periods of holiness, and, no matter how strong the determination not to fall from grace, one could never be sure about the future when it came to the spiritual life. 'The spirit is willing but the flesh is weak'; 'there but for the grace of God go I' – such expressions were a constant accompaniment for every Catholic boy who imagined he had a vocation to the priesthood or thought he was special. The empty chair at breakfast often as not was a sign that we had lost another of our contemporaries, never to be heard of again, cast into the outer darkness before he could entice any of us to drop our commitment to otherworldly pursuits. When Stephen Dedalus in *A Portrait* feels he is flying too high spiritually, he seeks out the smell of dung and tar or 'the odours of his own person' (*P* 151). Conversely, in Bella Cohen's brothel, the thought pricks him in his drunken stupor that 'Spirit is willing but the flesh is weak' (*U* 15:2531).

Each new academic year promised much. Freshly polished corridors, the familiar made familiar again, and a step up to a new class. For names of year-groups, we employed not 'lower' and 'third lines' as is the case in *A Portrait* but a fully fledged conceptual matrix culminating in rhetoric: Elements, Lower and Upper Rudiments, Grammar, Syntax, Poetry and

Rhetoric. It was a period of waiting, the years spent in queues outside the refectory, the classroom, the 'jakes' (as we called the toilets), or the dormitory. We were called but not yet chosen; hence for now we must wait in line, with every expectation that one day we would get to work in the harvest for then the harvest would be ours. *Spes messis in semine*, the hope of the harvest is in the seed, was the College motto, but the only joke we ever cracked about seeds concerned King Solomon who, with all his wives, never lost any. The innocents that we were, we never ever connected *semine* with seminary in that sense. An ejaculation was simply a prayer. Hope, however, didn't always sustain me. My worst year was 1962–3, and in particular the period after Christmas, when, the snow slow to clear, I felt every day like a week, every week like a month. I had no appetite for study, for friends, or for any joint activity, and nothing could shake me out of Coleridge's 'viper thoughts', a mood which, on reflection, must have been a form of teenage depression. It was the same winter in a flat in London, an hour away, that Sylvia Plath committed suicide. So much for the swinging sixties.

The honesty of *A Portrait* always impressed me. Ibsen's honesty is that of a miner, undermining bourgeois life. Joyce's is riskier for it is closer to the record of the self. Such writing courts sentimentality if not properly handled. It also invites the typical patronizing attitude of those who control a society's literary and cultural outlets but, against his scoffing contemporaries, the conscience-driven Joyce pitted himself and his experience of the world. Drawing a line is what I did once I realized I was not among the chosen, but Joyce was braver, re-entering his childhood and youth as if they could be rescued from the Church. The authenticity of some of his experiences, however, I never quite accepted. I don't believe Stephen or Joyce would have gone with a prostitute in his early teens. Never during my teenage years did I entertain visiting prostitutes or red-light areas. Perhaps Joyce was more street-wise living in metropolitan Dublin in a lower-middle-class family which was financially on the way down. Prostitutes I still imagined wore a chain round their ankle and, unlike the 'Monto' district in Dublin, there were no known red-light areas in my perfectly sealed provincial world. But going with a prostitute would threaten the sanctity of the self and risk external reality overwhelming the carefully constructed interior scene. Voyeurism and masturbation were the conventional recourse for the young Catholic boy, books, magazines or in my case films. Most of my confessions were fairly banal where sins against charity or of omission could be admitted almost with a sense of achievement, but when I had done something I was ashamed of, as when on holiday going to see an Ingmar Bergman film about flagellation (which I thought might include naked women), I would try and ensure the priest was someone who wouldn't recognize me. Once shriven, I would proceed to negotiate with as much good grace as I could muster the transition from confessional to pew.

The classical writers imagined *errare est humanum*, to err is human, but Joyce was wiser. To fall is human, and Joyce, like Dostoyevsky, is a writer for those who have fallen, a writer who never stops writing about falling and the fall. In Joyce's first printed story 'The Sisters', the scrupulous priest drops the chalice, a sign of his fallen state and taken as an omen by his sisters. Like Lucifer and Icarus, Stephen Dedalus, usurped of his inheritance and his future, returns unexpectedly from Paris and continues on a downward course in *Ulysses* until, knocked to the ground in a brothel, he is temporarily rescued by the modern-day Odysseus, the fallen hero Leopold Bloom. With the whole of human history for a canvas, Humpty Dumpty's fall from the wall at the beginning of *Finnegans Wake* occurs at the moment the first of the thunder words erupts. It is a God-like, meaning-defying word that captures something of the plight of humanity after the collapse of the Tower of Babel, a plight that begins with the childlike rumble of a consonant and a vowel and that ends with an exclamation mark, and all enclosed within a bracket. The bracket is itself inserted into a humorous story about the fall of a 'wallstraight oldparr', old Parr being the celebrated centenarian Thomas Parr (1483–1635) who was apparently charged at the age of 100 with being unfaithful to his wife and forced to do penance in front of his parish church in Shropshire:

> (bababadalgharaghtakamminarronnkonnbronntonnerronntuonnthun-
> ntrovarrhounawnskawntoohoohoordenenthurnuk!) (*FW* 3:15–6)

Through language and alcohol, Joyce imagined he could 'psoak-oonaloose' himself any time he felt so inclined (*FW* 522:34), but I wasn't ready in my teenage years for the fallen, apostate writer to undertake any psychoanalysis on me. I recoiled from seeing the world I believed in scrutinized in such a detached and, I considered, profane way. Here was someone attempting to come between my soul and my creator, and Joyce was company I could do without. So I left Joyce on one side and read other writers who allowed me space to enter the world on my own terms. Only much later, after university, did I return to the author who died six years before I was born. It took me a considerable time to catch up with him, and by that I mean write about him. What could I say about his work that Joyce hadn't thought himself? How could I supplement his writing, if to supplement was the role assigned to the critic? What could I bring except my own similar background, which he had already captured so brilliantly?

Displacement, not identity, this is what I get from Joyce. When I moved away from the folds of the Church, the last thing I wanted was identity. I abandoned black clothes, double-breasted blazers, detached collars, ties and neatness, and ceased thinking of myself as special. Brought up on a diet of Thomist philosophy, on a way of thinking which possessed little currency in the modern world, I had no intellectual system or mentor I could turn to. As it was for Joyce at a similar age, Latin at that time was my second language, but who wanted to read what I had composed in a dead language about the difference between *esse* (being) and *potentia* (potency), a distinction that had absorbed Aristotle and Aquinas but virtually no-one else since? Who wanted to spend any time reflecting on the Latin adage *ex nihilo nihil fit*, how out of nothing nothing comes? What was nothing when you could have everything? To combine two quotations from T.S. Eliot and Yeats, After such knowledge, not what forgiveness, but, the more insistent, what then? I would have liked to have been forgiven for taking the wrong path, but I looked in vain for someone to bless me or wish me God speed as I lit out for the new territory. Displacement could have issued in despair, but it didn't. I sold my trunk-load of theology books in Brighton for the paltry sum of £20, and took to reading in modern literature to catch up on what I had missed and to put space between an outdated philosophy and what I assumed was a hostile new environment. When I went up to university, the course that influenced me the most was Adrian Cunningham's 'Nineteenth-Century Religious and Atheistic Thought'.

When Joyce departed with Nora for the continent in October 1904, he carried with him a storehouse of memories and a culture not entirely defined by the Church. Like William Wordsworth, Joyce is one of the great writers of memory. In one sense, memory in Joyce is all 'memem-ormee' (*FW* 628:14), as he puts it in the tribute to his 'cold mad feary father' in the closing moment of his last work. But in another sense it is his means of salvation. Through memory, he could reconfigure or come to terms with his displacement from home, country and Church. Moreover, following John Henry Newman, through memory he could provide an *apologia pro vita sua*, the necessary justification for his own life. With Wordsworth, memory enables the poet to attain a higher form of unity for the self; with Joyce, it is closer not so much to recuperation of the self as to salvation, at once looser and more intense for more is at stake. There is no steady focus or filter as there is in Wordsworth to recover the past. Switching consciousness is a favourite device in *Ulysses*, while in *A Portrait* Joyce is quite merciless in pursuit of the original experience, beginning with a very young child's perception of the world: 'his father looked at him through a glass: he had a hairy face' (*P* 7). Here the colon, a highly sophisticated punctuation mark in English, registers precisely one of the earliest stepping-stones on the way to consciousness, where two impressions for the child are brought into active relationship by a single mark, one dot above another.

Memory is like a room which can be entered at will and with pleasure, full of scattered thoughts, little notebooks and filing-systems, but all the time in Joyce it is a discourse on displacement. I, now in Trieste, Rome, Zurich or Paris, am no longer there in Bray, Drumcondra, Dublin, or Clongowes Wood. This is what appeals to me in Joyce, the association of memory with displacement, which is never better captured than in the final scene in 'The Dead' when the Dublin journalist Gabriel Conroy suddenly realizes the importance of a former lover for his Galway bride Gretta. Given the overlap between my own background and Joyce's it might be thought I would stress the concept of identity, but I tend to flee in the opposite direction. I rarely feel at home in any discussion centred on identity, which, for example, reads *A Portrait* as a story simply about a Catholic boy growing up or which treats *Ulysses* as a discourse on modern marriage and its difficulties. If Joyce is now company, it's not because I walk in his footsteps but because I understand what propelled him to think of himself – rather grandly as Shem puts it – as 'self exiled in upon his ego' (*FW* 184:6–7). Unlike Joyce, however, I had no wish to level with anyone.

## Outline

*Joyce and Company* is a collection of interwoven essays on Joyce in the company of others. Conventional wisdom places him in his own company, perhaps with classical Homer, or in the company of the great modernists Eliot and Ezra Pound or among his fellow Irishmen such as Yeats and Samuel Beckett. This book draws on a somewhat wider sense of company, one that includes the eighteenth-century Yorkshire writer Laurence Sterne and the contemporary Irish novelist Jamie O'Neill, author of *At Swim, Two Boys* (2001), the weekly magazine *Tit-Bits* and Thomas Arnold's *A Manual of English Literature* (1897), and the fiction of Alfred Döblin and Virginia Woolf. In the company of others, Joyce assumes some of their colouring, displays another side to his own achievement, and at the same time reveals something of his vulnerability and his limitations.

In keeping with Joyce's own work, this study deliberately moves back and forth across several fields and historical periods. Joyce was an Irish writer on the European stage, who took what he needed from popular and highbrow culture to write himself into the history of the modern world. It's not simply because he's perverse that Joyce names at some point in *Finnegans Wake* perhaps all the rivers of the world, for, from the Liffey to the Limmat, the Yssel in the Netherlands to the Seine, all belong to the river of time and to the emergence of civilization along its banks. 'Yssel that the limmat?' (*FW* 198:13). Is that the Sihl or the Limmat, the two rivers which flow through Zurich and which are sometimes confused by visitors? Isn't that the limit! Indeed. His city is Dublin but his reach is global. The first actual reference to Dublin as a placename in *Finnegans Wake*, his book of 'Doublends Jined' (*FW* 20:16), of double ends joined, is to Dublin in the state of Georgia in North America.

The book is structured in eight chapters under four headings 'Joyce and History', 'Joyce and the City', 'Joyce and Language' and 'Joyce and the Contemporary World'. In the first part, Joyce is placed in the context of two historical periods, in Chapter 1, with touch in mind, against the eighteenth century, and in Chapter 2, the late nineteenth century alongside the idea of erudition. In the second part, 'Joyce and the City', I examine in Chapter 3 the portrayal of Dublin in 1904 with particular reference to the 'Wandering Rocks' episode of *Ulysses*, and in Chapter 4 I bring together Joyce and Woolf under the umbrella of the metropolitan imagination. Chapter 5, in the third part on 'Joyce and Language', affords some general observations on the issue of translation, Chapter 6, a detailed analysis of the Overture to the 'Sirens' episode of *Ulysses*. The final part is devoted to 'Joyce and the Contemporary World'. Chapter 7 explores the significance of *Ulysses* before and after the fall of the Berlin Wall in 1989. Chapter 8 tackles the debts contemporary Irish writers display to Joyce. Each of the chapters, while sharply focused on particular concerns, contributes to the argument of the book as a whole, that Joyce is best understood in the company of others.

The book opens with an exploration of touch and with the fascination for transgression in Joyce and his eighteenth-century predecessor Sterne. Not a little of the humour in their writings springs from the sense of touch, for touching presented problems at once for the good Irish Catholic boy and for the wayward Church of England married parson. In *Ulysses*, Joyce attempts a pastiche of Sterne in 'Oxen of the Sun', making reference to 'the little picture which I have so long worn, and so often have told thee, Eliza, I would carry with me into my grave' (*Sentimental Journey*, 3):

> With these words he approached the goblet to his lips, took a complacent draught of the cordial, slicked his hair and, opening his bosom, out popped a locket that hung from a silk riband, that very picture which he had cherished ever since her hand had wrote therein. . . . I declare, I was never so touched in all my life. God, I thank thee, as the Author of my days! (*U* 14:752–63)

The passage is not among the best things Joyce ever attempted. 'Author of my days' sounds distinctly unlike the eighteenth-century author, while 'had wrote therein' is plain ugly, regardless of whether or not it is cast as imitation. But there is enough of Sterne here to signal his importance to Joyce as a carrier of English prose style. The allusion to 'opening his bosom' recalls John Hamilton Mortimer's *A Caricature Group* (1767), a lively portrait of Sterne amid his contemporaries, where a grinning Sterne does indeed somewhat garishly bare his chest to reveal a heart-shaped locket. The caricature also includes a toast of what looks like a watered-down cordial being raised by Dr Thomas Arne to the celebrated writer who, in whatever company he found himself, would insist on showing a miniature of his lover Eliza Draper. For the mocking Joyce, this leads quite naturally to 'touch': 'I was never so touched in all my life'.

When he began composing *Finnegans Wake*, Joyce, we know from a conversation with Eugene Jolas had Sterne in mind, for the *Wake* too was an attempt 'to build many planes of narrative with a single esthetic purpose. Did you ever read Laurence Sterne?' (Jolas, 12). Whenever Sterne is mentioned in *Finnegans Wake*, he is invariably in the company of Jonathan Swift, most famously when he is linked with other Irish writers in a list which invokes a tradition: 'your wildeshaweshow moves swiftly sterneward' (*FW* 256:13–4). Equally, Joyce was the first person to suggest what now seems obvious, that in the scheme of things Sterne and Swift had been assigned the wrong surnames, for Swift is stern, and Sterne is swift. Joyce and Sterne have been frequently linked in terms of their radical contribution to a shared literary tradition especially in the fields of modernism and postmodernism. In the company of Sterne, Joyce reveals a way of writing which, when it first arrives on the scene, looks strikingly new, but which in retrospect seems to belong to a longer tradition of writing. Such writing then reminds us of something more central, a tradition of experimental fiction, as Joyce's question to Jolas perhaps implies, a tradition to which we might now add the names of Gabriel García Márquez, Guillermo Cabrera Infante, Milan Kundera and Salman Rushdie. When Viktor Shklovsky famously remarked that *Tristram Shandy* is 'the most typical novel of world literature', the Russian Formalist, his eye trained on formalist matters rather than on historical frames, did Sterne a service but Joyce and Sterne a disservice, for *Tristram Shandy* and *Ulysses* are indeed the most typical novels of world literature (Shklovsky, 57).

The following chapter on Joyce and erudition is designed to address the building-blocks in his intellectual formation. Joyce is a difficult writer but there is no reason to exaggerate this for today's reader. In some areas his erudition seems less like erudition and more like an acknowledgement of his familiarity with popular culture and of his undergraduate exposure to manuals of English literature. With the help of the weekly magazine *Tit-Bits* and Thomas Arnold's *A Manual of English Literature* (1897), my aim is to suggest how some of Joyce's erudition might be traced back to certain late-nineteenth-century contexts which have been insufficiently noticed. *Tit-Bits*, which was launched in 1881, was part of the general education and culture in the Joyce household. All kinds of fragments surfaced in its pages: curiosities of advertising, the danger of cold baths, betting on a certainty, big swindles, the daily life of the Chinese Emperor, comin' through the rye and what that phrase means, a candid confession, eccentric customers, faults of great men, the infallibility of gas meters, how to tell a man's character by his hands, what is love, matrimonial advice, how a lady gets on the omnibus, practical joking in the Middle Ages, quinine as a cause of insanity, why women look under the bed.[1] Leopold Bloom seems to step out of its pages, for Bloom is the advertising agent curious about adverts, the married man anxious to see in 'Lestrygonians' a stylish woman getting up into a carriage outside the Grosvenor Hotel, the common man who imagines he has a practical, scientific cast of mind reflecting on things not dissimilar to the danger of cold baths, the infallibility of gas meters and why women look under the bed. *Tit-Bits* makes its first appearance in *Ulysses* in the 'Calypso' episode when Bloom in the 'jakes' notices 'Matcham's Masterstroke', a prize-winning story by Philip Beaufoy. In the 'Circe' episode Beaufoy re-appears to accuse Bloom of being a 'soapy sneak masquerading as a *littérateur*' (*U* 15:822–3). I begin with the identity of Beaufoy and move on to consider Joyce the writer in the company of a prize-winning *littérateur*.

If we take popular culture seriously, there are implications here for a discussion of Joyce and erudition. *Tit-Bits*, which portrays a world in fragments waiting to be re-assembled, constitutes a project unified by fragments – precisely how we might describe a central strand of Joyce's aesthetic project. In the second part of this chapter, another potential source for Joyce's work is examined, this time within the more familiar confines of an educated context or high-brow culture. Joyce's erudition owes something to his English teachers both at school and university, as becomes clear re-examining the neglected textbook of one of his university professors, Thomas Arnold, the overlooked brother of the English poet and critic and one-time close friend of Cardinal Newman. In the space of some 650 pages, *A Manual of English Literature* (1897) affords even today a readable survey of English literature from the Anglo-Saxons to the late nineteenth century. Arnold's brief remarks on Sterne are not only apt but must have found a ready response in his pupil, who, too, would go on to write in *Ulysses* one of the great comic novels in the language, a novel where plot is downplayed and character emphasized, a novel which also displays in the monologues of Bloom and Molly 'unexpected transitions and curious trains of thought': 'His novel *Tristram Shandy* is like no other ever written; it has no interest of plot or of incident; its merit and value lie, partly in the humour with which the characters are drawn and contrasted, partly in that other kind of humour which displays itself in unexpected transitions and curious trains of thought' (Arnold, 419–20).

Exploring Joyce in the company of Arnold reveals a writer who not only responded directly to the texts in the culture but who also took account of how those texts were being interpreted and filtered. *Agenbite of Inwit*, the fourteenth-century devotional tract referred to by Stephen in *Ulysses*, receives a full paragraph in Arnold. Shakespeare's 'midway' position, midway that is between extremes, is precisely the one advanced by Stephen in the Library episode. The reference to 'stately lines' in Arnold's commentary on Tennyson's poem 'Ulysses' could have acted as a cue for the opening stately lines of Joyce's own epic. If at times Joyce sounds impossibly erudite, some of this must be ascribed to his teachers at university, who bequeathed to him not only an historical view of the subject but also something to reflect on, play with and if necessary undermine.

The first chapter of Part II, 'Joyce and the City', begins with a series of comparisons between *Ulysses* and Alfred Döblin's much-admired novel *Berlin Alexanderplatz: The Story of Franz Biberkopf* (1929). Joyce and Döblin were both involved in reading the modern city, for both realized an essential truth about the modern city, how in the words of Peter Fritzsche in *Reading Berlin 1900* (1996) it is not so much a built city as a 'word city'. Fritzsche concentrates in part on newspapers and street hoardings, but, following Joyce, I survey a variety of reading matter: titles to books, quotations from books and songs, advertisements, tram tickets, implied reading activities such as telling the time and reading the city through history.

One of the peculiar characteristics of Joyce's city, which is missing from Fritzsche's analysis, is that, like writing, it is strewn with errors. That this isn't itself a category mistake is in part confirmed by the way Joyce described the stories that were to become *Dubliners* as 'a chapter of the moral history of my country' (*Letters* II, 134). Unusually for a writer on the city, the categories of both morality and epistemology accompany or shadow his portrait of Dublin, and the two inevitably criss-cross. Although it is often construed in terms of his temperament and personality, description for Joyce in fact serves a higher purpose. As if he set them in train himself, factual errors repeatedly surface also in the work of later commentators and annotators, and the case of Bernard Vaughan S.J. is instructive in this regard. My comments on Vaughan in turn lead into some reflections on Joyce in the company of the Jesuits. The larger critical question addressed in this chapter is how we are to interpret Joyce's portrait of his city, and whether or not such a portrait belongs to the *Dubliners*' (morality) theme of paralysis or to (epistemological) images of a modern labyrinth.

Joyce and Woolf are two writers whose dates completely coincide, 1882–1941. Chapter 4 pairs them in a wide-ranging discussion of the metropolitan city and the modernist imagination, beginning not with familiar streams of consciousness but with the issue of power. Although not often expressed in such a stark way, it is the case that forms of power inform their work, just as on Bartholomew's contemporary maps of Dublin and London, once noticed, what stands out are the number of army barracks. But, while in London barracks tend to be sited near royal palaces and state buildings, in Dublin they are not only more prominent but positioned throughout the city. What their presence indicates is that Dublin was a city effectively occupied by the colonial power, whereas London was a city at the centre of an Empire not yet in decline where power – at least at home – was exercised in more diffuse, less obvious ways. For Joyce, it was impossible not to envisage his city as unfree; for Woolf, this was not the case, but she chose to provide a critique of power which stressed its high visibility in terms of ritual and public life and its pervasiveness in terms of ideology and control over private life. For Joyce, satire was a more appropriate trope, for Woolf, irony. None of this prevented either of them from celebrating their native cities, and I continue by reflecting on the similarities and differences they share with E.M. Forster and other writers on London such as Dorothy Richardson and the neglected Irish novelist Kathleen Coyle. Neither Joyce nor Woolf could live without their native cities. Like most exiles, Joyce, whether his European city was Trieste, Rome, Zurich or Paris, never cut the umbilical cord, while 'cockney' Woolf, as she described herself when marooned in Sussex during the Blitz, rarely moved outside its sphere of influence even when she sets her novels away from the capital.

Both writers, however, considered themselves outsiders from the order of things, Joyce on account of Church and State – the 'two masters' that Stephen Dedalus refers to in the opening episode of *Ulysses* – Woolf on account of her class position and her understanding of the way gender and patriarchy work against women. The disturbances in their writings display their own character. From a background of ease, where every connection ended in a subsequent connection, Woolf repeatedly fastens onto things that disrupt and disturb. In *Between the Acts* (1941), the novel that in one sense gives us the destination for her whole work, the author who more often than not conveys the impression of living on borrowed time is haunted by the image of aerial bombardment and the possibility of an end to English history. There is little sense of premonition in Joyce, while the patterns of Irish history, especially evident in the skirmishing in *Finnegans Wake* between the warring brothers Shem and Shaun, enabled him to retain to some extent his status as a contemporary. Equally, he came from a family where, to adapt Woolf's famous remark from her essay 'Modern Fiction', if they looked within they did indeed discover life was like this, a downward spiral towards increasing penury, moonlit flits and the pawnshop. Joyce's disturbances are 'local' in the sense that I describe in Chapter 6 but they are also, as the argument of my book as a whole suggests, cumulative. Even more than the compulsive Woolf, he invested in a critique that refuses to stop when the point is made.

The first chapter of Part III, 'Joyce and Language', is concerned with the issue of translation. The translation I have in mind is not only linguistic translation but also Joyce's translation to Europe and the issue therefore of language and identity. I begin, however, by touching on the translated look of Joyce's writing. In the opening story of *Dubliners*, we are confronted with 'gnomon' and 'simony', words which bear the scars of their origins in Greek and Latin and which seem designed to stop readers in their tracks. In his last work, *Finnegans Wake*, Joyce carries this confrontation a stage or two further by asking the question which in one sense most readers ask: 'Are we speachin d'anglas landadge or are sprakin sea Djoytsch?' (*FW* 486:12–3) (Are we speaking the English language or are speaking Dutch/German?). Languages are not only 'acquired' as Stephen Dedalus notices in his discussion with the Prefect of Studies in *A Portrait* over the word 'tundish'; they are also folded into each other in such a way that sometimes their character – also evident when words from different languages collide – never quite beds down into its new surroundings. As a student of European languages, Joyce reminds us not so much of the etymological roots to modern English in the Romance and Germanic languages or indeed in some anterior Ur-language, as of what happens to the subject in language. It was a lesson he learnt in childhood. The young Stephen begins confidently enough with fixed ideas of his place in the world, graphically recorded on separate lines in *A Portrait* as 'Stephen Dedalus / Class of Elements / Clongowes Wood College / Salins / County Kildare / Ireland / Europe / The World / The Universe', but he is then confronted with the unsettling truth that God in French is *Dieu*.

Chapter 6, on the 'Sirens' episode of *Ulysses*, explores the issue of language from a different angle. Initially, my probing takes the form of how the company of Joyce translators tackle the sounds in a phrase such as 'Imperthnthn thnthnthn' from the Overture to 'Sirens'. The sounds here are often detached from meaning, or their meaning is deferred until later in the episode, or we realize that their semantic field or phonological system is peculiar to English. With the help of translations from French, Spanish, German, Italian and modern Greek, we can see how 'Joyce and Company' rightly extends beyond the Anglophone community. In wrestling with Joyce's texts, translators remind us of what I describe as 'local disturbances' which surround not only the Overture to 'Sirens' but Joyce's language in general. I then complicate my argument by suggesting a possible parallel in 'Sirens' – an episode which is sometimes read in terms of the 1790s when the United Irishmen attempted to break the connection with the United Kingdom and which includes repeated pointed references to the 1798 song 'The Croppy Boy' – between local disturbances in language and local disturbances in Irish history.

This book closes with Part IV, 'Joyce and the Contemporary World'. Can Joyce be turned to engage with the course of modern European history? This is the question posed in Chapter 7 'On Reading *Ulysses* After the Fall of the Berlin Wall'. The chapter begins with an Overture, with a select list of references to walls in *Ulysses* (which for copyright purposes I have paraphrased). If walls divide communities it's sometimes reassuring to know that walls have other functions. On the other hand, there's something subversive about such listing, as I discovered in Münster in 1997 when my Overture prompted a dramatized dialogue between two German actors as if it were a chess match, complete with mock aggression, an egg-timer and a desk bell. The focal point of this chapter is a meditation on Joyce's reception in the German Democratic

Republic (GDR) and how this connected with the longer view of Joyce among the Left. What role does Joyce perform in different periods of history and under different social systems? In a wide-ranging survey I include a discussion of my own visits as an invited speaker to the GDR in the 1980s, the depiction of the GDR in the post-1989 fiction of Monika Maron, and the problem of commitment in the Southern African fiction of Doris Lessing and Nadine Gordimer. One recourse when thinking about 'Joyce and History' is to tie him into the contexts from which he emerged or the traditions to which he belongs, as can be observed in the opening two chapters and elsewhere in this book. But what emerges from this chapter is that Joyce in the contemporary world can be read in new circumstances with fresh insights, for there is merit in seeing him as a utopian writer committed to the future and the transformation of the present as much as to the evocation of the past.

With particular reference to Thomas Kinsella's collection of verse *The Pen Shop* (1997), O'Neill's gay novel *At Swim, Two Boys* (2001) and Aidan Mathews's witty short story 'Lipstick on the Host' (1992), Chapter 8, 'Joyce and Contemporary Irish Writing', explores the shadow Joyce casts on contemporary writing. Two thoughts inform this chapter. One is the towering presence of Yeats and Joyce for a later generation of Irish writers and how that influence is handled; the other concerns the more general predicament of belatedness and the continuing discourse on the end of history. As I write elsewhere: 'Blind, with a bloody bandage over his eyes, Hamm in *Endgame* (1958) sits in the theatre like some figure from a forgotten outpost of an abandoned empire, an image of the darkness now gathering to witness the endgame for the west' (Pierce 2005, 51). Arguably, Beckett more than Joyce transformed the way we think about ourselves and history, but this chapter explores how Irish writers find the means to continue writing after Joyce. For O'Neill, whose novel is set in Dublin on the eve of the Easter Rising 1916, 'after' is a sign of affiliation whereby Joyce's world is evoked through language, milieu and character. For Kinsella, 'after' is a temporal sign and signifies writing a generation or so after Joyce, where the image of a black refill suggests something of his relationship with the master. Mathews parades his debt to Joyce but his characters have a life of their own, talking like Molly about everything under the sun.

Of all modern writers the iconoclastic Joyce belongs in the company of others. Joyce gives the impression he is not only potentially everywhere in the culture but that, as implied by the figure of 'Here Comes Everybody' (HCE) in *Finnegans Wake*, he has potentially everyone in his sights. The playful mythological figure of Finn, as the wide-ranging survey conducted by James MacKillop (1986) indicates, crops up everywhere in placenames both inside and outside Ireland, and even if some of that history got lost or confused or, as often happens with placenames, corrupted, Irish *fionn* (white or fair) constantly taunts us. He can be identified for example in Fingal's Cave in Scotland and, perhaps, he lent his name to the capital of Austria, Wien or Vienna, where Finn acts as a historical reminder of the Central European roots of the Celts before their dispersal. More familiarly, Joyce in a daring act of appropriation, calls him the 'erse solid man' (*FW* 3:20), Finn that is speaking erse, once solid or perhaps only arse solid, and underlying the modern city of Dublin, his head pushing up in the Hill of Howth and looking for his 'tumptytumtoes' out in the Phoenix Park. Joyce needed little persuading that a characteristic of the protean Finn is not only playfulness but also permanence. Finn keeps rising and he does so in different guises and using different letters of the alphabet. Phoenix in Phoenix Park, which itself is a corruption if seen as a bird, also contains Finn in its first syllable in Irish, *fionn uisce* or clear water: it is the park of clear water rather than the park of the fiery bird, a park that is not only the largest city park in western Europe but one that has Finn in its name. Finn again. It is this protean aspect, Finn always having the capacity to come again, which is also especially marked in 'Finnegan's Wake', the nineteenth-century Irish-American ballad about the hod-carrier who falls from a ladder and breaks his skull. During his wake, as if to remind us of that word's proximity to 'awake', Tim Finnegan rises again when some whiskey is spilled over him by ill-tempered mourners. 'Bedad he revives, see how he rises', and his reply is suitably blasphemous 'Thanam o'n dhoul (your souls to the devil), do ye think I'm dead?' The title for Joyce's last work recalls this ballad but, without the apostrophe, it has the look of a statement or a threat. Take care when Finnegans, the Irish that is, wake. Do you think we're dead?

Unlike Ibsen's last play *When We Dead Awaken* (1900), which was much admired by the youthful Joyce and where Rubek the artist hero and his former model Irene climb to the peaks of a mountain to share death together, *Finnegans Wake* refuses to take the tragic path and celebrates, as does *Ulysses*, not only death but also life. At the end of *Ulysses*, Molly recalls memories sixteen years previously of love-making with Bloom on Howth and giving him seed-cake, then of Gibraltar as a girl and being called 'a Flower of the mountain', 'my mountain flower' (*U* 18:1602, 1606). It's a nice common touch to end on, with flowers and mountains and the unromantic thought as Bloom proposes to her 'well as well him as another' (*U* 19:1604–5). In the mocking cave of the 'Cyclops', Leopold ascends into heaven as 'ben Bloom Elijah' (*U* 12:1916), but Bloom also happens to be the name of a mountain in Ireland, Slieve Bloom, and in Irish mythology the mountain god Bloom has a daughter Coillte, who falls in love with Blath, Lord of all the flowers. Flowers and mountains, fathers and daughters, husbands and wives, sexual awakening, faithfulness and betrayal, myths and memories – all are here united in the meandering flow of Molly's untutored thoughts. Unlike Ibsen's last act, Joyce's mature vision, then, as is evident in the creation of his most winning characters from Bloom to HCE, from Molly to Anna Livia, is more down-to-earth, less intense, less threatening, and at the same time more inclusive of the whole river of humanity.

Away from rivers and mountains and universal themes, when Joyce is set against other more specific backgrounds, something equally interesting emerges. With Sterne, he reminds us of the continuity and the discontinuity of history and culture; with *Tit-Bits*, the way popular culture functions in his writings; with Thomas Arnold, the importance of his professors. Joyce we know has much to teach us about life in the modern city. Indeed, according to a recent commentator, *Ulysses* 'offers a more variously ample imagining of the city than any other modern novel' (Alter, 121). But what he teaches assumes a different complexion when Dublin is set against Döblin's Berlin or Woolf's metropolitan London. The difficulty he raises for translators produces its own kind of company but, even as they seek to ensure textual fidelity, the translated look and local disturbances of his own writing in English should never be overlooked. His relevance for the contemporary world can only be tested against specific examples of intervention. Translation is one example of intervention, a tangible sign of bringing into being different communities of readers. A second example is essentially political. In the light of 1989 the question worth addressing is Joyce's continuing relevance to those who have abandoned politics or to those who never entered it. A third example concerns strategies of independence. When contemporary Irish writers make use of Joyce in their work, they disclose ways of coming to terms with him as well as demonstrating that Joyce hasn't said everything.

This introduction began with identity and displacement. Ironically, Joyce's sense of displacement has ensured that he would eventually find the company of others. There is virtually no modern or contemporary Irish writer from Kate O'Brien to Edna O'Brien, from Flann O'Brien to John McGahern, from Sean O'Faolain to John Banville, or from Patrick Kavanagh to Seamus Heaney, who doesn't belong to his company. In continental Europe, he belongs with his Triestine friend the novelist Italo Svevo, with the post-war German experimental novelist Arno Schmidt, with Umberto Eco, one of whose books carried the title *The Middle Ages of James Joyce* (1989), and he has at least four cities anxious to claim him. In Britain and North America and in nearly every corner of the globe, his name stands for something. When he was buried in the Fluntern Cemetery in Zurich in 1941, war was raging in Europe and he had few friends to gather round his grave and mourn his passing. However, he was not alone because, as Nora humorously quipped, he had company from the lions in the nearby zoo. Interestingly, if he was ever woken by those lions, Joyce, who once imagined he had spent his life 'self exiled in upon his ego', would discover he was surrounded by writers and professors still busy about his business.

# Part I

Joyce and History

# 1

# Joyce, Sterne and the Eighteenth Century

### Introduction

Contemporary critical theory has sought to emphasize the body. However, this discourse is often characterized not by intimacy but by detachment, as if the body was not a living organism, dependent on the circulation of the blood and on oxygen to the lungs, but what one commentator has called 'a dematerialised textual object' (Seremetakis, 123). Only rarely, for example, are hands ever mentioned, and yet hands (more so than legs and feet) occupy an intriguing space between the body and the person, between the self and others, and between the human anatomy and culture. The eyes may give us a window to the soul, but the hands, as the gestures in Renaissance paintings constantly underscore, tell us something as well, not least about our personal intervention in the world and, more generally in terms of culture and history, about sense and sensibility. With their various gestures and continual agitation 'whereof we are ignorant or not willing them', Thomas Willis, the pioneering anatomist in the middle of the seventeenth century, refers to hands and arms as a 'wandering pair' (Pordage, 174). The phrase never caught on in that sense, but, as is apparent from looking at people when they are speaking, it might well have.

Touch in Joyce and Sterne is sentiment, sentimentality, the expression, intensification or repression of feeling; it is closer to the erotics of the mind than the Lawrentian sensuousness of the body; it is parody, play, satire, innuendo; it is, as the *Noli me tangere* (Don't touch me) of the Gospels reminds us, incontrovertible, a warning, but also suggestive, impossible to ignore; it is excitable, communicative, ductile, given to lingering in the eternal present; it is pressure, the hand, a gesture, additional, rarely simply functional, the release of memory. In that sense there is nothing it doesn't touch, and it is invariably the light touch which is most transgressive.

Separated by a century and a half, Joyce and Sterne act as bookends to the novel as a form, and they continue to fascinate anyone interested in the common ground that links or stretches across different historical periods. If Sterne responds to the Enlightenment and to the advances in the seventeenth and eighteenth centuries in understanding the physiology of the body, what intellectual framework or paradigm does Joyce confront or seek to address? After insisting on the physicality of touch and the common ground Sterne and Joyce share, this is the question I pose in this chapter. Like Joyce, Sterne is swift, someone who, in the words of Sterne the sermon writer, 'finds no rest for the sole of his foot' (Sterne 1760, 12).[1] Their work is full of paratextual and textual devices such as blank and marbled pages, blue covers and signed copies, dashes and asterisks, delayed prefaces and dropped full-stops, challenging footnotes and obtrusive emblems, newspaper subheadings and flourishes of one kind or another. They delight in such 'pop-up' games in writing, games which they also play with narrative voices.

Thus the anonymous Arranger in *Ulysses*, who intervenes not as a third person narrator but as a slightly unnerving, supra-personal figure, 'arranges' things, cautioning or advising the reader as for example when we encounter in 'Sirens' the phrase 'As said before he ate with relish the inner organs' (*U* 11:519–20). This particular reference the reader first encountered some 175 pages before when in the opening lines of 'Calypso' we learn that Bloom did indeed eat 'with relish the inner organs of beasts and fowls' (*U* 4:1–2).[2] At one point in 'Sirens', soon after Boylan strides into the Ormond Hotel, we read 'Not yet. At four she. Who said four?' (*U* 11:352). The first two sentences alert us that we are inside Bloom's increasingly agitated consciousness as the hour approaches when Boylan is to make love to Molly, but who we might well ask says 'Who said four?'? It could be Bloom rummaging in his mind for some comfort or mental distraction, but the voice sounds like the person who earlier in the episode inserts 'O'clock' on a separate line at the end of Boylan's exchange about the timing of the Ascot Gold Cup:

– What time is that? asked Blazes Boylan. Four?
O'clock. (*U* 11:385–6)

'Who said four?' contains a distinctly mocking aspect to it, but it can also be read as Joyce's direct question to the reader. Stay alert. Who said Boylan would meet Molly at four in the afternoon? As for 'O'clock', this sounds like a person, with his 'O' like an Irishman, perhaps an Irish jockey in the Gold Cup, riding in the same race as 'O. Madden', the mount of Sceptre, 'a game filly', as Lenehan, with his insistent, crude taste, cannot help noticing for us. And it is 'O. Maddden' not O'Madden, yet more insistence by the Arranger or Berlitz tutor to stay awake.

Sterne comes at us from a different direction and his knowingness is invariably showy and sometimes smutty but never sinister. Who, we might well ask, is the person in *Tristram Shandy* who slips in and out of conversation with us and tells us not only what kinds of readers there are in the world but also how to read the book we have in our hands, who informs us that 'Writing, when properly managed (as you may be sure I think mine is) is but a different name for conversation' (*Tristram Shandy*, 125)? Is this figure Sterne as convivial host beside his fire in Shandy Hall, Sterne as critic justifying his own work, Sterne as whimsical narrator, Sterne as postmodernist novelist playing with the conventions of novel writing?

However we feel about them, such pop-ups, unlike the ones that appear in the corner of a computer screen, are an integral part of the reading experience and are not meant to be blocked by the reader. The sense of touch in their writings, especially in relation to transgression, is another kind of pop-up. The aural and the visual in Joyce and Sterne have received due recognition but the sense of touch has tended to be neglected. In their writings touch is invariably transgressive in nature and effect. In *Ulysses* Molly recalls going to Confession and telling Father Corrigan: 'he touched me father and what harm if he did where and I said on the canal bank' (*U* 18:108). More high-mindedly, the narrator of *Tristram Shandy* asserts that 'nothing which has touched me will be thought trifling in its nature' (*Tristram Shandy*, 9). Touching protuberances or areas adjacent to protuberances, whether they are noses or Uncle Toby's wound to his groin, constitutes part of the recurring humour or wit in *Tristram Shandy*, while in *Ulysses*, though less given to wit, touch, too, is humorous, and often accompanied by narrative delay as when Bloom half-formulates the thought 'All that the hand says when you touch' (*U* 13:1198), or when he scurrilously thinks 'Women all for caste till you touch the spot' (*U* 5:104).

Like sight, touch is frequently a reciprocal affair. But while one can see without being seen, touch involves something more or something else. Hence the oddness of Bloom's thought that you don't know who will touch you after death, for then the body can be touched without you knowing it (*U* 6:18). Some senses, as Laura Mulvey reminds us in connection with the male gaze, are more active than others in distinguishing between subject and object. When the short-sighted Stephen, who spends Bloomsday without his glasses, links eyes with touch – 'Touch me. Soft eyes.' (*U* 3:434–6) – touch is here being used in a transposed way, a mode so normal we sometimes forget it is in fact a metaphorical usage. As Sterne points out in one of his sermons, a piece of music can touch 'the secret springs of rapture' (Sterne 1760, 34).[3] Bloom is right to concur with Mr Kernan's suggestion that the line delivered in English at the Church of Ireland's funeral service *I am the resurrection and the life* 'touches a man's inmost heart' (*U* 6:670). By contrast, in the Catholic service, *In paradisum* merely sets Bloom thinking about whether *In* should be translated by 'to' or 'in' (it's in fact neither, the translation being 'into' as in the hymn 'May the angels lead you into paradise'). When Yorick in *A Sentimental Journey* visits his beloved Maria, a character Sterne gave the world in *Tristram Shandy*, she is 'much as my friend [Mr Shandy] described her' (*Sentimental Journey*, 114) and in mourning because her lover has abandoned her. Yorick feels her loss as real and at one point reaches for the language of touch to guarantee the truth of the moment: 'And is your heart still so warm, Maria? said I. I touch'd upon the string on which hung all her sorrows' (*Sentimental Journey*, 116).

## Joyce

We can begin with the mind in the Library in *Ulysses*. The assembled group are discussing paradoxes in the context of authorship. 'It's the very essence of Wilde, don't you know. The light touch' (*U* 9:529–30). Richard Best is recalling Wilde's story-essay 'The Portrait of W.H.' (1889) and the proposition that Shakespeare wrote his sonnets for the boy-actor Willie Hughes. Best's comment is lifted in part from Wilde himself who has Algernon in *The Importance of Being Earnest* declare: 'The very essence of romance is uncertainty' (Wilde, 255). In one of those unsettling markers that distinguish the 'Scylla and Charybdis' episode, the disgruntled Stephen Dedalus thinks to himself: 'His glance touched their faces lightly as he smiled, a blond ephebe. Tame essence of Wilde.' This is clever and puts Best in his place alongside Haines with his 'smile of a Saxon' in that other tower (or garrison) episode 'Telemachus', but the pun on Wilde's name, if it's not directed at Best being Wilde's tame essence, is a little obvious, and what exactly is essence when Wilde is all performance? Perhaps the intention on Joyce's part is for the comment to rebound on Stephen, for Wilde is not so much tame as external, all brilliance, someone who, as with 'the very essence', empties intensifiers of their meaning but who also challenges us to distinguish affective and affectatious. As for Wilde's 'light touch', in the context of Willie Hughes, this is presumably a *double entendre*, perhaps unintended on Best's part and not pursued by Stephen, but one capable of being registered by Joyce's ideal, 'wideawake' reader, more so today in the light of O'Neill's *At Swim, Two Boys* (2001), a novel which brings out the latent homosexual theme in *Ulysses* and which is discussed in more detail in Chapter 8. So Wilde's light touch is both metaphoric and literal, both witty and physical in nature, capable of being appreciated and at the same time rejected by polite society, a midway position that is revealing for those who have eyes to see and blind or deceptive for those who don't.

At the beginning of the day, Molly innocently informs Bloom that for the upcoming concert she is to sing 'La ci darem la mano' (Give me your hand) from Mozart's *Don Giovanni* and 'Love's Old Sweet Song', two songs that never stop rebounding on Bloom and his predicament as a husband about to be cuckolded. On her own Molly is more wised up about her part in the narrative and has little doubt that the touch of 'la mano' by a man is both sensuous and transgressive. Part of the pleasure for Molly derives from being touched where she shouldn't be touched, and, somewhere, she knows, or has been told, being touched is sinful. The reply to her priest that she was touched on the canal bank is reminiscent of the constant innuendo in *Tristram Shandy* surrounding Uncle Toby's groin injury or of jokes which confuse place and position as in the standard joke about the pilot being asked for his height and position by air traffic control and replying something like 'six feet two and at the front of the aircraft'. With aeroplanes that get into difficulties, it's essential to know height and position but there's something intrusive about the celibate priest's inquiring into where a man placed his hand on a woman's anatomy even if it is to determine whether the sin is mortal or venial. When obliged by her confessor to supply details, Molly becomes confused, and in that confusion – or, if 'canal bank' is a reference to the female body, her linguistic slippage – she reveals for the reader not so much her foolishness as the Church's limitations in the area of sexual morality, especially when that conflicts with tact and what elsewhere might be considered a leading question designed for some ulterior motive or vicarious pleasure. Even in its most private moments, either at the time or in the privacy of the Confessional, touch is potentially public, so that while it is conducted between two people, a third, in the guise of conscience, the Church, the courts or the press, is always present. There is a necessary tension here, but the scene being described by Molly is not a crime scene and her answer is innocent, so innocent that it lifts the burden of guilt away from her and onto the priest, whose inquisition would seek what amounts to a forced entry into intimate encounters between men and women.

Molly's fascination with what is happening on the other side of the gender fence leads her at one point to imagine what it might be like to be a man: 'I wished I was one myself for a change just to try with that thing they have swelling up on you so hard and at the same time so soft when you touch it my uncle John has a thing long' (*U* 18:1383–5). The addition of 'for a change' is a light-hearted cry against necessity as if a sex-change could be treated like an excursion to the seaside. It is followed by 'just to try', a phrase denoting experiment and an attempt at persuasion, as if she were seeking the use of her friend's new gadget or sex toy. In contrast with the canal bank reference, her thoughts here are more private but whether they are a frank expression of feelings or simply the playing out of a rolling imagination remains an open question. This is not something she would confess in the Confessional, but, again, touch complicates matters, for as soon as she comes to hard / soft she slips, her memory takes over and she recalls a delightfully filthy children's street rhyme about 'my uncle John has a thing long ... my aunt Mary has a thing hairy'. Molly's imagination is so graphic and linguistically rich that it requires readers frequently to pause, as when they encounter 'on' and not 'in'. Picture that! Bodies touch, but touch is not so much gender-ambiguous as gender-distinct, for it promises union but delivers separation, more so with coitus interruptus. The boundary that Molly transgresses, therefore, is not so much a boundary but more like a series of contradictory impulses, where touch is graphic in that it is written down but where taboo words are translated into something else, a substitute, that thing.

Stephen by contrast is an innocent when it comes to touch. In *A Portrait of the Artist as a Young Man*, he pines for the soft touch: 'The soft beauty of the Latin word touched with an enchanting touch the dark of the evening, with a touch fainter and more persuading than the touch of music or of a woman's hand' (*P* 244). In the shape-changing episode of 'Proteus', the same tune can be heard again, this time a little more insistently: 'Touch me. Soft eyes. Soft soft soft hand. I am lonely here. O, touch me soon, now. What is that word known to all men? I am quiet here alone. Sad too. Touch, touch me' (*U* 3:434–6). Like the Aeolian harp Stephen waits passively by the Attic shore for the wind to blow and set him tingling. The waves break and as they do so his thoughts also alternate with the rhythm, changing from her to him, from soft eyes to soft hand, from eyes to I, from I to all, from too to touch.

Appropriately, she has soft eyes (all eyes are this) and she belongs to the modality of the visible, which is itself, as we have learnt from the opening to the episode, 'ineluctable' – unless, that is, you have trouble with your eyes like Joyce or Stephen his fictional counterpart. Later in the novel, in 'Circe', Stephen brings a lighted match to his eye and recalls the incident in 1888 when his glasses were broken on the cinder track. The repercussions for Stephen in *A Portrait* are dramatic, but here in 'Circe' his brain only just manages to discover through the alcohol a thread for his thoughts: 'Must get glasses. Broke them yesterday. Sixteen years ago. Distance. The eye sees all flat. (He draws the match away. It goes out.) Brain thinks. Near: far. Ineluctable modality of the visible. (He frowns mysteriously)' (*U* 15:3628–31).

However, in general, the visible is ineleuctable while touch is 'eluctable'. Sheltering the eyes, looking modestly downward, looking away, staring, eyeing, being eyed – all these remind us that the visible, whether operating in a world of female tease, the male gaze or male shame, is always to some extent part of a world that is both avoidable and ineluctable. Stephen desires she touch him for, like Bloom whose own emotional landscape is anticipated in this scene, he too is lonely. The phrase is not 'It is quiet here' but the even more locked-in 'I am quiet here'. There is nothing 'touchy-feely' about any of this, in part because identity lies elsewhere. Touch acts as an imagined transforming agency and perhaps relates to the word known to all men, part of a universal language. In keeping with the overall theme of 'Proteus', Stephen's emotion is deeply felt in personal terms but he seeks through repetition an identity with forces larger than himself and through touch a merging with the Other.

The untouched woman, as the Bawd in 'Circe' reminds us, attracts a higher (commercial) value: 'Ten shillings a maidenhead. Fresh thing was never touched' (*U* 15:359). And, in a comment that links Jesus and the author of *Tess of the d'Urbervilles*, the Nymph adds, fixing Bloom, 'You are not fit to touch the garment of a pure woman' (*U* 15:3458). Bloom, on the other hand, has already made up his own mind: 'Women especially are so touchy' (*U* 6:753–4), where 'touchy' is a word that now rarely means 'sensitive to touch' but is more likely to signify hyper-sensitive and hence irritable, keep off, avoid, don't touch. As for Bloom himself, 'There's a touch of the artist' about him according to Lenehan, who's always interested in whether he can touch someone for something, and he continues: 'He's a cultured allroundman ... not one of your common or garden' (*U* 10:581–3). But in the very next paragraph we read: 'Mr Bloom turned over idly pages of *The Awful Disclosures of Maria Monk*, then of Aristotle's *Masterpiece*. Crooked botched print' (*U* 10:585). Clearly, if we imagined Lenehan was referring to culture as high-brow we would be mistaken, for one text concerns an ex-nun's dramatic revelations about her Order, while the other title has nothing to do with the Greek philosopher from antiquity but was a popular *vade mecum* or guide for midwives and others in the eighteenth and nineteenth centuries. The phrase 'allroundman' sets Bloom in the company of Homer's *polytropos*, the many-sided Odysseus, but 'touch of the artist' points in a different direction. For Stephen, art is a high calling and it needs protecting from what Joyce referred to in his 1901 pamphlet as the 'rabblement' (see Mason and Ellmann 1959). When attacked by Mulligan for not toning down an adverse review of a book by Lady Gregory, Stephen concedes he doesn't have Yeats's capacity to dissemble: 'She gets you a job on the paper and then you go and slate her drivel to Jaysus. Couldn't you do the Yeats touch?' (*U* 9:1159–61). Untouched, touchy, touch of, the (Yeats) touch – the run would be incomplete without a reference to touched, meaning mad. And *Ulysses*, a novel about touch, doesn't disappoint us for, as Bloom suggests about Fanny Parnell and indeed the whole Parnell family: 'All a bit touched' (*U* 8:513).

Each of the three main characters in *Ulysses* is defined in part by touch. Stephen is in search of a body and for him touch is intense, an intensity which is in inverse proportion to his not finding a woman to touch or be touched by. Molly's view of her body involves a lot of touching. When she thinks of places like the Gaiety Theatre, her thoughts revert to touching and not just touching but also to what happens in the dark: 'a lot of that touching must go on in theatres in the crush in the dark' (*U* 18:1039–40). The deictic marker in 'that touching' signifies a mixture of knowingness, fascination and proper distancing. Touch, as Molly confirms, is part of culture. When discussing 'Penelope' with Frank Budgen, Joyce, who rarely allowed anyone outside the family to call him by his first name, explained that the word 'yes' signifies 'cunt', 'bottom' is 'womb' and 'because' is 'arse'. As for Molly, *Ich bin der Fleisch der stets bejaht* (I am the flesh that always affirms) (*Letters* I, 170). Memory, language, the body – any nature in Joyce is rarely conceived as a space in opposition to culture. 'Cunt' is both physical and part of a world of signs and language, linked by Joyce in 'Penelope' with obscenity and denial but also with affirmation, the signal that most young men hope for from a woman. Here it is two men – the same two who had been involved in a scene of seduction with Martha Fleischmann in Zurich in 1918–19 – discussing a fictional creation and in the process reminding us that 'Penelope' belongs as much to male talk as to a woman reflecting for herself alone.

Bloom is a mind in a body rather than a body in search of a mind as he has sometimes been portrayed, and, like Molly, he, too, spends not a little time reflecting on touch. For Bloom, the body occupies not so much a private as a social space and it needs watching therefore. He is free to think what he likes in a profoundly Catholic country but other suitors, other bodies, invade his consciousness. He lacks Boylan's confidence and in the appropriately named 'Nausicaa' episode reverts instead to touching himself watching a woman lift her skirt for him. In contrast, at the Ormond Hotel, Boylan, the man who is about to cuckold him, 'touched to fair miss Kennedy a rim of his slanted straw' (*U* 11:346). To make matters worse, Bloom is conscious for much of the day of what people are or might be thinking about him – 'greaseabloom' (greasy, grey sea, Bloom) is one of many terms of abuse that bestrew his path in the 'cruelfiction' (*FW* 192:19) of 'Sirens'.

There is another side to this question. As a father Bloom enjoyed physical contact with his daughter Milly. In 'Nausicaa' – and the post-masturbation context here is important – when he recalls her letter, his thoughts seem to cross over from intimacy to something more decidedly sexual: 'Dearest Papli. All that the hand says when you touch. Loved to count my waistcoat buttons' (*U* 13:1198). The language of flowers in *Ulysses* operates more securely as part of a system of exchange, but the language of touch, partly because of its frequently compromised and guilty nature, operates differently. In this respect, touch has the capacity to alter the flow of things – witness the shift here from Milly's terms of endearment, recalled by her father from earlier in the day, to general, evasive, thoughts about the hand touching, to a third sentence about buttons (her mother had a thing about these) and idly counting: 'Loved to count my waistcoat buttons.' This sequence could be entirely innocent, but the language of touch prompts more suspicious readings. 'All that the hand says when you touch.'

At its most innocent, the hand communicates through touch. It is more than Malinowski's phatic communion, though it often is simply that, simply another way of saying hello. The hand also possesses its own form of communication, a sign that you belong to the same tribe.

When the customers enter the Ormond Hotel in 'Sirens', they greet the barmaid by the hand in a show we might think today is a little too free, a little too familiar. By contrast, the slightly flustered Miss Douce bows to the 'suave solicitor' George Lidwell and holds out a 'moist' hand for his 'firm clasp' (*U* 11:562–4). Bloom, on the other hand, his senses awakened, recalls Molly's 'cool hands' among the rhododendrons at Howth (*U* 11:582). 'All that the hand says when you touch.' And what does it say? For everything speaks in its own way in *Ulysses*. As an adolescent Stephen is 'thrilled' by Cranly's touch when he 'pressed Stephen's arm with an elder's affection' (*P* 247), an incident which is recalled in 'Telemachus' in a remark that pops out at the reader: 'Cranly's arm. His arm' (*U* 1:159). How we interpret this returns us to 'all that'. At one level it is Stephen associating Mulligan with a school friend and, in an episode about dispossession, with obligation towards his native country, but it also perhaps reminds us of something else, of touch as delay, as a homosexual come-on, as personal satisfaction, as a moment of resistance, as a reminder of the need for the embattled intellect to be on guard against his contemporaries, a reminder that is of all that the hand indeed says when you touch.

## Sterne

In her essay on gender and power in *A Sentimental Journey*, Melinda Alliker Rabb rightly points out that

> Most of the important 'events' of the journey are enacted by hands: exchanging snuffboxes, trying on gloves, feeling a pulse, holding a sword, wiping away a tear, pulling a cord, pointing to *Hamlet*, distributing *sous*, stretching out from bed, or, of course, holding a pen. (Rabb, 542)

Every woman Yorick meets in *A Sentimental Journey* presents him with an opportunity to take her hand. The first occasion occurs with a woman he encounters when hiring a carriage to take him to Paris:

> The impression returned, upon my encounter with her in the street; a guarded frankness with which she gave me her hand, shewed, I thought, her good education and her good sense; and as I led her on, I felt a pleasurable ductility about her, which spread a calmness over all my spirits– (*Sentimental Journey*, 16–17)

The tongue-in-cheek prose is here to be relished. A 'pleasurable ductility' is precisely what Bloom would have liked from the woman getting into her carriage outside the Grosvenor Hotel. It is equally becoming that Yorick's woman is not forward but, conventionally, has an attractive 'guarded frankness'. Supposedly, it is just an ordinary encounter, implying nothing sexual. There are no secrets either, for this is writing that eschews those kinds of devices. What have good sense or good education got to do with extending a hand to an unknown stranger? Yorick's motivation is plain for the reader to observe, and his whimsical character is in keeping with a narrative that also doesn't quite get going. Yorick does, however, have an extended opportunity to compare the conduct of sexual mores and advances in France. '[A]nd as I led her on, I felt a pleasurable ductility about her, which spread a calmness over all my spirits–'. As Wilde might well have agreed, what is touch but uncertainty, the essence of romance. Calm is soon restored and it spreads over all Yorick's 'spirits', a word we might agree is closer to the pagan body than to the Christian soul.

The sentence also ends in a dash. Such a punctuation mark in Sterne is akin to a conversation marker, suggesting a pause for thought or breath, a dramatic flourish, a twist in the narrative. Like its author, the dash delights in concealment and mischief, and perhaps it was Sterne's practice which in a reverse kind of way prompted Joyce to use honest dashes instead of dishonest quotation marks. Joyce, we know, thought inverted commas 'perverted' for they imply they aren't the author's words; in *Finnegans Wake*, the 'poor joist' even imagined he was 'constitutionally incapable of misappropriating the spoken words of others' (*FW* 108:35–6). In some editions, following Victorian editors who tended to shield the world from obscenity, *A Sentimental Journey* ends not with a blank space but with a dash or a full-stop. A blank space allows for all kinds of interpretation, and not just the smutty. John Warner argues that a typographical absence provides a cyclical marker to recall the text's opening discourse on death (Warner, 120). Modern critical theory, ever alert to gaps and aporias, can also make something of the dash, for the dash signifies not absence but something real, 'that thing' as Molly might have called her own vagina. Invited in to share a farmer's house for the night, Yorick somehow manages to find himself sleeping next to a young woman and when he reaches over in the dark it is her dash or blank space or full-stop, her backside or end-stop, he accidentally grabs hold of: 'So that when I stretch'd out my hand I caught hold of the fille de chambre's'(*Sentimental Journey*, 125). Touch and titter, then, dashes and ductility, empty spaces and end-stops, belong together in Sterne's playful, pop-up world as he strikes out against the deadening hand of mid-eighteenth-century English propriety, against those like the Scottish Presbyterian James Fordyce who railed against 'the general run of Novels' and their altogether improper 'scenes of pleasure and passion' (Fordyce, 149).

Later, in Paris, Yorick stops at a glove shop and another opportunity presents itself:

> Any one may do a casual act of good nature, but a continuation of them shews it is a part of the temperature; and certainly, added I, if it is the same blood which comes from the heart, which descends to the extremes

(touching her wrist) I am sure you must have one of the best pulses of any woman in the world– Feel it, said she, holding out her arm. (*Sentimental Journey*, 52–3)

Yorick begins as if he were William Harvey (1578–1657) explaining the way the body works, tracing the flow of blood from the heart to the extremes of the body, but almost at once he becomes familiar with his 'patient', taking her wrist and then feeling her pulse. As he touches her wrist he discovers one of the best pulses of any woman in the world. This is yet another recourse by Yorick to ridiculous subterfuge, ridiculous because no-one would believe him if he claimed he was involved in a scientific or medical inquiry and ridiculous also because one could never obtain the evidence to prove she did indeed possess one of the best pulses in the world. When her husband returns and discovers Yorick holding her hand, he passes no remark; Yorick on the other hand is bemused and puts it down to cultural difference.

Yorick is a parson, not a medical man, yet behind Sterne there was an ongoing medical revolution which brought together not so much two professions concerned with the well-being of the individual as a way of thinking about the body and relationships which impacted on the two professions in question. As Roy Porter has underlined, Sterne 'was aware of a fresh emphasis upon nature as living and active, and the new physiological importance of the nerves, organisation, sensitivity and sexuality' (Porter 2003, 303–4). It was Thomas Willis (1621–75) who, in *Cerebri Anatome Cui Accessit Nervorum Descriptio Et Usus Studio* (1664), introduced the word 'neurology' into the language, and in other studies such as *Pathologiae Cerebri et Nervosi Generis Specimen* (1667) he outlined what he considered the origins of epilepsy and other neurological disorders. Willis gave fresh impetus to studies in localization, in identifying, that is, areas of the brain or nervous system which caused or housed sensation, how laughing – to take an example which itself has its funny side – was 'caused by the fifth conjugation of the nerves'. However, not without some justification has George Rousseau recently claimed that the long eighteenth century was 'the Age of Willis as much as the Age of Locke' (Rousseau, 25), that is, an Age devoted as much to the body as to the mind.

Willis stressed the 'corporeity' of the soul, the idea of the animal soul, the soul, that is, which is common to both animals and humans, a soul which also has something bodily in its make-up, something on the way to the modern interest in 'corporeality'. At the beginning of Chapter 2 of *Tristram Shandy*, as if he had been reading Willis on the animal soul and the nervous system, Sterne refers to the HOMUNCULUS that is Tristram in the womb and to the fear that 'his own animal spirits' might be 'ruffled beyond description,— and that in this sad disorder'd state of nerves, he had laid down a prey to sudden starts, or a series of melancholy dreams and fancies, for nine long, long months together' (*Tristram Shandy*, 3). The train of thought is 'curious', to invoke Arnold's word, and playful but, like Willis, Sterne sought through a consideration of the body's origins and pathological states not eccentricity or freakishness but order and humanity. As Willis's translator, Samuel Pordage, notes in his 'Table of Hard Words' (see below), man is not a 'single' but 'a curious machine', precisely what Sterne never stops emphasizing.

Sterne's curious mind took him almost inevitably to the moment when the body starts life, when personality traits are made therefore or revealed, and, later, to the occasions when things go wrong for the body. Willis's language is still imbued with a medieval vocabulary of souls and their rank-ordering, but as a natural philosopher his mind is decidedly turned to describing the world in its own terms. Sterne is a system-refuser and delights in systematically undermining and showing the limits of natural philosophy. Hence the deliberately imprecise phrase 'ruffled beyond description', which reminds us more of the person suffering than the medical condition. Similarly with 'sad disorder'd state of nerves', which, through the introduction of the adjective 'sad', shifts attention from the scientist's laboratory and the professor's anatomy class to the world outside and how people speak about such conditions and the state of their nerves.

Willis drew on the pioneering work of William Harvey, whose discoveries about the circulation of the blood in the seventeenth century introduced a scientific basis for the language of flow and made possible among other things the great Sternean metaphor of circulation. Harvey introduced a new paradigm, and with him, as Richard Sennett has suggested, 'A new master image of the body took form' (Sennett, 255). Willis shared Harvey's interest in circulation, only now it is the animal spirits flowing through the nerves: 'Indeed, the animal spirits flowing within the nerves with a living spring, like rivers from a perpetual fountain, do not stagnate or stand still; but sliding forth with a continual course, are ever supplied and kept full with a new influence from the fountain' (Pordage, 126). As is discernible from Sterne's hymn to Sensibility, quoted below, the image of the fountain conveys a particular force. 'Velut aquarum rivi à perenni fonte' (Willis, 176–7), like rivers of water from a perpetual fountain, is Willis's Latin, a language and style that takes up into it a world beyond the body, for Willis could be writing about a river basin for example or anticipating Sterne and the concept of Romantic inspiration itself.

When Pordage translates Willis into English in 1681 – in this sense 'neurology' entered the language in 1681 – he often reproduces the metaphors intact as if Willis's Latin retained the look and not just the word-order of its first language. But whether as metaphor or translation, the language calls attention to itself and to its potential for interpreting the world anew:

The nerves themselves ... are furnished with pores and passages, as it were so many little holes in a honey-comb, thickly set, made hollow, and contiguous one by the other; so that the tube-like substance of them, like an Indian cane, is everywhere porous and pervious. (Pordage, 127)

The image of nerves as hollow tubes recalls the continuing influence of Galen on medical thinking, but the phrase 'like an Indian cane', 'cannae Indicae' in the Latin (Willis, 180), is such an unexpected comparison that it evokes almost at once not so much the body as the East India Company and the opening up of another world in the second half of the seventeenth century. Meanwhile, the adjectival phrase 'porous and pervious', easier on the eye and ear than 'porosa ac pervia', has all the qualities of arresting, poetic prose.

*A Sentimental Journey*, and the same can be said of *Tristram Shandy*, is nothing if not about circulation and exchange, about not stagnating or standing still. Circulation signifies an ongoing process of touching and separating; every encounter raises the prospect of touch and circulation. 'Feel it,' as the woman interjects. As with circulation, so with touch: there is a constant switching between the physical and the figural, just as there is in Willis. The metaphor is pointedly grounded in the physiological aspect, so that when Yorick feels pulses he is in touch with both his own feelings and the life blood, animal soul or corporeity of another person. This can be approached from another angle. Like the blood flowing round the body from the heart or the never-ending flow of the animal spirits through the nerves, Sterne's narrative never stops pulsating. Think of La Fleur's delightful movements in *A Sentimental Journey*, his appearance in a blue satin waistcoat with gold embroidery which had been 'touch'd up' (another example of circulation), the agitation he betrays in getting Yorick to write a letter for him (and the letter has been used before), or the debonair French captain in the street showing Yorick the way to seduce a woman. However, while the blood and the animal spirits circulate round the body, Sterne's narratives pulsate but provide no return, no Joycean *ricorso*. In this sense Sterne seems intent on bringing his narratives into line with the pilgrim body, there in the world, ready for encounters and exchange, conscious of frailty but not of that overused modern word 'closure', a journey without end, to be cherished for what life is.

Sterne's world is upheld by circulation. Interruption, the hallmark of his work, is but a reminder of this metaphor, an interruption, that is, in the circulation. Circulation is about changing places and the development of a sympathetic imagination. It is appropriate that Yorick's initial antipathy toward the mendicant monk at the beginning of *A Sentimental Journey* is followed by the exchange of snuff-boxes. Exchange and circulation remind us not of the organicist tradition which came to fruition in the English Novel in the nineteenth century – the image of the web in George Eliot's fiction has a representative quality in this regard – as of something more lively, less integrated, where the pattern is less insistent, there for the taking if you want it. What Sterne grasped from his student days at Cambridge when his lungs filled and he 'bled the bed full', as he informs us in his letters, was that his body was always going to speak to him in a direct physical way (he must also have realized he would never see old age).[4] Willis was interested in experimentation and at Oxford in the 1650s he became a leading expert in both chemistry and anatomy – one of the fullest entries in Pordage's 'Table of Hard Words' is on urine. Sterne, too, is an investigator, but in his case his attitude and stance is not so much experimental as responsive: he is a great listener to his own body and he traces his feelings back to their source in 'the eternal fountain of our feelings'. For Sterne, history is your own heartbeat, to quote the title of a volume of verse by Michael S. Harper.[5] So the only sort of pattern he attended to in earnest was the precarious one which led from one encounter to another. Nothing was more fitting than to construct a European Grand Tour which, unlike Tobias Smollett's *Travels Through France and Italy* (1766), never proceeds effectively further than France, a tour which was based on nothing more than and nothing less than a series of encounters, which has nothing to say about the quality or circulation of the water from place to place, and which ends in a dash or a blank space.

The importance he assigned to the idea of circulation supplied Sterne with something else. Sterne's argument is with the materialism of his age, not the materialism of Marx or Leopold Bloom but the mechanistic materialism of Baron d'Holbach, the atheism as propounded by mid-eighteenth-century Encyclopaedists in France, and the empiricism of John Locke. For Sterne, the body is not a machine and the mind is not a *tabula rasa*. *Tristram Shandy* takes particular delight in noticing that the entry into the world is anything but straightforward. Thus, Tristram's nose is cruelly squashed when touched by the forceps in the birth canal. As with the nose so with its male counterpart, the penis. With no chamber pot nearby in the upstairs bedroom, the housekeeper Susannah resorts to getting her charge, the five-year-old Tristram, to urinate out of the window, but while he is doing so the sash window, which was not 'well hung', gives way and 'Nothing is left,—cried *Susannah*,—nothing is left—for me but to run my country' (*Tristram Shandy*, 449–50). The moment, impossible not to visualize, is well-captured in Michael Winterbottom's film *A Cock and Bull Story* (2005). Susannah would find sanctuary with Uncle Toby, but the phrase 'for me' can perhaps also be read as Susannah identifying with Tristram, whose phallic loss is linked humorously by Sterne with the exercise of power in adult life.

As Sterne recognized, life is dependent not only on winding up the clock but also on the flow of blood and the movement of the animal spirits or 'very subtil little bodies' (Pordage, 127). It also had a life of its own as it were, so the body was never simply nature as opposed to culture and, moreover, it was subject to accidents which Providence might or might not have prevented. The 'sensitive' body, the soul that man shares with 'brutes' – as opposed to the rational soul – has involuntary movements or is subject to 'reflex action', a phrase that enters the language with *Cerebri Anatome*. Willis was intrigued, for example, not only by the 'wandering pair' but also by the fact that, when asleep, a person scratches himself. Three generations later, Sterne reconfigures yet again the relationship between the cognitive faculty of the mind and the realm of the imagination, for, like Leopold Bloom, he understood the interdependence of mind and body: 'Rumple the one, you rumple the other' (189), as we read in *Tristram Shandy*. In a world of accidents, Sensibility, not the dispassionate God of the Deists, is Sterne's natural recourse, and the hymn to Sensibility quite naturally also includes a reference to touch and the effect of the weather on people with a disorder of the nerves:

> Dear sensibility! source inexhausted of all that's precious in our joys, or costly in our sorrows! thou chainest thy martyr down upon his bed of straw—and 'tis thou who lift'st him up to HEAVEN!—eternal fountain of our feelings!—'tis here I trace thee—and this is thy divinity which stirs within me—not, that in some sad and sickening moments, '*my soul shrinks back upon herself, and startles at destruction*'—mere pomp of words!—but that I feel some generous joys and generous cares beyond myself—all comes from thee, great—great SENSORIUM of the world! which vibrates, if a hair of our heads but falls upon the ground, in the remotest desert of thy creation.—Touch'd with thee, Eugenius draws my curtain when I languish—hears my tale of symptoms, and blames the weather for the disorder of his nerves. (*Sentimental Journey*, 117)

## Concluding Remarks

Joyce is not Sterne, Sterne is not Joyce. That much is certain. In *Ulysses*, there are no specific references to corporeity or corporeality, to that seventeenth-century debate that clearly interested the eighteenth-century parson, as the spiritual world began to recede in the face of new material, and to some extent more powerful, explanatory concepts. Porter has rightly argued that *Tristram Shandy* is 'the first novel to bear the weight of a major philosophical shift. Its comedy made the new interiority of Lockean and Humean man – a creature of confused subjectivity – seem normal and even sympathetic' (Porter, 303–4). If Sterne provides a sustained engagement with empiricism and materialism, then what intellectual system does Joyce reflect, give expression to, or, more properly, satirize? One possible answer is the medieval world that Rabelais also satirized. Joyce, we might recall, is 'middayevil down to his vegetable soul' (*FW* 423:28), medieval not just down to his animal soul but to his even

lower soul, the vegetable one. It is a view which receives further confir-
mation in the 1903 notebook newly acquired by the National Library of
Ireland in which we see the young man carefully transcribing sentences
from his intellectual master St Thomas Aquinas. According to Bakhtin,
'Rabelais's task is to gather together on a new material base a world
that, due to the dissolution of the medieval world-view, is disintegrating'
(Bakhtin, 205). Change Rabelais to Joyce and medieval to capitalist and
Bakhtin's comment resonates across the centuries and through different
historical periods.

Like Rabelais, Joyce is a gatherer, an orderer, someone given to a non-
transcendent view of the universe, to the Aristotelian / Thomist view that
there is nothing in the intellect which doesn't come through the senses.
The issue is complicated not least because his Jesuit masters ensured
the medieval world was not only contemporary but also constituted a
valuable weapon in the Catholic armoury against the modern world. So
Joyce's new material base betrays both a confident attachment to and
a distrust of modernity. Like Rabelais, Joyce's sense of the grotesque
– used here not as in Southern grotesque but in its original meaning
as mixed in form, a departure from the classical viewpoint, not logical, as
when in art or sculpture a reed supports a roof – involves 'a blurring of
distinctions ... a riot of incompleted forms' (Parrinder, 8). Joyce's mixed
response stands in contrast with the Protestant clergyman Sterne, whose
satire on Roman Catholicism – as in his mockery of the form of excom-
munication or of the proposal to baptize distressed infants in the womb
by injection – is singularly confident, sharp and 'enlightened'. When 'any
thing, which he deem'd very absurd, was offer'd' (*Tristram Shandy*, 78),
Uncle Toby took to whistling half a dozen bars of *Lillabullero*, the Orange
tune guaranteed to antagonize Irish Catholics.

In attitudes to the dead and the afterlife, Joyce betrays both modern
and medieval ways of thinking. His interest in corpses and in wakes
is thoroughly Irish and traditional, but his curiosity in how the dead
are treated in different cultures also reflects developments in modern
anthropology. In *Finnegans Wake*, a book in its own way about the
dead, he makes constant use of Ernest Budge's *Book of the Dead* (1901)
concerning ancient funerary customs in Egypt. To counter the gloomy
cultural diagnosis of *The Waste Land*, a text which is also indebted
throughout to anthropology, Joyce finds hope in the many-layered
connection between corpses and crops: 'Life, he himself said once, ...
is a wake, livit or krikit, and on the bunk of our breadwinning lies the
cropse of our seedfather' (*FW* 55:5–8). This is also the place to recall the
moment when the amateur ethnographer Bloom steps into All Hallows
Church in an episode devoted to modern lotus-eaters and witnesses Holy
Communion, 'the thing', being distributed: '*Corpus*: body. Corpse. Good
idea the Latin. Stupefies them first' (*U* 5:350–1). Joyce is intrigued by this
proximity between corpus or body of Christ and corpse, between words

from a dead language (Latin) and what implications this might have for Christian theology. Indeed, if customs are best appreciated by outsiders, so too is language.

For Sterne, the body has feelings and these are wired to a complex fretwork of pulses, arteries and nerves. In one of his most lyrical passages in *Tristram Shandy*, in which he comes close to a form of natural religion, the narrator declares: 'True *Shandeism* ... opens the heart and lungs ... forces the blood to run freely thro' its channels, and makes the wheel of life run along' (*Tristram Shandy*, 401). In Joyce, the body is less vulnerable and made of stronger stuff, and, in spite of his studying medicine for a short while in Paris, his image of the body – and this also includes the eyes – almost invariably gives the impression of being closer to culture than nature, closer that is to Henri Bergson's emphasis on lived experience as a counter to nineteenth-century positivism. In a famous remark from *Matter and Memory* (1896), Bergson declares: 'The brain is part of the material world; the material world is not part of the brain' (Bergson, 4). Sterne didn't know what Joyce's generation knew, that, as *Tit-Bits Monster Table Book* (1902) informs us, 'At each beat of the heart (about 72 per minute) about 6 ozs. of blood is driven into the aorta from the left ventricle, and the same amount driven from the right ventricle into the pulmonary artery' and that 'The whole of the blood in the body ... passes through the heart in 32 beats' (62). Joyce could have made more of this, but, like Bergson, he seems more interested in mind over matter, in the Bloomian mind's capacity, for example, to compare the dead heart to a rusty pump.

Even when the body is no longer alive, Joyce still clings to culture, treating the dead as if they still belonged to the living rather than to the earth or nature. It is partly for this reason that 'Hades' constitutes one of the funniest episodes of *Ulysses*. When at the beginning of 'Aeolus' we read the headline in capital letters 'IN THE HEART OF THE HIBERNIAN METROPOLIS' with its allusion to the centre of the tramway 'circulation' system, if it weren't for the previous episode 'Hades', we might spend little time reflecting on the condition of the heart. The subheading reminds us more of a newspaper than of the heart and more of the transposed literal meaning of 'centre' rather than of anything connected with the body. Conversely, when we begin 'Aeolus' with 'Hades' in mind, the HEART resonates against the image of 'rusty pumps' and the reference to the 'breakdown' of Paddy Dignam's heart, which, significantly, takes place as the cortege passes Nelson's Pillar. But resonance works differently in Sterne. When we encounter 'the wheel of life', we sense the comic viewpoint has been excluded, for Sterne, in serious mode, insists that life is dependent on a good pair of lungs and strong circulation. When Bloom, who knows very little about the game, is leaving the cemetery at Glasnevin after the funeral, he (wrongly) uses a cricketing metaphor as if to put space between himself and the dead: 'They are not going to get me this innings' (*U* 6:1004).

In the case of Stephen, the body is opposed to the mind, for Molly the body presents itself as a storehouse of memories and adventures, and for Bloom it belongs to determination and is closer therefore to a rational discourse strongly influenced by reductionism and modern forms of associationism. In the various journeys between the body and the mind that *Ulysses* constructs, there is nothing stranger than McCoy's 'medical' inquiry of Bloom, 'How's the body?' (*U* 5:86). However, unlike in Sterne, there is no great 'SENSORIUM of the world' and no hymns to a higher being, no exclamation marks in this sense. Arguably, the closest Joyce gets to the divine is the mind which perceives the world, perhaps most strikingly expressed in Stephen's image of the 'strandentwining cable of all flesh' (*U* 3:37) or 'the word known to all men'. Surprisingly, when a survey is conducted into the use of 'lips' in their writings, it transpires that Sterne is often better than Joyce at conveying a sensuous pressure behind the word.

Sterne's is a more vulnerable world, but, leaving aside his eye problems, unless we are afflicted with poor health, Joyce's is generally closer to the one we inhabit. This is a world in which an upbeat consumerism and late modernity have problematized the idea of free choice. Yorick enters a shop in Paris which is not unlike someone's front room. The encounter is personal, face-to-face, quiet. The world in Joyce is noisy, noisy with information, with printing presses, the clatter of trams, ringing bells, horses' hoofs, creaks on the bar floor from tan shoes. All the sounds fit or speak, nothing is there by chance, and, as Bloom notices, some shops have winning shop assistants and others more surly ones. Against the anonymity of modern life, Joyce sets down a realistic marker, but it is at a price, for it can be argued he returns us to a discourse on design that belongs to a religious age. Dublin in 1904 is clearly not the best of all possible worlds, but if everything fits, as my remarks on 'Wandering Rocks' in Chapter 3 'Reading Dublin 1904' suggest, what room exists for individual freedom or precarious encounters or social visits to characters drawn from other novels? That tension, that openness to experience, more often than not connected with something beyond himself, is always there in postmodernist Sterne, but in modernist Joyce, at the same time as we witness an increased complexity in realistic texture, there is a narrowing down as if the Arranger couldn't let go of paring his fingernails.

But Joyce is also a carrier, and he carries with him the eighteenth-century interest in cultural difference, nineteenth-century forms of reductionism or determinism, as well as the whole era of Romanticism, and, especially in the Irish context, the ideal of nationalism. He witnesses the emergence of modernism, the development of modern psycho-analysis, and in the field of politics the march of Fascism. When Sterne and Joyce are compared to bookends to the novel, we shouldn't overlook the excluded middle. As the hymn to Sensibility or the image of the trapped starling in *A Sentimental Journey* suggest, Sterne anticipates the full-blown Romantic era as well as the French Revolution; Joyce inherits that world. But in both the anticipator and the inheritor, there is a concern with freedom, with the nature of feelings, with articulation and with cultural norms. In novels such as Henry Mackenzie's *Man of Feeling* (1770), there was an attempt to draw back from the unsettling image of feelings as portrayed in Sterne.[6] Joyce faced similar attacks from the arbiters of taste whether that was in the columns of literary journals or in the courts of law. What Sterne and Joyce share is a history of oppression, an attention to the body, and an awareness of the special properties and cultural codes inherent in touch. Whether the topic is satire and the novel, body and mind, matter and memory, medievalism and modernity, postmodernism and modernism, or eighteenth-century materialism and twentieth-century consumerism, touch and its supporters still have work to do.

# 2

# Joyce, Erudition and the Late Nineteenth Century

In his Introduction to *The Books at the Wake*, James Atherton cites a remark by Robert G. Kelly on the nature of Joyce's intelligence: 'Whatever else might be against him he would exceed in intelligence all his rivals. ... He became a literary antiquarian. ... He delved into medieval tracts, studied learned discussion of conscience (*Agenbite of Inwit*) by forgotten monks, and memorised quaint old ballads suitable to his musical taste and abilities' (Atherton 1974a, 19). Kelly supports his comments by citing an observation made by Oliver St John Gogarty, how 'No man had more erudition at so early an age'. Atherton questions Kelly on his assumption that Joyce's knowledge was that *recherché* but to my mind he might have gone further.

Two lines of compression or argument run through this chapter and overlap. One concerns Joyce's erudition in general; the other is at once more specific and speculative, and concerns his possible debt to Thomas Arnold's *A Manual of English Literature* (1897). With the first, my intention is to re-examine what is meant by erudition in Joyce, beginning with something that doesn't in itself qualify as erudition, namely material and excerpts from *Tit-Bits*, and then moving on to some general remarks about the nature of erudition in our culture. With the second, I want to propose that some things which sound erudite in Joyce belong to his education at the hands of the Jesuits (which has been covered elsewhere) and to his tutor for English at university (which has been perhaps overlooked). As indicated in my Introduction, Joyce is a difficult writer, but there is value in not adding to his difficulty. In his use of popular culture or in his knowledge of English Literature – the two topics I deal with here – he betrays he is a product of late-Victorian Ireland where borders were in dispute and where nothing, not even erudition, was safe.

## *Tit-Bits*

The issue of erudition is a complex one. The annotator of a Joyce text needs to possess considerable knowledge but s/he also needs a knack in tracking down sources which the passage of time has obscured. On the surface, you don't need erudition to understand or make sense of the reference to Philip Beaufoy in *Tit-Bits* (this was its original spelling, not *Titbits* as it appears in *Ulysses*) which Bloom comes across while in the outhouse in 'Calypso'. But if you were familiar with *Tit-Bits* from that period you might be persuaded that the character of Bloom steps out of its pages, and not only his character, for, as the Physiological Table in *Tit-Bits Monster Table Book* (1902) reminds us, Bloom, at 5 foot 9½ inches in height and 11 stone 4 pounds in weight is close to the average height and slightly more than the average weight of an Englishman (5 foot 9 inches and 10 stone 10 pounds) at the turn of the century. Some items in *Tit-Bits* magazine, such as a report in the issue for 26 August 1899 about men luring women through the columns of a newspaper, have distinctive Bloom markings: 'A private gentleman, aged 40, of education, wealth and more than average good looks, wishes to meet a lady of good private means with a view to matrimony.' On inquiring further the woman receives the reply: 'MADAM – I am highly honoured by your most amiable letter, and shall be delighted to make your acquaintance. You have all the qualities I seek in a wife, but unfortunately I am too busy to arrange a meeting at present. Meantime I can add materially to your fortune by my system of investment. ...' Bloom's advert is more succinct: 'Wanted, smart lady typist to aid gentleman in literary work' (*U* 8:326–7), and the ruse worked in Bloom's case even when he had strayed beyond the bounds of propriety: 'Answered anyhow' (*U* 5:65). The *Tit-Bits* correspondent kept her money and *Tit-Bits*, which was generally sympathetic to the plight of women whether single or married, added that she 'prefers to remain single'.

Some articles such as 'Why Are Women So Addicted to Postscripts', which appeared in *Tit-Bits* on 6 August 1904, the summer Joyce was courting Nora in Dublin, are germane to this discussion, especially the suggestion that the postscript represents not only the social position of women, 'the necessity commonly laid upon her of obtaining her wishes by indirect persuasion', but also 'the literary equivalent of the kiss she blows from her finger-tips when she turns after having said farewell'. In her reply to Bloom, Martha is both forward and direct, as if she knows exactly the convention she is using: 'P. S. Do tell me what kind of perfume does your wife use' (*U* 5:58). We'll never know if other articles such as 'The Life of a Sandwich-Man' on 9 July 1887 gave Joyce ideas, in this case for the H.E.L.Y'S advertisement which eels its way through *Ulysses*. When thinking of Bloom's fondness for 'the inner organs of beasts and fowls' (*U* 4:1–2), if we knew it, we might recall the advertisement for

Yorkshire Relish on 22 July 1899, relish which 'Enriches the Daintiest of Dishes, and makes palatable otherwise unappetising food'. Or take an item that appeared in 10 July 1886 under the heading 'Raising the Wind', precisely the subheading that appears in 'Aeolus' ($U$ 7:995). J.J. O'Molloy, the impoverished lawyer, is looking for a loan from Myles Crawford, but the editor pleads poverty himself. If he could get the money, raise the wind that is, he would: 'With a heart and a half if I could raise the wind anyhow.' In the *Tit-Bits* piece, an impoverished old man is busking in the East End but he doesn't have enough 'wind' to compete with the cold December winds. An unknown passer-by, noticing 'the poor flutist's efforts to raise the wind', takes up the instrument and proceeds to 'blow out a liquid flood of melody', bidding the old man to hold out his hat to passers-by. When the flute is returned and the old man wishes him a share of the 'windfall', the 'rubicund Orpheus' declines. The beautifully constructed *Tit-Bits* piece is a good Samaritan story, but there is little generosity in 'Aeolus', an episode that is rich in other forms of exchange as is suggested by references to pawnshops, Ireland's submission to Rome or the Crown, and what the island received in return (plum-stones is one reading of Stephen's Parable of the Plums). What the two scenes, however, share is a chord, how a phrase can be worked repeatedly, especially between title and story, until it yields a poetic density all its own, until, that is, we're not sure if we're reading a story or an example of how to write a story, rhetoric being the art of 'Aeolus'.

The format and tone of *Tit-Bits* must also have appealed to the author of *Ulysses*. The question-and-answer format of 'Ithaca', for example, resembles a similar format in *Tit-Bits*, as miscellaneous questions (taken from a single issue) such as the following remind us: 'Which country has the most women preachers?' or 'What is the largest sum ever given for a mouse?' or 'Which jockeys in this country had most mounts and wins in the season of 1900?' or 'In which city is it necessary for a man to obtain the consent of his wife before he can go up in a balloon?' (19 January 1901). The subheadings in 'Aeolus' belong not only to tabloid newspapers, as I mention in Chapter 3, but also to the pages of *Tit-Bits*. On one page of *Tit-Bits*, little incidents were collected and recorded with a heading which acted as a commentary on the story that followed. Some headings are straightforward and informative such as 'THE WORLD'S HOURS' or 'A DREADFUL ACCIDENT'. Some are tongue-in-cheek such as 'READING QUITE UNNECESSARY' or 'BETTER THAN ORTHOGRAPHY' (reminiscent of ORTHOGRAPHICAL in 'Aeolus'). Some are beautifully inflated such as 'A CRUSHING REPLY' and 'INJURED INNOCENCE'. And some are decidedly ironic such as 'QUITE DIFFERENT' and 'SHE AGREED WITH HIM' (see 7 December 1901, 4 and 18 January 1902). One heading was 'GOOD—AND VERY GOOD'. Which recalls 'CLEVER, VERY' ($U$ 7:674). It is in keeping that Joyce spoofs the convention, but without such cues to his imagination he might not have travelled as far as he did when at the end of 'Aeolus' he describes, thus, the weakness of the two middle-aged women who are the focus of Stephen's Parable of the Plums: 'DIMINISHED DIGITS PROVE TOO TITILLATING FOR FRISKY FRUMPS. ANNE WIMBLES, FLO WANGLES—YET CAN YOU BLAME THEM?' (*U* 7:1069–71) In turn, the headings in *Tit-Bits* come to resemble those in 'Aeolus' as with 'A WONDERFUL EMBROCATION' (about growing cows' tails) and 'INCONVENIENT OBEDIENCE' (about a young sentry arresting his superintendent) (31 May 1902).

If you were not a research student but familiar with the pages of *Tit-Bits*, there would be a question-mark over your reading habits or how you had spent your youth (or, more flippantly, with Bloom in the outhouse in mind, what kind of toilet paper the family used). For Joyce's father, 'That *Titbits* paper' was the only one he read for 'general culture' (Stanislaus Joyce, 106), and *Tit-Bits* we learn was also read by Virginia and Vanessa Stephen as girls in London (Squier, 13). On the other hand, to Miriam in Dorothy Richardson's novel *Backwater* (1916), *Tit-Bits* is simply associated with confinement whether socially or culturally: 'That dreadful room with the dreadful man hiding in it and staying in bed and reading *Tit-Bits* on bright Sunday mornings' (Richardson, vol. 1, 311). For those brought up in the 1890s, then, for those who became the first generation of *Ulysses* readers, the reference in 'Calypso' might well have required no gloss, no exercise in erudition. It is later commentators who struggle, and some, such as the late Don Gifford, through their labours in libraries and elsewhere become erudite.

Beaufoy himself requires separate treatment. Prompted no doubt by Stanislaus Joyce (106), Gifford and Seidman state that Beaufoy was 'A real person who contributed (terrible?) stories to *Tit-Bits* in the 1890s' (Gifford and Seidman, 81). Actually, in the 1901 Census for England and Wales there are 151 people with the name Beaufoy (and this across the whole country) but there is no mention of 'P. Beaufoy', so one suspects Beaufoy, which half-rhymes with Purefoy, the name Joyce assigns to the woman in labour in 'The Oxen of the Sun' – 'Mrs Beaufoy, Purefoy' Bloom thinks in 'Nausicaa' (*U* 13:959) – is a pseudonym for a real person(s) (that is, unless the person was outside the Census and resided elsewhere, in France or Dublin for example). If it was a pseudonym, this was contrary to *Tit-Bits*' policy, which insisted that 'The correct name and address of the sender *must* be distinctly written upon every competition, for publication in the event of success' (*Tit-Bits*, 16 July 1887).

Beaufoy's address has also escaped critical attention. Gifford and Seidman contrast Beaufoy's name with his 'fashionable' London address (which isn't given by Joyce; the annotators infer the address from 'Playgoers' Club'). In the 23 December 1899 issue, Beaufoy's address is given as the Strand, but in other issues the address of the Playgoers' Club is 6 Clement's Inn or simply Clement's Inn. Clement's Inn Passsage is just off the Strand, so perhaps the slight alteration in the address is not significant. Whatever the case, the address isn't particularly fashionable. The Club itself certainly wasn't. It was relatively new at the time, open to men and women (so P could conceivably stand for Philippa), and catered especially for the literary profession, itself a problem term. We might have inferred the term's problematic status from Beaufoy's insistence in 'Circe' on a fee for acting as a prosecution witness during Bloom's arraignment, the cash-conscious clerical worker, that is, struggling to make a living and using what he thought was a fashionable address.

In the years around the turn of the twentieth century, Beaufoy was a regular contributor to *Tit-Bits*, signing himself at first Philip and then simply P. Beaufoy. In 'Circe', as mentioned in the Introduction, Beaufoy accuses Bloom of being a 'soapy sneak masquerading as a *littérateur*' (*U* 15:822–3), but his own identity has something of the masquerade and *littérateur* about it, even when he claims he is famous: 'The Beaufoy books of love and great possessions ... are a household word throughout the kingdom' (*U* 15:825–7). Library and other catalogues record a Philip Beaufoy, author of the title story in a children's book of stories *The Dosing of Cuthbert* (1928), a Philip Beaufoy Barry, author of *The Mystery of The Blue Diamond* (1925), one of the children's Captain series, and a P. Beaufoy, author of *The Red Book of Boys' Stories* (1927). P. Beaufoy also wrote 'The Magic Matchbox', a story which was anthologized in *The Grand Adventure Book for Boys* (1940) and which sounds not unlike P. Beaufoy's 'Matcham's Masterstroke'. This person might be the same as Percy Beaufoy, author of 'The Story of an Alarum Clock', which appeared in *Boy's Own Paper* in November 1903. What is not in doubt is that 'P. Beaufoy' had an enviable knack for attracting a popular audience, winning several prizes for stories printed in *Tit-Bits* including 'My Last Card: A Baritone's Story' (2 January 1897), 'A Reading Room Romance' (6 March 1897), 'Jack Langley's Overcoat' (10 April 1897), 'A Marble Bill Sykes' (31 December 1898), 'A Handshake with Death' (an anarchist story) 22 April 1899, 'Dick Darrell's Victoria Cross' (23 December 1899), 'The Reservist's Chum: An Incident of the Boer War' (10 March 1900), 'The Split Button' (21 April 1900), 'The Finale of Act 2: An Actor's Story' (9 February 1901), 'Wilfrid Mason's Engagement: A Story of the Stage' (17 August 1901), 'Billie Scott's Eva' (28 December 1901), which I discuss in more detail below, 'Dick Armstrong's Sacrifice' (14 June 1902), 'A Mysterious Post-Card' (7 November 1903), which begins like 'Calypso' with a breakfast scene and the delivery of an upsetting post-card on which is written 'Prepare to Die Before the End of the Year', 'The Counsel for the Defence' (30 January 1904) and 'Mr Renshaw's Typist' (31 December 1904). The stories are the work of a *littérateur* and have strong plots which turn on coincidence, chance and mistakes, and which lead in turn to the happy reversal of fortunes for hero or heroine.

How many of Beaufoy's stories did Joyce know? Did he deliberately include Beaufoy in his prose masterpiece to tease his high-brow reader? Bloom uses one of his stories as toilet paper but, to my mind, we would be wrong to imagine such action represents Joyce's opinion of Beaufoy. Joyce was almost certainly conversant with 'Billie Scott's Eva', Beaufoy's story about gambling on horses which appeared in the 28 December 1901 issue and which was reprinted in *Fifty Prize Stories from Tit-Bits* (1902). Billie is an inveterate gambler; his fiancée Eva wishes he wasn't. Billie decides to reform and on the upcoming Saturday will place his last bet, the remaining £100 from his father's £5,000 legacy, on a horse in the Chesterfield Cup. Unfortunately, Billie is involved in a traffic accident and knocked unconscious. On regaining consciousness in hospital he is anxious not to miss betting on the race, so hands Eva the betting slip to take to the telegraph office. Eva mislays the slip but recalls Billie had mentioned the horse bore her name. The problem is which name, Eva or Chesterton? All ends well because Eva (mistakenly) places the bet on her first and not on her second name and a 'hopeless outsider' wins the race and £3,000 for Billie and Eva. This may be a 'terrible' story but that's really beside the point. The relevance of such a story to *Ulysses* needs little insisting on – not the Ascot Gold Cup but the Chesterfield Cup, a bet with a name misunderstood or mislaid, a win not for a hopeless but for 'a rank outsider' (*U* 12:1219), and an anxious exclamation about the hour: 'Ha! Four o'clock! The results would be out by this time.'

All these are mere details in a little-known story, ready to be consigned to the waste bin of history along with yesterday's news, and yet for the student of Joyce they are like 'portals of discovery'. But in the context of a discussion about erudition what do they tell us? It would be difficult to conclude that Joyce's erudition shines through any of this. Simply that he (possibly) made use of a story in *Tit-Bits*, a weekly that invited 'Litterateurs', as an advert puts it in the 22 December 1888 issue, to submit their story. And where does the erudition lie in my digging out a copy of an issue of the same weekly magazine and suggesting a possible source text for *Ulysses* overlooked for over seven decades by commentators and annotators alike? Is that really erudition or simply the engineered serendipity of a compulsive truffle-hound? Or is it entirely coincidental and that Joyce never knew the existence of such a story? Or, conversely, could it be that in his portrait of Bloom he had unwittingly written himself into the prize-winning pages of *Tit-Bits*?

## *A Manual of English Literature* (1897)

Erudition, it goes without saying, involves an issue of surface and depth. As his notepads suggest, Joyce is a schemer, an orderer of the world, someone given to arranging the monads in the world into a series of taxonomies where high culture, unable to protect its cherished position, finds itself colliding ceaselessly with popular culture. The sheer variety and the dazzling sense of order can convey the impression of erudition, but I would hesitate before calling it this. *Tit-Bits* reminds us that Joyce's project is essentially heterodox or mischievous; at its simplest, it is designed to outflank the reader, or to remind the reader of a different way of ordering the world, or to show the reader that this is indeed the way the world is. His use of popular culture serves as a reminder that he sought to undermine culture as high culture, piercing its ideological or protective armour, gathering the world anew. The contrast with Forster's Arnoldian novel *Howards End* (1910) and the portrait of Leonard Bast *acquiring* culture is at its sharpest here, and it is a topic I return to in Chapter 4. But there is another side to this. Joyce isn't really a literary antiquarian, and if he did delve among the cobwebs of libraries it wasn't for long. So, with regard to his studying obscure works by forgotten monks – and this takes me into my second line of argument – we should perhaps recall that Joyce almost certainly would have encountered a title such as *Agenbite of Inwit* while at university. Joyce read modern languages at the Royal University in Dublin (now UCD), and studied under Matthew Arnold's brother Thomas Arnold (1834–1900), who was Professor of English Language and Literature. Little is made of the role of Arnold in Joyce's intellectual formation, where pride of place is usually assigned to the Jesuits and not to the English Anglican convert. But I would like to propose in this chapter that Arnold and his *A Manual of English Literature* (1897), the first edition of which appeared in 1862, have perhaps been overlooked as a source and as an example for Joyce. As *Tit-Bits* also reminds us, erudition in Joyce, therefore, belongs to something closer to home.

Arnold concludes his section on the Norman period with '*Ayenbite of Inwyt*, or Remorse of Conscience' to give it the title and modern translation as it appears in *A Manual*, where it is described as a translation of a French treatise 'Le Somme des Vices et des Vertus' and done into Kentish dialect, 'and exceedingly rough' according to Arnold. The inclusion of the English translation, together with its characterization as 'rough', points to how the text is used by Joyce in *Ulysses*. The medieval text is first mentioned in 'Telemachus' when Mulligan takes Stephen to task for not washing and when Haines suggests he intends to make a collection of Stephen's sayings: 'They wash and tub and scrub. Agenbite of inwit. Conscience' (*U* 1:481–2). Stephen's train of thought runs on to the Elizabethan period and Lady Macbeth's inability to wash the guilty blood off her hands. It would be difficult to agree with Kelly that this is a 'learned discussion of conscience'. Indeed, the phrase was a late insertion at page proofs stage (see Groden 1978a: Gathering 1, 16). Moreover, you can hear a tutor in a Literature survey class making the Shakespearean link for the student, and you don't need to be a professor to recognize the destructive power of guilt. What is intriguing is the fundamentally unEnglish original translation *Ayenbite of Inwyt*, as if Dan Michel, the Kent translator in the 1340s, wanted nothing which sounded French, as if his intention was to wash the language of its guilty past. I suspect it's this linguistic aspect which also fascinated Joyce, especially usable in an episode about dispossession. Later, in 'Wandering Rocks', Joyce also draws attention to the odd, awkward genitival construction of the phrase: 'Agenbite of inwit. Inwit's agenbite' (*U* 10:879). In the context of this particular episode, where rocks constantly threaten to block smooth passage, it is appropriate that the phrase resurfaces to remind Stephen of his mother's death, and, as before, the phrase is not in italics, not a book that is, but something with a more personal application, precisely what the medieval author, Kelly's 'forgotten monk', no doubt intended.

If we move forward to the nineteenth century, the historical period has changed dramatically but not the connection I have been drawing here. Thus Joyce's admiration for Newman's prose style, evident from Stephen's remarks in *A Portrait* (80), is also perhaps indebted to Arnold, who in *A Manual* writes: 'For all the ordinary purposes of prose style, Dr Newman's manner of expression, considered as a singularly direct and lucid medium of thought, has probably never been surpassed' (Arnold, 505). In Joyce's novel there follows what looks like a non-sequitur: '– And do you like Cardinal Newman, Stephen?' Stephen has just asserted the superiority of Newman's prose, but Nash wants to know if he *likes* Newman – as if such a qualification frequently accompanied a discussion about Newman in Dublin circles at that time. The sequence, however, makes perfect sense in the context of Arnold, who also expressed a mixture of admiration and reservation about Newman. In *A Manual* Arnold ends his section on Newman, the person who was largely responsible for his own conversion to Rome and for his initial academic appointment in 1856 at the Royal University (see Bergonzi, 91–7), with a barbed comment: 'In recent years Cardinal Newman sanctioned the collection and repub- lication – in some cases with corrective notes – of nearly all his earlier writings.' On Newman's death in 1890, he confessed to his daughter Frances: 'To the *mind* of how many of us has he been of service! to the character not so much' (Bertram, 224). What disappointed Arnold was the way Newman's consistency assumed a frozen quality, how after his conversion to the Church of Rome in 1845 he lost his sparkle, 'almost to fold his arms', and how he proved incapable as Cardinal of Westminster of leading English Catholicism out of its dullness.

When it comes to the finest poet in English, Stephen has no doubt that accolade belongs to Byron, defending him against his rival Heron's charge that he was 'a heretic and immoral too' (*P* 81). Arnold, too, is fulsome in his praise of Byron, and also rushes to his defence as an individual. Unlike eighteenth-century unbelievers such as Hume and Gibbon, Byron suffered on account of a mind which 'shudders at the moral desolation which scepticism spreads over its life' (Arnold, 453). Arnold also admired Byron for his representative status, and it is this that raises his stature as a poet: 'Byron represents the universal reaction of the nineteenth century against the ideas of the eighteenth.' According to Arnold, the secret of Byron's charm 'was, and still is' '[t]he turbulent, haughty, passionate, imperial soul', a description the youthful Joyce could not, one suspects, but respond to positively. A little earlier, with Byron sitting on his pen, Stephen begins a poem to his sweetheart 'To E—C—' (*P* 70). In *Ulysses*, Byron and the profession of love is continued when Bloom makes a present to Molly of a book of Byron's verse (*U* 18:185).

The case is altered when it comes to Tennyson. Called by Stephen a 'rhymester' (*P* 80) and ridiculed in *Ulysses* as 'Lawn Tennyson, gentleman poet' (*U* 3:492), Tennyson is admired by Arnold but not without qualification, as his unflattering remarks on 'Ulysses' suggest:

> 'Ulysses' is enveloped in antique heroic dignity, as with a halo. The chief 'motif' is the thought expressed in those lines of Goethe in the *Wilhelm Meister* (Carlyle's translation), –
>
> To give space for wandering is it
> That the world was made so wide.
>
> A few stately lines contain a perfect estimate of the less glorious work and less heroic energy of the *respectable* Telemachus. 'He works his work, I mine.' (Arnold, 492)

To describe a poem as 'enveloped in antique heroic dignity' is not the same as saying it conveys or expresses heroic dignity – 'heroic dignity' is the phrase used by Maud Gonne in a letter to Yeats on the Easter Rising (Yeats 1954, 613), and she meant it. The adjective 'antique' robs the poem of what the poet is trying to achieve, while the quotation from Goethe merely serves to underline the 'less glorious work' of Telemachus and, by association or innuendo, of Tennyson himself. For readers of *Ulysses*, the presence of the phrase 'stately lines' in a discussion of Ulysses and Telemachus will strike a chord, as will the reference to *Wilhelm Meister* and the related Hamlet theme. Could this be a conscious or unconscious association Joyce had in mind when he composed the opening line to *Ulysses*? Of course, 'stately' was, and to some extent still is, a conventional adjective to describe lines of verse – De Quincey's verse is described as such by Edward Minto in *A Manual of English Prose Literature* (Minto 1886, 50) – but Joyce has some other purpose in mind when he begins his epic with 'Stately, plump Buck Mulligan'. Arnold had already entered a caution in *A Manual* by linking 'stately' with 'less glorious'. In *Ulysses* this is taken a step further, not only because Mulligan is not Odysseus, but also because 'stately' is applied to a person and almost immediately qualified by 'plump', a word the narrator has fun with later in 'Sirens' in connection with Ben Dollard's bulky form and manner. No antique heroic dignity here, but a style which serves to undercut Victorian pretension and at the same time bring up to date the story Homer gave the world. The gentleman poet comes in for more rough treatment later in *Ulysses*. In the windy episode of 'Aeolus', Joyce quotes the phrase about 'windy Troy' from Tennyson's poem (*U* 7:910), while in 'Lestrygonians' the mock heroic prose is applied to Bloom who does not drink life to the lees as Tennyson has it but 'drain[s] his glass to the lees', an action accompanied by yet more downward pressure, this time from his bladder (*U* 8:834).

The image of Shakespeare that emerges from the account in *A Manual* is of someone who occupies the temperate zone, who is conscious of the inevitability of the tragic process but equally aware that passion is '*vincible* by conscience and reason' (246). According to Arnold, Shakespeare never went through a 'storm and stress' period, and, by way of explanation, he adds with his characteristically sharp eye that 'the burgher blood which ran in his veins was not favourable to it' (236). The view of Shakespeare as a calculator is spelt out in the Library scene in *Ulysses*: 'He was a rich country gentleman, Stephen said, with a coat of arms and landed estate at Stratford and a house in Ireland yard, a capitalist shareholder, a bill promoter, a tithefarmer' (*U* 9:710–12). At thirty years old, the author of *A Midsummer Night's Dream* 'was capable of giving adequate expression to the most profound and various conceptions', 'the elasticity of his wonderful mind' intact (Arnold, 229). 'The intellectual strain under which he must have worked during his middle period' took its toll and, after amassing a fortune in the theatre, he retired to Stratford. Arnold's Shakespeare is a man of the theatre, not so much a systematic philosopher as someone in touch with his various audiences. Again, this view is not dissimilar to Stephen's, how 'All events brought grist to his mill' (*U* 9:748). Arnold is impressed with *Richard III*, with its popularity both as a printed text and as a play in performance. *Henry VIII* is a 'piece of gorgeous court-pageantry' (Arnold, 243), a play that can be dated to the reign of James I because of the King's Spanish sympathies and not to the reign of Elizabeth because of the treatment of her mother Anne Boleyn. The emphasis on purgatorial pain in the Ghost's speech in *Hamlet* would have satisfied an audience brought up in the old faith. Solecisms and other syntactical irregularities are admitted, but for Arnold these are 'mostly licenses, not faults – far less vulgarisms' (246). Again, we are back with Stephen in the Library and, by extension, his oft-quoted remark: 'A man of genius makes no mistakes. His errors are volitional and are the portals of discovery' (*U* 9:228–9). On *Hamlet*, Arnold's comments are succinct but include reference to *Wilhelm Meister* and Goethe's criticism, which for its enthusiasm and freshness Arnold recommends above all others. Appropriately enough, 'Scylla and Charybdis' begins with *Wilhelm Meister*, an episode which centres on Stephen's 'midway' interpretation of Shakespeare. For Stephen, Shakespeare walks through life meeting himself, he is the ghost and son of his father, Hamlet and Hamnet, the artist in dialectical relationship with his material whether as father, son, brother, husband or grandfather, a man of the theatre who rests after his labour. Stephen has a theory to prove and all is grist to his mill, but the reader never forgets that it is a theory, a theory which on the one hand takes seriously the argument about a midway position and which on the other hand indicates the distance he had travelled from the time spent in Arnold's temperate zone.

When he attempts a summary of Shakespeare's achievement, Arnold falls back on his own inadequacy in the face of Milton's 'great heir of Fame' and refers modestly to his *A Manual* as 'unpretending' (243). Reading Arnold on Shakespeare has a certain liberating effect. Here are the plays, this was the period and these are some of the interpretations the plays provoke. However, Arnold does not labour things, so that the student could quite legitimately deduce that the object of reading Shakespeare is to discern what hasn't been noticed before. Arnold's is an encouraging form of criticism which mixes appreciation and explanation, and, if something doesn't fit, the literary historian should not try and explain it away. Against the one-dimensional view of the French Gallic critic Hyppolyte Taine that passion carries all before it, that nothing can curb it, that 'the conduct of its subject-possessor is *inevitable*' (244), Anglo-Saxon Arnold quietly proposes that this doesn't apply to every Shakespearean character, and he instances the banished Duke in *As You Like It*, Isabella in *Measure for Measure*, and Miranda in *The Tempest*, characters who refuse extremes and rely on reason and conscience to guide their behaviour. According to Stanislaus, in an assignment awarded a high mark by Arnold, Joyce had attacked *Macbeth* for its formal deficiencies (Stanislaus Joyce, 113). In what sounds like petulance, though on whose part isn't easy to determine, Stanislaus continues by observing that his brother considered Shakespeare a 'time-server' and disliked in him 'his total lack of faith ... an all-or-nothing devotion to something'. Certainly, this was one reading that might have begun to form itself under his liberal humanist Professor – 'temperate' and 'temporising', while semantically apart, share an initial syllable – but, as is particularly evident from Stephen's thesis advanced in the Library or Joyce's careful chronology of Shakespeare's life reproduced in *The James Joyce Archive* (Groden 1978b, 323–48), it wasn't the one which held sway in a novel indebted throughout to *Hamlet*.

We know that Joyce had a copy of George Saintsbury's *A History of English Prose Rhythm* (1912) in his library of books in Trieste and that, as Atherton shows, he employed it when writing 'The Oxen of the Sun' (Atherton 1974b, 313–39) – part of the evidence stems from Joyce reproducing an Anglo-Saxon sentence translated by Saintsbury himself (Atherton 1974b, 316). There is no direct evidence that Joyce used Arnold's *A Manual*, so all we can do is build up a picture along the lines

I have suggested here. In spite of his prodigious memory, Joyce needed the passages from Saintsbury to write 'The Oxen of the Sun' episode, but he didn't need by his side a copy of *A Manual* to feel Arnold's presence. Arnold gave Joyce something prior to Saintsbury, which can be best summarized as the sweep of English literature, its historical contours, and its sites of special interest. Above all, unlike for example Minto's *A Manual of English Prose Literature* which focuses on style at the expense of history, or Saintsbury's 'style-history' (Saintsbury, 230), which ironically cannot account for changes in style, Arnold's historical imagination imparted a broadly conceived 'processional' view, so important to Joyce, who invariably starts his fictions with a time in the past and then proceeds down the ages to the maturity of the present. Arnold gave to Joyce something else – the wherewithal to undermine the processional view. As Eliot, in conversation with Virginia Woolf in September 1922, recognized, *Ulysses* 'destroyed the whole of the 19th century. ... It showed up the futility of all the English styles' (*A Writer's Diary*, 56–7).

On the matter of history, it is worth recording that both Arnold and Joyce set their face against condescension. Arnold's attitude toward Irish writers, for example, is instructive. The Irish are mentioned throughout *A Manual*, in contrast, say, to a modern equivalent such as David Daiches's *A Critical History of English Literature* (1969), where Irish writers are largely overlooked. In this regard also the Hibernophile Arnold needs to be distinguished from Saintsbury, who is up-front about his imperialism, refusing to apologize for the 'vulgar patriotism' in claiming that 'we have the most glorious ornate prose in Europe' (Saintsbury, 219). Arnold's portrait of nineteenth-century English Literature includes discussion of Maria Edgeworth, Tom Moore, Gerald Griffin, Charles Lever, William Carleton, Samuel Ferguson, Aubrey de Vere, even Cardinal Wiseman, and he shows how all these Irish figures belong to the single story. His insights are not always accurate but they are nearly always of interest. While sympathetic to her peasantry, Edgeworth 'does not seem to have realised the terrible situation which the course of history and the Penal Laws had created for her country' (479). In his two-page discussion of Moore, Arnold notices the political relevance of *Lalla Rookh* and how the Irish too, like Ghebers or the fire-worshippers of Persia, are a persecuted race who yet managed to preserve the faith of their forefathers and their ideal of nationality (466). The fact that the 'stern Englishman' Arnold – unlike his brother Matthew, whom the deaf gardener resembles – does not seem to have been guyed or satirized by Joyce in any of his works we might see as testimony to the shy courtier's ability to present an even-handed picture of English Literature, even-handed meaning open to the Irish contribution as integral to the story, not an added extra, and not there as a storehouse of collectible sayings.[1]

Joyce also shared something of Arnold's low estimate of certain English writers. The most venomous passage in *A Manual* – reminiscent of Yeats's remark about her 'distaste for all in life that gives one a springing foot' (Yeats 1955, 88) – occurs in a discussion of George Eliot's *Mill on the Floss*:

> [T]he story is unpleasing and tedious; and when posterity, not recog-
> nising, as we do, living and familiar features, shall ask what there is so
> very interesting in these samples of cramped, warped, uncultured, human
> nature, it is doubtful whether the response will be so unhesitating as it is
> at present. (498)

The great English novelist is missing from the great Irish novel. In *Finnegans Wake* Joyce repairs some of the damage with humorous play on the titles of a series of mid-Victorian books that includes Sheridan Le Fanu's *House by the Coachyard* (for Churchyard), John Stuart Mill's *On Woman* and then '*Ditto on the Floss*' and 'a stone for his flossies' (*FW* 213:1–3). Dickens receives only cursory treatment as a writer of low life (593) and as the inventor of comic characters: 'high average quality' (482) is how Arnold describes the long series of novels from *Pickwick Papers* to *Our Mutual Friend*. The Leavises dubbed Dickens 'the Shakespeare of the novel', but there is no hint of such esteem in either Arnold or Joyce. The fortunes of John Donne, to take another example, did not begin to revive until Herbert Grierson's edition of his poems in 1912, a decade or more after *A Manual*, where Arnold speaks of the 'repulsive harshness and involved obscurity' of Donne's style. But Arnold does notice Donne's poem 'Metempsychosis, or The Progress of the Soul' (1601), a satirical poem Donne later regretted and one which might have caught Joyce's eye as a student – it would certainly have fitted in with the theme of the 'Proteus' episode of *Ulysses*, and it was after all a word and concept that is all Greek to Molly in the episode which follows 'Proteus'.

## Concluding Remarks

Let me end this chapter on a slightly different note, one that relates to the issue of erudition but glimpsed now from another angle. In its historical focus and processional viewpoint, Arnold's *A Manual* is a quintessentially nineteenth-century text. To understand an object or indeed a subject the student was encouraged to examine its origins. With language this involved in particular the study of etymology and in the nineteenth century it was accompanied by the whole expansion of historical linguistics. Fittingly, Joyce as a very young man insists in 'The Study of Languages' (1898–9): '[T]he study of any language must begin at the beginning' (Joyce 1966, 27). With literature the same principle could be observed; start at the beginning with Anglo-Saxon writing and then, in Arnold's case, proceed to the present. Running through my remarks here has been Arnold's midway position, his emphasis on the temperate zone, the way extremes in attitude and awkwardness in style were avoided, overcome or smoothed out. In this he shares Saintsbury's 'pebbles of style' view (Saintsbury, 115), how English prose rhythms were washed and polished through the centuries. Speaking broadly, the crucial distinction between history and function was rarely made in the nineteenth century, and in the field of linguistics, to continue with this example, it was left to the disciples of Ferdinand de Saussure to insist on such a distinction, which in their case turned on the difference between synchronic or horizontal and diachronic or vertical relations. Henceforth, language and languages could be studied without (constant) recourse to history. This much is broadly familiar to most students of humanities.

Joyce begins in the nineteenth century but instead of distinction he moves in a direction marked 'conflation'. Instead of separating out history and function, he insists on the 'collideorscape' as he puts it in *Finnegans Wake* (143:28), the kaleidoscope. Shake the kaleidoscope and words collide and from that collision new meanings escape or arise. The future bias is already there in *Ulysses* and it is already there in *A Manual*, a manual which contained a Critical Section classifying English Literature into its various forms and genres and which could therefore serve as a *vade mecum*, a helpful guide, for critical or creative writing students. With his stress on ornateness and balance, discussion of ink-horn expressions and Euphuism, and repeated recourse to the imagery of music, Saintsbury confirms this impression that style could slip its historical moorings. Tennyson's heroic style, for example, or Walter Scott's medievalism suggested time-frames could be altered or invoked through style. Indeed, running through the pages of *A Manual* is the mock-heroic aspect, something that also appealed to Joyce, as can be observed throughout *Ulysses*. In the bar of the Ormond Hotel, for example, Lenehan 'quaffed the nectarbowl', Boylan 'bespoke potions' and enters, according to Lenehan, as 'the conquering hero'; in relation to one of the barmaids, the narrator quips, 'Fair one of Egypt teased' (*U* 11:263, 349, 340, 383). Part of the humour of this kind of style, which at this point we might notice is inseparable from erudition, lies in its inappropriateness, its inflation, its 'over-adequacy' or what Hugh Kenner, with his fine ear for the language, elsewhere calls 'impertinence' to a given situation (Kenner, 45), its mixture of different time-frames.

When we turn to *Finnegans Wake*, we can discern a collapse of distinctions so that whatever was is, or as Joyce puts it 'waz iz' (*FW* 4:14). The historical record no longer holds its shape. Stephen in *Ulysses* recalls the incident in the Middle Ages when whales were stranded in Dublin Bay and he thinks of the savagery of the citizens at the time, and then stops: 'Their blood is in me, their lusts my waves' (*U* 3:306–7). But in *Finnegans Wake* this kind of rationality or ability to see *sub specie aeternitatis* (in the light of eternity) gives way to various forms of conflation: not *in* me but me, 'not *about* something: *it is that something itself*', as Samuel Beckett inimitably puts it (Beckett, 14). One kind of conflation we might liken to shorthand. The 'Willingdone Museyroom' (*FW* 8:10) is not so much a war museum as an awful shorthand for war, for the Duke of Wellington – willing done – is the terrible soldier who, without pause for thought, does the bidding of his master. Another kind of conflation, which, again, has implications for how we view erudition, is sheer coincidence, perhaps akin at some level to the coincidence of opposites as propounded by Nicholas of Cusa and others such as Bruno of Nola.

One effect of such coincidence in the modern period is simultane-ously to invoke and deny historical perspective. Thus in a sentence such as 'Eireweeker to the wohld bludyn world' (*FW* 593: 3) we can hear Earwicker, perhaps like the Pope at Easter, addressing the whole bloody world. But the context is also the Easter Rising ('Easter Week'; 'were you out in Easter Week' became common expressions). Eire is addressing the world, a world which in 1916 was indeed bloody. In such a set of many-layered coincidences, Joyce was also lucky in having another ready-made coincidence: *éirí* in Irish is rising. Behind 'bludyn' we might also decipher an anagram for Dublin, and, more remotely, we might also hear in the word 'blood-dimmed', the adjective used by Yeats in 'The Second Coming'. So the Eireweeker sentence hints at or alludes to several contexts – the Church's salvation history, the Irish insurrection of 1916 and Pearse's address from the General Post Office in Dublin, the Great War and its aftermath, as well as to the plight of Earwicker himself. But we would be hard-pressed to assign priority to any of the allusions. If the sentence is erudite, then it is because it operates within a text or a kaleidoscope which allows it to be so.

This kind of conflation is reminiscent of substitution exercises in foreign language teaching. *Ulysses* resembles at times an extraordinary illustrative manual for understanding English syntax, for example how prepositions or possessives work (as in 'Agenbite of inwit. Inwit's agenbite'), or what meaning resides in morphemes or prefixes (Arnold's use of '*vincible*' in the quotation above suggests a similar interest), but in *Finnegans Wake* Joyce extends this idea to ring the changes on particular words and phrases. Thus a portmanteau phrase such as 'foenix culprit' (*FW* 23:16) contains not only the references to Finn and 'clear water' and to the Phoenix that rises from the ashes, which we noticed in the Introduction, but also the following associations: the Church's resur-rection motif *felix culpa* or happy fault; the Phoenix Park where the Chief Secretary to Ireland was murdered by the Invincibles in 1882; the culprit responsible for a possible murder in Le Fanu's intriguing novel *The House by the Churchyard* (1863); 'the feelmick's park' (*FW* 520:1); perhaps the language of children's comics 'Foe knicks culprit'; 'Feenichts Playhouse' (*FW* 219:2) where admission is free. The phrase also betrays a doubt as to whether or not there has been a crime committed, whether or not there is either a foe or a culprit, a pair who are separated in this instance by nix, nichts, nothing. Unlike substitution exercises, which are set out on the one page, in *Finnegans Wake* the substitutions are encountered throughout the book but on each occasion we are reminded of all the other occasions the phrase can be heard. The effect of this kind of internal quotation is to layer the text with yet more examples of what can sound like erudition. Deconstructing such portmanteau words or phrases is a necessary obligation for the annotator but in an odd way it runs counter to the central importance Joyce in *Finnegans Wake* attaches to conflation. 'O foenix culprit!' contains all these associations, all these possible associations and all this history. This is how language works; there is no word which isn't already part of something else, some other potentially portmanteau word. In his Berlitz classes, to reinforce a particular syntactic construction, Joyce would set his students the task of filling in the blank spaces in a sentence. The process was given to repetition and constituted a machine-like approach to language learning. As he had remarked in his 1898–9 essay, studying Grammar is like studying tables in Arithmetic and to be undertaken 'surely and accurately' (Joyce 1966, 27). In *Finnegans Wake* he fills the blank space with repetition whose chord-like meaning accumulates with each subsequent note. But, again, in a strange way, what Joyce's erudition leads us to is not the mind that created it but the world and the languages that made it all possible.

'When I'm dreaming back like that I begins to see we're only all telescopes. Or the comeallyoum saunds' (*FW* 295:11–12). In *Finnegans Wake* Joyce telescopes history, one moment turning it into a distant object, the next quickening it from within. Moreover, it is the males of the species who are the telescopes, a claim almost at once denied by the come-all-ye of the next sentence, the sound, that is, not of Yeats's dead person dreaming back through a living person, but of humanity as a whole. When we insert the concept of erudition into this discourse, we realize that some rules no longer apply. Normally, quotations hold the world in place or reinforce the solidity of our understanding of culture. 'April is the cruellest month', the famous opening to Eliot's *The Waste Land*, invokes Chaucer's *Prologue* and the beginnings of English Literature. Eliot's ambition is to (re)write himself as an individual talent into that tradition, to shore himself against his ruins or history's end-stop. In contrast with Joyce, as an early commentator insightfully recognized, Eliot's exclusiveness (and snobbish appeal) relies 'chiefly on ability to recognise allusions; much less on ability to manipulate linguistic elements' (Schlauch, 249). Joyce's quotations in *Finnegans Wake* are like conflations, or rather his conflations contain all kinds of material some of which can be identified as quotations from the tradition, tradition which in the 1920s had been newly added to by Eliot himself. Thus, Eliot's title in Joyce's hands becomes 'the wastobe land' (*FW* 62:11) and linked to 'lottuse land', the land which Joyce the emigrant had left but which always remained for him somewhere a was-to-be-land, a lotus land but also empty, a lot-of-use-land. Joyce also plays on the man who was 'transhipt from Boston' (111:9) and at one point he calls him disparagingly 'Tansy Sauce. Enough' (164:22). Erudite readers pick up on such phrases and often without prompting. Eliot wrote for the *Boston Transcript*; TSE is another variation of Joyce's playing with three initials in *Finnegans Wake*, most notably with HCE. But Joyce is doing something different to Eliot. His work is full of fragments, half-heard comments or phrases, but arguably there are no ruins in Joyce and nothing that resembles or could be considered a shoring up against a hated modernity. If Joyce learnt anything from Arnold it was to go beyond a processional view of tradition. Equally, perhaps it was Arnold, along with his other teachers, who gave Joyce a shorthand to that tradition, so much so that while there is value in gathering together the books at the wake, and showing enormous erudition in the process, this perhaps gives too much credence to the view that Joyce was a literary antiquarian whose erudition exceeded all his rivals.

# Part II

## Joyce and the City

# 3

# Reading Dublin 1904

## Examples of Reading Matter in 'Wandering Rocks'

1. Titles of Books
*Le Nombre des Élus; Old Times in the Barony; The Woman in White* (*U* 10:147–8, 161–2, 368).

Imagining the title of a book by Bloom: *'Leopoldo or the Bloom is on the Rye'* (*U* 10:524).

Name of a novelist worth reading: 'Mary Cecil Haye' (*U* 10:372).

Titles of secondhand books: *The Awful Disclosures of Maria Monk; Aristotle's Masterpiece; Tales of the Ghetto; Fair Tyrants; Sweets of Sin* (*U* 10: 585–6, 591, 601, 606).

Titles Stephen notices: *The Irish Beekeeper; Life and Miracles of the Curé of Ars; Pocket Guide to Killarney* (*U* 10:838–9).

Reference to Bloom buying a book on astronomy (*U* 10:525–8).

Mr Kernan wants to borrow 'the reminiscences of sir Jonah Barrington' (*U* 10:782). Stephen imagines discovering one of his school prizes on the bookstall with an inscription in Latin, *'Stephano Dedalo'* (*U* 10:840).

References to 'Thumbed pages' of the 'Eighth and ninth book of Moses'; 'How to win a woman's love' (*U* 10:844–7). 'Chardenal's French primer' (*U* 10:867–8, cf. 1228).

2. Quotations from Books and Songs
Line from the Preface of the Mass: *'Vere dignum et iustum est'* (*U* 10:4).

Quotations from history: Cardinal Wolsey (*U* 10:14–16).

Line from a Church textbook on sexual morals: *'eiaculatio seminis inter vas naturale mulieris'* (ejaculation of seed within or between the natural organ of a woman) (*U* 10:168).

Lines from the popular song, 'The Death of Nelson' (*'For England, home and beauty'* *U* 10:232–5).

Parody of the first line of the Lord's Prayer: 'Our Father who art not in heaven' (*U* 10:291).

Singing a song from William Balfe's opera, *The Siege of Rochelle* (*U* 10:557).

Mr Kernan recalls a line from John Kells Ingram's ballad, 'The Memory of the Dead', and a line from 'The Croppy Boy' (*U* 10:790, 793).

Medieval manual of virtues and vices recalled: 'Agenbite of inwit' (*U* 10:879).

Quotation from *The Merchant of Venice* (*U* 10:980).

References to other texts: Stephen on *Hamlet*; Swinburne; Julius Pokorny (*U* 10:1058–9, 1073, 1077–8).

Reference to the music-hall number, 'My Girl's A Yorkshire Girl' (*U* 10:1242).

### 3. Writing Books
Possible book about Jesuit houses (*U* 10:162).

Historical account to be written by O'Madden Burke (*U* 10:410).

History book being written by the Reverend Hugh C. Love about the Fitzgeralds (*U* 10:438–9).

Stephen 'is going to write something in ten years' (*U* 10:1089–90).

### 4. Reading Advertisements
Church announcement in Great Charles Street. 'The reverend T. R. Greene B.A. will (D. V.) speak' (D. V., Deo volente, God willing) (*U* 10:69–70).

Newsboards on North Strand Road (*U* 10:89).

Business titles: 'H. J. O'Neill's funeral establishment' (*U* 10:96).

Advertising hoarding: Mr Eugene Stratton (*U* 10:141, 1273).

Advertising card: *'Unfurnished Apartments'* (*U* 10:250).

Advertising boards: 'H.E.L.Y'S' (*U* 10:310, 1237–8; with a full-stop after the 'Y' in some Shakespeare and Company editions).

Advertising poster: Marie Kendall (*U* 10:380, 495, 1141, 1220; including one outside Dan Lowry's).

Shop window display: 'a faded 1860 print of Heenan boxing Sayers' (*U* 10:831–2).

### 5. Reading Items
Blue tram ticket (*U* 10:115).

Pounds, shillings, pence (*U* 10:11, 116–17, etc.).

List of engagements and appointments: Corny Kelleher's daybook (*U* 10:207).

Police Constable's identity: 57 C (*U* 10:217).

Books for pawning at the pawnbroker's (*U* 10:260).

Throwaway (*U* 10:294–7, etc.).

Writing an address (*U* 10:320).

Tram destination: Dalkey (*U* 10:357).

'Recipe for white wine vinegar' (*U* 10:844–7)

Legal writ (*U* 10:945).

Fifty guineas prize for boxing match between Dublin pet lamb and Portobello Barracks bruiser (*U* 10:1133–5).

### 6. Associated or Implied Reading Activities
Reading the time: Conmee's watch (*U* 10:1–2).

Telling the time from Marcus Tertius Moses' office and O'Neill's clock (*U* 10:508–9).

Posting a letter (*U* 10:46–53).

Secretary typing in an office (*U* 10:375).

Secretary scribbling a telephone message (*U* 10:393).

Sermons: Father Bernard Vaughan (*U* 10:33–5).

Musical score (*U* 10:363).

Reading disks: 'Turn Now On' (*U* 10:483).

Reading the language of clothes: Conmee's silk hat; Boylan's trousers; 'the cut of her blouse'; 'a concertina skirt'; Mr Kernan's stylish coat (*U* 10:30, 324, 327, 384, 743).

Suggestive language: 'May I say a word to your telephone, missy' (*U* 10:336).

## 7. Newspapers

Reference to a sporting newspaper: the *Sport* (*U* 10:394).

Talking about the news in the street: Mr Kernan on the *General Slocum* disaster (*U* 10:725–33).

Newspaper office: the *Mail* (*U* 10:973).

Becoming a possible item of news in a newspaper (*U* 10:1159–60).

## 8. Reading Habits

Priest reading the office from his breviary (*U* 10:184).

Capel Street Library (*U* 10:368).

Bloom perusing secondhand books (*U* 10:585 ff.).

## 9. Reading the City

Names of streets, squares, rows, malls, walks.

Names of shops and offices.

Map of the city repeatedly alluded to.

## 10. Reading the City through History

1798 constantly mentioned: Robert Emmet; Sir Jonah Barrington; Edward Fitzgerald; Ingram's Ballad, 'The Memory of the Dead' (*U* 10:764, 782, 785, 790).

English history: Wolsey; Mary Queen of Scots; Death of Nelson (*U* 10:14, 65, 232 ff.).

St. Mary's Abbey, 'the most historic spot in all Dublin' (*U* 10:409).

## 11. Reading Marks on the Page

Use of asterisks to separate sections (arranged in a triangular pattern, '\*\*\*', in Shakespeare and Company edition).

Humorous use of abbreviations:

- &c.: 'Maginni, professor of dancing &c' (*U* 10:56).
- (D. V.): 'The reverend T. R. Greene B. A. will (D. V.) speak' (*U* 10:69-70).
- 'strings' in the final section, as in 'Gerald Ward A. D. C.', answered in the following sentence by 'D. B. C.' (*U* 10:1223–4).

Possibly humorous use of initials, as in the 'reverend Hugh C. Love' (*U* 10:437) ('you see love').

Use of italics, especially of foreign words.

12. Reading Languages other than English
French: '*Moutonner*' '*idée fixe*' (*U* 10:182, 1068).

Italian: in the Almidano Artifoni section (*U* 10:338–66).

Latin: the language of the Church. 'D.V.'. Also names, as in 'Marcus Tertius' (*U* 10:508).

Spanish / Spanish-Arabic: '*Se el yilo ...*' (*U* 10:849).

Irish language: 'Damned' (*U* 10:1011).

13. Encountering Weighty or Confusing Latin and Latinate Words
Conmee describes human sexual activity as 'tyrannous incontinence' (*U* 10:171).

Final sentence of the first section: '*verbis*' or words help defend Conmee from the snares of the world (*U* 10:205).

'*An imperceptible smile*' (*U* 10:616) is a phrase that Bloom encounters in *Sweets of Sin*.

'*Coactus volui*' (literally, having been forced I was willing) (*U* 10:1113). (Cashel Boyle O'Connor Fitzmaurice Tisdall Farrell's remark expresses more than the reader can at first, or even on reflection, understand.)


## The Word City

As is evident from perusing the list above, Joyce's city is a city of words, a city not only saturated in printed matter, but almost impossible to conceive without language. After hiding a copy of Wilkie Collins's *A Woman in White*, which she has borrowed from the Capel Street Library, Miss Dunne innocently types on her keyboard the date that has since become celebrated '16 June 1904'; within hours, news of the *General Slocum* disaster in New York finds its way onto Dublin street hoardings, inviting a response three thousand miles away from Mr Kernan and other passers-by in the city; later than he should, the Jesuit priest, in superior mode, quietly reads from his breviary the hour of Nones; Boylan, buying some flowers on his way to Molly, roguishly enquires of the shop assistant: 'May I say a word to your telephone, missy' (*U* 10:336). From the shout outside the classroom that Stephen hears in 'Nestor' to the 'sllt' that periodically punctuates the episode in the newspaper office, there is no aspect of life depicted which exists or could exist outside of language: no sexual adventure or innuendo, no chance encounter or arranged meeting, no throwaway thought or indeed half-thought, no memory or envisaged moment, no prayer or slice of interior life, no shot of the city exists which is not already clothed in language.

The modern generator of so much printed matter, the printing press, is the image par excellence of a city of words. But, characteristically, in the newspaper episode of 'Aeolus', where Odysseus in Homer's epic tacks and veers according to the direction of the wind, the narrator returns technology to a human dimension: 'Almost human the way it sllt to call attention' (*U* 7:175–6). Similarly in 'Lestrygonians', after a paragraph of empty political slogans, Bloom, hearing the noise of trams passing one another 'clanging', runs them all together: 'Useless words' (*U* 8:477). This is a measure of Joyce's achievement, not simply to show the reach and pervasiveness of language, but, more significantly, to capture the transfiguration of a built city into language, to produce not so much a city of words but Peter Fritzsche's compound word or phrase, a 'word city'.[1] In a previous employment Bloom was a traveller for blotting paper. This, too, affords a suggestive image of the 'word city' where the city's ink is dried on Bloom's consciousness, where 'the cracked lookingglass of a servant' (*U* 1:146), which was Stephen's image of Ireland in 'Telemachus', is supplanted by another mirror, which is not so much cracked as designed to be read backwards.

In *Reading Berlin 1900* (1996), Fritzsche focuses on the great nineteenth-century Prussian metropolis, but in some respects – if we leave aside his emphasis on the fugitive or transient city – he could be writing about the 'word city' that is Dublin, the Hibernian metropolis. While Berlin is a created, industrial city, built for the most part in the nineteenth century, the modern city of Dublin, dating largely from the eighteenth century, was a commercial rather than an industrial city. Joyce's Dublin is evoked rather than constructed, and it is evoked partly through maps. Joyce had a map of the city in his head which he accessed constantly in his fiction to give us in turn a prospect of his city. In Bartholomew's 1900 map of Dublin, reproduced on the endpapers of the hard-back edition of my *James Joyce's Ireland* (1992), the new tramway system, the most dramatic change to the city streetscape, was in place and its routes marked, and with the help of this map we can follow these and other routes taken by his fictional characters. Indeed, the map constitutes not only one of the best guides to *Ulysses* and *Dubliners* but also an excellent vantage-point for observing the city.

Unlike conventional paintings of Dublin, the map provides a bird's eye view of the city from above as it were. The eye travels across the page, up and down, from south to north, west to east, noticing the various landmarks, the river's role in dividing and joining the city, the ten bridges across the Liffey, the flanking role provided by the Customs House and the Four Courts, the city enclosed within the North and South Circular Roads, the number of barracks scattered throughout the city. There are no clumps of trees or overhanging branches to frame the perspective, no people in it, no dogs, no horses, no hats, no gestures as you might encounter in James Malton's *A Picturesque and Descriptive View of the City of Dublin* (1791). But, like *Thom's Directory* of Dublin, the map is waiting for the artist to lay claim to it, and this is in effect what

Joyce did in *Ulysses*. 7 Eccles Street was empty, so he occupied it with the Blooms. The map belonged to no-one and was empty, so he decided to people it and set it in motion for one day in the year. The transformation didn't stop there, for Joyce's map is not unlike an adult boardgame, ready to be played by anyone who cares to pull up a chair.

Trams feature prominently in Joyce's writings, and give the impression of a city, a body, in motion. In this regard, the contrast with Alfred Döblin's novel *Berlin Alexanderplatz: The Story of Franz Biberkopf* (1929) is worth noticing. Döblin's naturalistic novel begins with a journey by tram from the prison at Tegel into the centre of Berlin. Biberkopf, who has been in prison for four years, leaves unprepared for the new sensations about to bombard him. Outside the prison gates he is directed to the tram by the warder. At the tram stop he waits. 'Die Strafe beginnt', not the open-ended 'die Strasse beginnt', the road begins, but 'die Strafe beginnt', 'his punishment was only beginning' as Joyce's friend Eugene Jolas translates this sentence (Döblin 1930, 12; Döblin 1978, 11). The tram races off, leaving Biberkopf with his head turned back toward the red wall of the prison. The journey by tram 41 is short but significant, and it acts as a stem or basis for the novel as a whole, for, throughout the novel, the narrator returns to this tram ride to remind the reader of Biberkopf's difficulty in finding a place in polite society and how close he remains therefore to the prison he has left behind but not completely abandoned, his head turned back like some figure in an older form of narrative. At the beginning of the Second Book, Döblin humorously rehearses the story of Adam and Eve and then creates another picture of Biberkopf's entry into the city, only this time marked by a series of miniature woodcuts plus adjacent headings to represent the fate or box that awaits him. First comes the city's heraldic animal, a defiant black bear on its hind legs, then an image of factory chimneys alongside 'Trade and Commerce', followed by 'Street Cleaning and Transport', 'Health Department', 'Underground Construction', 'Traffic', 'Municipal Savings Bank', 'Gas Works', 'Fire Department' and, finally, 'Finance and Credit' (45–6). The city stands over against him, the flow of the narrative interrupted by a series of ten images (which are not unlike medieval decorative intitials or stations of the cross), every area of his life catered for, with only his soul free to fall.

Joyce works differently. The Old Testament stories weave their way enticingly in and out of *Berlin Alexanderplatz*; Joyce uses Homer as his civilizing guide to life in the modern city. Bloom never confronts the city as some huge backdrop to his fate. Moreover, there is never a suggestion in Joyce of the prison overshadowing the city – paralysis has a different origin – and nowhere does he use a tram journey to convey a change in fortunes or new hope for an individual. Each morning Mr Duffy would catch the tram into the city from Chapelizod, and after he had 'dined moderately in George's Street and read the evening paper for dessert', the creature of routine would walk home (*D* 112). Maria's journey by tram in 'Clay' merely confirms something we already know about her, namely her naivety; as if she were waiting for others to mould her, as it were. As I suggest in the next chapter, Dublin is an occupied city but not an imprisoned one, and it would take a later Dublin writer such as Brendan Behan in *The Quare Fellow* (1956) to make something of the connection between post-Independence Ireland and prison.

The significance of trams in Joyce's reading of Dublin in 1904 lies elsewhere. Trams were new and must have been adjudged at the time as a symbol not of backwardness or of times past but of modernity itself. What impressed both Joyce and Döblin was their speed and how this would impact on a new, emerging consciousness. Biberkopf is swept along from the outset by the tram, as if his destiny was already being laid out for him: 'The tram took a bend; trees and houses intervened' (Döblin 1978, 11). Because of their speed, trams were not only exciting for the traveller but also dangerous for the pedestrian. The blind stripling in Dawson Street needs Bloom's assistance to cross the road. Even round tight bends, trams were fast; the road might be clear as Bloom tells him but Dawson Street was short. Later that night, Bloom himself 'trickleaps to the curbstone' after narrowly avoiding a tram in the dark, and he receives a suitable admonition from the motorman, who includes a reference not to an Irish game of hats and turd, as Gifford and Seidman suggest, but to what I assume is a contemporary magician's disappearing act: 'Hey, shitbreeches, are you doing the hat trick?' (*U* 15:195). Such a remark is more in keeping with the aggressive tone of Döblin's novel than the one which has its origins in Joyce's classical temper. Should he report him is Bloom's first thought, but then his humanitarianism gets the better of him: 'Tension makes them nervous'.

Interestingly, the newly discovered films by Mitchell and Kenyon of industrial Lancashire in the early years of the twentieth century suggest people treated the streets as theirs, and they only gave way to approaching trams at the last minute not out of cussedness but because the streets were where they gathered naturally, not yet accepting their confinement to the pavement as pedestrians.[2] The slow world is also there in *Ulysses*, as we witness with horse-drawn carriages of one sort or another, but the novel wouldn't be the same without the new electric trams. Equally, if he had set his novel ten years later, the author of 'After the Race' might have made more of the motor car, for Joyce liked to give the impression he was up to date with the latest means of transport and the latest technology. After all, in Bloom's municipal heaven, there would be 'Electric dishscrubbers' and 'Saloon motor hearses' (*U* 15:1687–9).

As for permanent landmarks, we might select one small area on Bartholomew's map for comment, the upper half of Sackville Street (now O'Connell Street). The street had been laid out according to plans approved by the Wide Street Commissioners in the second half of the eighteenth century, and we can witness Joyce repeatedly returning to it in his fiction. Gresham's Hotel, where Gabriel and Gretta Conroy spend an unhappy night in 'The Dead', is marked on the map, as is Nelson surveying the colonial city from the top of his Pillar and awaiting the visit of the stone-throwers Anne Kearns and Florence MacCabe, whose ventures are recalled in 'Aeolus' under the heading 'The Parable of the Plums'. Inside the buildings and monuments mentioned on the map, an inner drama is recorded by Joyce. As a result, a certain modification in the relation between the built city and the human city occurs, with Joyce at once reflecting and conveying the imprint of human consciousness on the city. This constitutes another form of ownership, one consequence of which is that, today, we have difficulty not seeing Joyce when we have a visitor's map of Dublin in front of us, as if he had taken on the role of freshening up his city as the Commissioners had done two centuries before. The Spire, however, which now occupies the place formerly occupied by Nelson's Pillar (and, more recently, by 'the floozy in the jacuzzi'), serves as a reminder that not everything in Dublin belongs to Joyce. More significantly – and I discuss this more fully in Chapter 8 in connection with O'Neill's *At Swim, Two Boys* – because of its association with the Easter Rising of 1916, the most famous building on O'Connell Street today is the General Post Office, a site which had to wait until the opening to the final section of *Finnegans Wake* before being properly addressed by Joyce.

Under the impact of ongoing nationalism, street names had begun to alter – Sackville Street to O'Connell Street for example – but the essential fabric of the city in 1904 was all as it was when Joyce made his first visit to the city as a child in the 1880s. In *Berlin Alexanderplatz*, people walk on planks when pavements are ripped up to build the underground; in London 'a boom in tubes' was, according to the 1904 Ward Lock *Guide to London* (56), in process, but in *Ulysses* there is little to suggest a city under construction or, indeed, destruction. The foundation stone of Parnell's statue at the top of O'Connell Street, which the funeral cortege passes in 'Hades', acts more as a reminder of a debt to the past than a pointer to the future. In her 1931 essay 'The Docks of London', Virginia Woolf speaks of '[i]ndefatigable cranes ... dipping and swinging, swinging and dipping' (Woolf 1982, 10–11). The only crane mentioned in Joyce's novel – which is surprising given that every day in his ten-year sojourn in Trieste he must have seen them at work along the busy harbour wharf – occurs in 'Circe' when Bloom's Hungarian father Virag 'cranes his scraggy neck forward' (*U* 15:2571–2). But, equally remarkable is the way Joyce figures or configures the city as a Daedalian workshop and then invites the reader to share his novelist's art or perception (for these last are, in Joyce's case we realize, close to being identical).

To the social historian, Dublin in 1904 is synonymous with stagnation and poverty. It was a city where child mortality rates were among the highest in Europe, where the job market was dominated by the general labourer and the domestic servant, and where one of the largest employers was a biscuit factory. In demographic terms, as Joseph O'Brien reminds us, stagnation also left its mark. The population of Dublin in 1901 was 290,000, only some 15,000 more than in 1891 (O'Brien, 39). By way of contrast, in the thirty years preceding the Great War the population of Greater Berlin doubled from two to four million (see Fritzsche, 7, 30), while, according to an article on the modern Babylon in *Tit-Bits* on 25 March 1893, London's population, which by 1901 reached over 6.5 million, grew by '200 souls a day', tacking on, according to *Tit-Bits* on 18 June 1902, the equivalent of a Brighton in a single year. But to Joyce, the under-capitalized city, which he never conceived in Babylonian terms, was not so much in decline as at once frozen in time and in ceaseless movement. Moreover, his city was an already built city, always there, and he felt no pressure as a wordsmith to invent something that existed long before he came along to put it into words.

Dublin possessed no Potsdamer Platz, no Brandenburg Gate, no Hausmann boulevards, no ancient gates into the city, only the largest park and one of the widest streets in Europe. The 'most historic spot' was St Mary's Abbey, but this reference in 'Wandering Rocks' resembles an answer to a question for a Christmas quiz in *Tit-Bits*. THE HEART OF THE HIBERNIAN METROPOLIS, according to the grand-sounding, capitalized subheading at the beginning of 'Aeolus', is not the Bank of England or Trafalgar Square as the equivalent would be if London were the metropolis, but the area outside the General Post Office where trams departed to every part of the city and beyond, only to return. It is this unpretentious quality which has made Dublin appealing to writers from Joyce to Roddy Doyle and which they have never stopped exploiting. But such a quality is conjoined in part with something less appealing, which Joyce needed little prompting to latch onto and satirize. Dublin was not only a village, it was a city historically committed to keeping its people in their place as the warning contained in its verbless motto reminds us: *Obedientia Civium Urbis Felicitas*, the obedience of the citizens constitutes the happiness of the city, or happy the city where citizens obey. It was a motto waiting to be sent up by the burgher son of a one-time rate collector for Dublin Corporation, perhaps most wittily in the tongue-tied, h-less phrase in *Finnegans Wake* which reads 'the obedience of the citizens elp the ealth of the ole' (*FW* 76:8–9).

Dublin was also a city which understood emigration better than immigration. When Biberkopf gets to see the centre of Berlin for the first time after four years, his thought is a simple one: 'Berlin ist groß', 'Berlin is big' (Döblin 1930, 16; Döblin 1978, 14). It is immediately followed by the immigrant's thought that size is opportunity: 'Where a thousand live, one more can live' (Döblin 1978, 14). Such a way of thinking is foreign in Joyce's Dublin. Equally, if there is a Central European dimension to

*Ulysses*, it resides more in the story of Bloom and his Hungarian Jewish family than in the city's streetscape. Bloom's story is frequently portrayed in comic, and therefore essentially human, terms, as in 'Calypso' with his trip to Dlugacz, the pork-butchers, to buy a pork kidney for his breakfast. Dlugacz is named after Moses Dlugacz, a Zionist rabbi who was taught English in Trieste by Joyce. Bloom stares at the window display, at 'the hanks of sausages, polonies, black and white', and breathes in 'tranquilly the lukewarm breath of cooked spicy pigs' blood' (*U* 4:143–4). In the queue he thinks of 'Prime sausage' and how women like sizeable policemen. He notices the woman ahead of him and is anxious to get served and catch up with her in order to see her 'moving hams'. Bloom and the 'ferreteyed' Dlugacz have Jewish names, but the meat they sell and consume is strictly forbidden; in that sense they are not good examples of their adopted city's motto either. Equally, we never for a moment imagine the shop is in Central Europe, in Trieste, for example, the main port of the Austro-Hungarian empire, or in Zurich where 'Calypso' was written, or on Bleibtreustrasse in Döblin's Berlin, a street which housed a company investing in land in Turkey that catches Bloom's eye. In incorporating such references – never far from stereotypes – into his Irish capital, Joyce not only insists on a European dimension to his novel but he also reminds us that a city exists to cater for personal needs and wants, bodily desires and satisfaction. The city is in this sense a 'domestic' city, one which harbours an attachment more to inside stories and non-conformity than to imposing vistas and neat thoroughfares. This, too, constitutes the heart of the hibernian metropolis, a city which was more at home with comforting stereotypes than with the challenge of difference.

To someone familiar with European capitals (and to those who weren't), Lady Morgan's 'Dear Dirty Dublin' lacked a certain grandeur, and perhaps it is for this reason that Joyce made much of the generous river flowing though the city's arteries. If, by comparison with Paris or London, you had only a small number of things to show off, you had, in addition to a new tram system, a river, and it was not just a river to carry the Guinness barges to the North Quay or the city's effluence out to sea but the mythological river of time. The merciful Anna Livia, who is commemorated in a lyrical passage from *Finnegans Wake* that begins 'O / tell me all' (*FW* 196:1–2) – the washerwoman listening like a confessor to the sins of Dublin's males – acted as a counter to the chauvinism he must have heard as an exile and a reminder of subterranean feelings for the native country he left as a twenty-two-year-old. Unlike Berlin, 60 per cent of whose population in 1905 had been born elsewhere (Fritzsche, 265), Joyce's city is a constant, renewing itself from within. 'Cityful passing away,' thinks Bloom, 'other cityful coming, passing away too: other coming on, passing on' (*U* 8:484–5). In this context the addition of 'too' is worth noticing, the individual and his or her generation not unique but part of a series, a sober reminder that for Joyce the transient city pre-dates modernity, just as philosophical reflection – in this case by an immigrant from Central Europe – predates sociological inquiry and the growth of modern European capitals.

In a parallel way, Joyce's city functions independently of the reader, but at the same time it is dependent on the reader for the flow to be noticed and information processed or retrieved. All these are ironies, asymmetries, stretched comparisons, even points of contradiction, an example of an economic base at variance with its ideological superstructure. Hence the frequency in accounts of 'Joyce and His Contexts' of counter-currents such as 'in spite of' and 'however'. But, without the imaginative leap which Joyce effected from the built city to the word city and from the word city to the built city, our view of the modern city would be perhaps seriously impoverished. Words like connection, networks, lines of communication, or even Raymond Williams's 'knowable community' (Williams, 202ff.), all seem slightly lacking in drive or edge to describe what is happening in Joyce's word city. In his frequently insightful account of the emergence of the modern metropolis, Fritzsche observes at one point: 'To read the newspaper was to consume the city and also to see oneself as a consumer or spectator' (Fritzsche, 158). According to *Tit-Bits* (see 25 June 1904), some 800 dailies came off the pressses in Germany and England in 1904, so there is some truth in this remark, but, again, Joyce refuses to shelter under such an observation. Instead, he undermines not just neat distinctions between reading and consumption, public and private, participant and observer but also most attempts at constructing a theory round the culture of consumption – or indeed the meaning of hybridity.

Scanning the 'inventory' in 'Wandering Rocks' underlines Joyce's combatively inclusive disposition as if he were a modern street fighter entering the lists. There is a nineteenth-century novel, Collins's 'sensationalist' *The Woman in White*, whose sensationalism escapes Miss Dunne (*U* 10:368); revelations of funny goings-on in a convent in *The Awful Disclosures of Maria Monk* (*U* 10:585–6); a life of a nineteenth-century French ascetic priest, the Curé of Ars (*U* 10:838–9); a tourist guide to Killarney, the most 'touristy' spot in Ireland (*U* 10:839); plays by Shakespeare, appropriately Stephen's *Hamlet* (*U* 10:1059; here it is the title of the play rather than the protagonist, as is the case in 'Telemachus') and Bloom's *The Merchant of Venice* (*U* 10:980); a French primer (*U* 10:867–8); a medieval manual of virtues and vices (*U* 10:879); the eighth and ninth books of Moses (*U* 10:844–5); Aristotle's *Masterpiece* (*U* 10:586), a popular illustrated *vade mecum*, first published in 1694 and used by midwives throughout the eighteenth and nineteenth centuries, offering, as already noted, supposedly authoritative counsel and remedies to child-bearing women; music-hall numbers, 1798 ballads, operas, lines from Church prayers and tracts, books on astronomy and cooking, on Irish beekeeping (*U* 10:838; in November 1903, Joyce worked as an assistant editor on *The Irish Beekeeper*, but for one day only) (Ellmann 1982, 141) – all these ensure that the cultural historian, post-colonial critic, or Ithacan cataloguer, if assigned the task of making sense of Joyce's city of words, would be kept busy for a not inconsiderable length of time.[3]

The list of examples of reading matter above also conveys something of the variety of reading activities in this episode, with advertising a central feature: Church announcements, advertising cards, leaflets, boards, posters and, perhaps most famously, the sandwichboard men, 'eeling' their way through the streets of the city. Jennifer Wicke makes the valuable point that

> No one understands the social reading of advertisement better than James Joyce, at least as manifested in the primer we could call *Ulysses*. ... Ads float free of this rootedness in the commodity ... as the throwaway ad exemplifies. Joyce sets individual ads floating down the river of the text as if they were bubbles of modernity inscribing the text with its material presentness, as the circulation of ads does in everyday life. (Wicke, 599)

In the context of a discussion about newspapers, the thirty plus 'interpolations' in this episode resemble the sixty-one subheadings of 'Aeolus', designed in part to interrupt the flow for the reader. Some items such as tram tickets, their destination emblazoned on the front, addresses, the language of commerce (£-s-d), the identity of a police constable by his badge, are there to be read as discrete items and have a function both inside the text and outside the text as it were. Associated, implicit or applied reading activities are also there to be noticed: characters read or tell the time; music scores are folded into batons (*U* 10:363); concertina skirts herald the music theme of 'Sirens' (*U* 10:384). Books are not only read but they are also going to be written – Conmee on the houses of the Jesuits, Stephen something in ten years time (*U* 10:162, 1089–90).

In some suggestive remarks on the 'metropolitan blasé attitude' that appear in 'The Metropolis and Mental Life' (1900), Georg Simmel claims that life in the metropolis has blunted discrimination and that consequently 'no one object deserves preference over any other' (Simmel, 414). This idea runs in and out of my account in this chapter, but it is worth recording that Joyce's deliberately inclusive project is designed not to blunt but, in a slightly perverse way, to heighten discrimination. Joyce's choice of material in 'Wandering Rocks' is suitably catholic. There is nothing in the list of books that amounts to a Great Tradition. We are in the rag-and-bone shop of Irish (and English) culture, sifting not through John Montague's 'shards of a lost tradition' (Montague, 108) but through the left-overs of the culture, ever-conscious of the work of the usurper, that figure announced in the first episode, and of living at a time, in Yeats's phrase from 'Easter 1916', 'where motley is worn'. But such an interpretation, even as it gains support by reference to pawnshops, auctionrooms and secondhand books, also needs balancing, for Joyce's satire characteristically cuts both ways. He mocks the movement of which Haines thinks Mulligan is part (*U* 10:1085), but in his rage for order he refuses to endorse the Arnoldian concept of culture, which seeks to discriminate at precisely the point where Joyce would want not just to include but to incorporate.

### Paralysis or Labyrinth?

In a review of Hugh Kenner's *Dublin's Joyce* in 1956, Sean O'Faolain summarizes what was once a common enough view of Joyce in general and 'Wandering Rocks' in particular. Joyce's work, we are reliably informed, is

> concerned with a city and its citizens and overtly describes only a series of individual lives; thematically they deal with – to put it bluntly – the Decline of the West, its collapse into the hideous chasm of the nineteenth century. Joyce was supremely fortunate in having been born in a city which still retained the last vespertine glow of the century of Swift and Burke; a city not indeed civilised, far from it, but echoing the voices of the dead, its life (the word should be put between quotation marks) an eloquent parody of the good old days before the beastly industrial and still more beastly romantic revolution. His city was a whispering gallery of the past. It teetered on the brink of the future. His father's memories and vigorous language, the grave buildings about him, the songs in the pubs, the eloquence of the commonest citizen, even the hollow and mechanical words of his teachers – priests turned policemen – evoked traditions of a time when not only Dublin but all Europe was still in and of Christendom. But it was only an evocation. The city was paralysed except in its mouth. Otherwise it was a corpse. An unpromising subject one might think – all those fate-blinded gasbags and gutters, however witty, however inspired as to the biting or colourful word. But what a theme if one were to place among them one steel-cold, clear-eyed observer to record satirically, yet not without passion or that love which always hides behind the mask of satire, the crisis – symbolically universal – of Sodom and Begorrah!
> (O'Faolain 1956)

'The city was paralysed except in its mouth' affords an apt rejoinder to those who insist on seeing nothing but paralysis in *Dubliners* and other Joycean texts. But, in general, the O'Faolain / early Kenner line, especially when applied to 'Wandering Rocks', has been persuasive. In one of his last essays, Bernard Benstock comments: 'If James Duffy were there to observe the event [the Viceregal cavalcade], he would not only have concluded that no social revolution was in the offing but no national revolution either' (Benstock 1994, 448). Technically and stylistically, 'Wandering Rocks', according to Charles Peake, 'suggests the purposeless activity of the Dublin streets' (Peake, 214). To Clive Hart, on the other hand, writing in 1974, the episode affords 'Joyce's most direct, most complete celebration of Dublin, demonstrating succinctly his conception of the importance of physical reality, meticulously documented, as the soil from which fictions may best grow' (Hart 1974, 181). For Ellmann, the episode affirms the personality which eludes Church and State, the twin forms of authority as represented by Father Conmee and the Viceroy (Ellmann 1984, 101). In an argument extending the concept of 'The Arranger' to apply to a figure he christens 'Jamesy', James McMichael has suggested that, as 'the most panoramic of Jamesy's cityscapes, chapter 10 discloses that he knows with certainty what every character in Dublin is doing, saying and thinking between the hours of three and four in the afternoon' (McMichael, 60).

To my mind, the city as portrayed in 'Wandering Rocks' is not so much paralysed or in varying states of being alive as error-strewn and closer therefore to the Homeric injunction to be on guard against the wandering rocks. Hovering around its title there is a warning-notice: 'No ship of men ever escapes that comes hither, but the planks of ships and the bodies of men confusedly are tossed by the waves of the sea and the storms of ruinous fire' (Butcher and Lang, 194). The adjective πλαγκτος (*plagktos*) means 'wandering', but in its transposed sense it means 'wandering in mind', 'distraught', 'unsettled'. A πλαγκτηρ (*plagkteer*) was a person who led one astray; but only in epics of the imagination can rocks wander. 'Wandering Rocks' is a plagkteer's text for analysis, a searching topic for study in a workshop, a forerunner of 1930s Mass Observation in Britain, a case study for the social scientist, an orchestration of the sounds and rhythms of a city, a map for the urban geographer, a guide book for walks off-the-beaten-track, a directory of a city derived from another directory of the city, a newspaper freshly inked with yesterday's news, a collection of tittle-tattle, an encyclopedia of items for a dealer or librarian to catalogue, a field-day for the private detective, a maze to trap or delight, a tease, a game for the long haul.

It is right for commentators to allude to the map of Dublin which Joyce had in front of him as he composed 'Wandering Rocks', or to the game of 'Labyrinth' which he played with his daughter Lucia at this time. Hart's fold-out diagram, recording the times and places of 'Wandering Rocks' (see Hart 1974, 216ff.), is a helpful reminder both of Joyce's meticulous attention to detail and of the Joyce critic's equally fastidious response. Twenty years later – partly, one suspects, in response to changes in contemporary critical fashion – Hart arrived at a different position: 'We can document only a tiny proportion of the life of an individual – let alone the life of a city. The most immediate expression of this limitation is to be found in "Wandering Rocks", which is very porous, almost all gap. Tiny scraps of action and text serve as the basis of an attempt at micro-history' (Hart 1993, 435–6).

Hart takes us so far. If he was right in his general drift, then *Ulysses* and 'Wandering Rocks' in particular would be like the sketches and feuilletons or feature articles in the new mass daily newspapers, whose 'attention to, and even celebration of, diversity and difference tended to undermine a coherent vision of the city' (Fritzsche, 94). In some respects, as my remarks on *Tit-Bits* in Chapter 2 indicate, *Ulysses* can be compared to a series of feature articles in a newspaper or weekly of the time. Its stories are not dissimilar to those in a newspaper, with putative titles such as 'Life from a Barmaid's Perspective' (as in 'Sirens'), or 'Funny Remarks Overheard in a Cemetery' (as in 'Hades'), or, more formally, with Mr Bloom in mind, 'A Day in the Life of a Space-Hound', or, as Bloom himself imagines, '*My Experiences*, let us say, *in a Cabman's Shelter*' (*U* 16:1231). Moreover, they have an integrity missing from the excised but essentially unquotable bits of newspapers to be found in the pre-Cubist collage paintings of Picasso and Braque. However, posing the issue in terms of a contrast between 'scraps' and 'microhistory', between diversity and coherence, invites or ignores a prior question, one which raises the point and direction of Joyce's narrative as a whole. What meaning could 'microhistory' have in a novel that centres on someone on the northside of Dublin queuing at a pork-butchers for his breakfast, browsing through a motley collection of secondhand books by the Liffey after lunch, and then later in the afternoon masturbating on the beach near the Star of the Sea Church at Sandymount? Summarizing the plot in this way merely serves to emphasize its parodic nature, that the story must be located in some other narrative, and not just the Homeric one, as my remarks on *Tit-Bits* in Chapter 2 suggest.

Differences therefore crowd in. *Ulysses* is a narrative, whereas a newspaper is not in itself a narrative (unless you were to say that the Murdoch press advanced an ideological line through all its various stories and features and that this constituted its grand narrative as it were). The columns of a newspaper contain narratives. The eye travels up and down and across the page to articles and advertisements, and the reader expects little or no connection or narrative cohesion across the page except to notice if it belongs to the front page news or is a business item or part of the sports section. Döblin, who begins as a naturalist writer but who is in reality a modernist with naturalist roots, originally intended to glue a passage from a newspaper into the manuscript of *Berlin Alexanderplatz*. This is not something Joyce, the modernist whose naturalist sensibility is never far from the surface of *Dubliners*, would have contemplated. Everything in *Ulysses* coheres. Even the subheadings in 'Aeolus', which afford another example of a pop-up mentioned in Chapter 1, are designed to be read and not, as they often are in tabloid newspapers, skipped. 'CLEVER, VERY' (*U* 7:674). In 'Wandering Rocks', Miss Dunne's '16 June 1904' is the only occasion the date is mentioned on which *Ulysses* is set, a small detail whose significance is deliberately underplayed by Joyce in a departure from novelistic convention. When Mr Kernan recalls a line from 'The Croppy Boy' in 'Wandering Rocks' he is helping to orientate the reader to the following episode of 'Sirens', where the 1798 song assumes particular significance, as I suggest in Chapter 6. The reference in the same episode to the music-hall number 'My Girl's a Yorkshire Girl' is actually an error on Joyce's part because the song was written after 1904, but, in terms of the novel, it anticipates the brothel scene in 'Circe' and at the same time recalls Bloom's predicament, married to a woman who's also involved in deception.

Without mentioning Joyce, Fritzsche stumbles on an important truth: '[T]he act of reading the entire city as a complete work was overwhelmed by the larger, ongoing process of just rereading and rewriting' (Fritzsche, 173). To take any one hour in the life of a city and to provide a cross-section of what takes place can, of course, only be done by 'retrospective arrangement' (*U* 10:783), a phrase that appropriately makes its appearance in this episode. The open-endedness, the chance sightings, the encounters in the street, the missed opportunities, are all absolutely precise. This is, of course, wholly unlike the actual experience of any single individual in a city, for none of us – as, incidentally, Joyce brings out in the Viceroy's misunderstandings of his loyal subjects – has access to a bird's eye view of a city. Contrast this with Carinthia Leicester's chance meetings in the opening chapter of Kathleen Coyle's novel *Piccadilly* (1923) with three individuals she has never set eyes on before: a Russian exile, who treats her to tea in a restaurant overlooking Leicester Square, a beautiful woman she later learns is Laura Price and a young artist Pelham Wace, who wants her to sit for him and who it transpires is in a relationship with Laura. Here the chance meetings are not so much precise as calculated, calculated that is by the novelist to suggest the beginnings of a journey of initiation for the unemployed female protagonist. That they occur in the centre of London amid the crowds and the streets adds a realistic touch as well as a sense of danger for a single woman alone in Piccadilly.

From all that has been suggested here, two ways of thinking about this episode need guarding against. One is this. In *Inventing Ireland* (1995), Declan Kiberd rehearses the standard view: 'Half-way through *Ulysses*, in a chapter of fragments, each of which represents *in parvo* a chapter of the book, Joyce adopts a god's eye view of Dublin, from which distance both men appear (like everyone else) as mere specks on the landscape' (Kiberd, 350). The other can be indicated through a remark in *Berlin Alexanderplatz*. In a comparable episode to 'Wandering Rocks' at the beginning of the Fifth Book, the narrator, impressed by all the crowds in the city, offers a qualification: 'To enumerate them all and to describe their destinies is hardly possible, we could manage only a few at most' (Döblin 1978, 174). Joyce shares something of this naturalist sensibility, but 'Wandering Rocks' is not essentially about the anonymity of the city or the selection of some individuals and not others to describe.

The point is worth pursuing. After 1889, from the summit of the Eiffel Tower, Parisians could see their entire city laid out beneath them, and for the first time the city assumed the form not so much of a labyrinth as of a flattened canvas, a perspective which Robert Hughes has linked with 'the characteristic flat, patterned space of modern art' (Hughes, 14). A generation later it was natural for Le Corbusier in his influential study *The City of Tomorrow* (1924) to celebrate the straight line and to describe the curve as 'a paralysing thing' (Le Corbusier, 16). Dublin possessed no such belvedere, and Nelson's Pillar, which could supply its citizens only with an ironic Pisgah Sight of Palestine or, more satirically, with a vantage-point for spitting out plum-stones on passers-by below, was no substitute. This is one reason labyrinth is such an apposite image for this episode, for Joyce's characters rarely get above street-level. Another reason is that a labyrinth is a maze, and a maze, which is about being lost or the possibility of being lost, is normally entered or negotiated from a position of security, precisely the position of the reader.

Adherence, then, to space-time co-ordinates in 'Wandering Rocks' is designed to show not the mechanical nature of the city but something else. What precisely that is has never been satisfactorily explained, but it seems to be related to the triumph of pattern over design and to an inquiry into the two time-space meanings of 'plot' – plot as in narrative plot and to plot as in a map or diagram. In contrast to Joyce's idea of pattern, Dorothy Richardson in *Revolving Lights* (1923), a novel published the year following *Ulysses* and the same year as Coyle's *Piccadilly*, makes an important qualification almost wholly missing from 'Wandering Rocks': 'How can people talk about coincidence? How not be struck by the inside pattern of life? It is so obvious that everything is arranged' (Richardson, vol. 3, 282). As for Fritzsche's use of 'overwhelming', this recalls the naturalist fear of the city as malevolent, a tradition that Joyce in part comes out of but which he largely escaped from. The only thing that overwhelms the reader in 'Wandering Rocks' is Joyce's inability to stop when the point is made.

Time, too, receives a serio-comic treatment, as if in response to the new consensus then emerging about the fate of individuals under synchronization and what one recent commentator has described as 'inner urbanisation' (see Fritzsche, 214). Simmel notices the 'universal diffusion of pocket watches' in the metropolis, and, while he has money in mind, his view has a more general bearing: 'If all clocks and watches in Berlin would suddenly go wrong in different ways, even if only by one hour, all economic life and communication of the city would be disrupted for a long time' (Simmel, 413). With trams to catch, busy streets to cross, crowds to be negotiated, shop-windows to draw the eye, newspapers to be read, coffee and tea to be consumed, people were conscious that the world in 1900 was speeding up. Hawking his necktieholders round the streets of Berlin, the reluctant street merchant

Biberkopf articulates a new truth, that people no longer have time on their hands. 'The romantic days are over and won't come back again' (Döblin 1978, 66), he shouts at passers-by. A generation or so earlier, in a celebrated passage on Old Leisure in her historical novel *Adam Bede* (1859), George Eliot addressed the transition from the late-eighteenth to the mid-nineteenth century, noticing how Old Leisure was 'free from that periodicity of sensations which we call post-time' (Eliot, 484). But what does Joyce do with what sociologists and others were discerning was a newly modern predicament affecting 'the sensory foundations of psychic life' (Simmel, 410)? The answer, it has to be conceded, is a bit of a let-down for, characteristically, Joyce turns the predicament into a theme. From Patrick Dignam's 'blooming time' (*U* 10:1129) to Micky Anderson's 'alltimesticking watches' (*U* 10:1215), the episode provides a Shandean meditation upon the aesthetics of space and time that is by turns playful, frustrating, profound and superficial. If Joyce brings order to the chaos of modern life, as T.S. Eliot famously claimed, he does so in a peculiar way, for in many respects 'Wandering Rocks' resists and refuses such high-flown ordering.

Appropriately, in the episode's opening sentence, Conmee resets in his interior pocket his smooth watch. But almost at once Joyce moves off away from time to another discourse. As he descends the steps to catch a tram to Artane, we are made aware of the distinction between time and eternity, between the sacred precincts of the Church and the ordinary world of the streets, between external reality and interior consciousness, between subject and object, but the image of the 'smooth watch' in the 'interior pocket' here reminds us that there is no depth, no immanence, no hierarchy of significance in 'Wandering Rocks', only a watch which tells the time. In an episode whose science is 'Mechanics', the image of a watch that tells the time affords another rye contribution to the discourse on representation and articulation in *Ulysses*. A watch possesses no natural rhythms, is neither attracted to nor repulsed by people and events, tells the time but recognizes no history, links people together in a synchronic embrace but accepts no connection, admits to no origin and no purpose, shares no destiny, lives for the present from which it cannot escape, moves according to an already existing order of things, tells and informs but never speaks or confides.

However, while the science is 'Mechanics', the people described are not robots following a meaningless course. Joyce eschews the connection between automata and the colonial subject. There is a purpose behind their every movement, an inner consciousness, a sign for others. At each point – in spite of the patterning – it is a human world that is emphasized. Auction room bells ring, coins are thrown into the street, a thousand casualties are reported on newspaper hoardings and names such as Hugh C. Love are played on. It is a world subject to chance, tragedy, providence and humour. Indeed, it is a Wellsian world of the 'timedulled chain' in the lapidary's window (*U* 10:801); of the shop assistant who knows how to play her part among the 'ripe shamefaced peaches' (*U* 10:305–6); of the secretary answering the phone and scribbling down a message; of the waitress unloading her tray; of the small man going to law to complain about being insulted by his fellow citizen; of peripatetic music teachers and commercial travellers. One of its most telling moments is when Dilly tackles her father for money in the street. Here perhaps we feel something of real time, of the family circumstances and pressure behind the writing, the improvident father who exposed his family to shame, but who also, as the closing moment of *Finnegans Wake* reminds us, bequeathed to his prodigal son the keys to the kingdom.

'Wandering Rocks' is also saturated with another kind of reading matter that is out of time. Conmee, who should have read Nones before lunch (*U* 10:191), is the author of *Old Times in the Barony*, his 'little book' on the local history round Athlone, a pamphlet first published by the Catholic Truth Society of Ireland in 1900 (Gifford and Seidman describe the pamphlet as a book). Joyce is remorseless in his pursuit of the figure of authority who was twice his superior, first as his Headmaster at Clongowes Wood College and then as Prefect of Studies at Belvedere College, Gardiner Street, Dublin. In 1898 he was appointed Superior of the adjoining St Francis Xavier Community, a position which in the first sentence of 'Wandering Rocks' is alluded to and immediately discounted by the lower case: 'The superior, the very reverend John Conmee S.J.'. Conmee finds truth in God's words (*U* 10:197), but even as he does so, the narrator cannot help noticing a young man and woman with a twig on her skirt appear from a gap in the hedge. Miss Dunne is bored by a novel which perhaps she assumed from its title would be more sensational and more straightforward (*U* 10:371). Bloom reads some sexy lines from *Sweets of Sin* and decides that this is a book to excite Molly (*U* 10:606ff.). Dilly Dedalus, reduced to begging from her father and to periodic visits to the pawnbroker, purchases Chardenal's French primer to learn French (*U* 10:867–8). Each character reads for his or her own purposes: edification, comfort, excitement, vicarious pleasure, acquiring knowledge or supposed knowledge, whether about other languages, cultures or history. But, in each case, there is a mismatch of sorts, so that the emphasis falls less on the subjectivity of experience and more on the gap between reader and world. As 'gnomon', a 'missing' word that appears in the very first paragraph of his first story of *Dubliners*, reminds us, Joyce is a gnomic writer. 'Wandering Rocks' is no exception. The chord it repeatedly strikes is incompleteness, precisely the note that ironically contributes to the narrative cohesion of *Ulysses* as a whole.

'Wandering Rocks' is a labyrinth of misses, many of which can only be discerned on several re-readings and recourse elsewhere to critics and guides. It is an episode which recalls the 'almosting it' of 'Proteus' and 'Lotus-Eaters', but here the world is decidedly less accommodating, and the image of the labyrinth enforces itself, ensnaring the acts of reading and seeing. The Belvedere boys 'sixeyed' Father Conmee (*U* 10: 49); Corny Kelleher 'glanced with his drooping eye' (*U*10:207–8); Boylan, who in the next episode 'eyed, eyed', here 'looked into the cut' of the shop assistant's blouse (*U*10:327); Miss Dunne stares at a poster of Marie Kendall and questions her good looks (*U*10:380–2); M'Coy 'peered into Marcus Tertius Moses' sombre office' (*U* 10:508); the shopman 'lifted eyes bleared with old rheum' (*U* 10:640); Dilly Dedalus looks accusingly into her father's eyes (*U* 10:671); the sun on the windscreen of a motor car prevents Mr Kernan from identifying Ned Lambert's brother (*U* 10:757–60). The city no longer displays 'Signatures of all things I am here to read' (*U* 3:2), but has become, as the Linati scheme reminds us, a 'Hostile Environment'. As Hart pointed out in 1974, the episode not infrequently throws a false scent. When Cashel Boyle O'Connor Fitzmaurice Tisdall Farrell strides past 'Mr Bloom's dental windows' (*U* 10:1115), we could be forgiven for thinking it is Leopold Bloom's window; there is a reference to Grattan's 'stern stone hand' (*U* 10:352), but, in fact, the statue is made of bronze; the Viceregal cavalcade passes not the Royal Canal bridge but the Grand Canal (*U* 10:1273); the '*Res*' and '*Sin*' that Father Conmee reads from his breviary (*U* 10:196, 204) refer not to the Latin word for 'thing' or to moral culpability, but to letters in the Hebrew alphabet.

Even expert readers of this episode continue to trip up, their errors serving to underline that in the eighty years or so since the publication of *Ulysses*, not all the 'reader-traps', as Hart calls them, have been uncovered. After his encounter with Mrs Sheehy, Conmee is reminded of Father Bernard Vaughan's 'cockney voice'. In their notes to this episode, both Gifford and Seidman and, following them, Jeri Johnson, adjudge that Vaughan, speaking with a cockney accent, must self-evidently have been a cockney (Gifford and Seidman, 261; Johnson, 867). And the reader might be tempted to concur, given the evidence: 'he thought on Father Bernard Vaughan's droll eyes and cockney voice' (*U* 10:33–4). But Vaughan, whom Joyce refers to familiarly in one of his letters as 'B.V.' (*Letters* II, 182), and who was, according to Stanislaus, the model for Father Purdon in 'Grace' (*Letters* II, 182, n.1), a preacher, that is, of Society Sermons, was not a cockney, and he only used a cockney accent for dramatic effect when preaching or acting out a scene from the Gospels. There is a relevant passage worth citing in full by his Jesuit biographer, C.C. Martindale:

> A far more weighty, or shall I say ponderous, objection was, that Fr. Vaughan used, when taking the layman's part, a deal of slang. It was not slang, but honest Cockney dialect. But, it was urged, sermons should be in as beautiful an English as possible. The so-called uneducated can quite well appreciate a good thing when they see or hear it. Certainly: Fr. Vaughan, who was later on to insist that soldiers, in camp or hospital,

could quite well recognise good music and ought to get it, would have been the last to deny that what you offered to anyone should be, if not the best of its kind, at least the best that you could give. But, he would continue, these Dialogues are not sermons, but as different as possible from sermons. Should it be said that none but the most pure English was ever suitable in church, he would quite simply have disagreed. He would have said that he could not have produced the effect he wanted so satisfactorily in any other way – he used business jargon freely in Manchester, and, though less freely, the idiotic slang of Mayfair, which was real slang, in that elect demesne. But Catholic doctrine, it was truly said, can be stated in the simplest, yet the most dignified language. No doubt: but whether the working-man's own thoughts can be so conveyed, may be debated. Fr. Vaughan wanted to produce his listeners thinking aloud, and to do that he had to take not only the thoughts out of their head, but the words in which they would have articulated them, could they have done so at all, out of their mouths. Thereupon the objection reduced itself to this – Would those have been their words; and if so, would not the hearers have held themselves insulted by the very accuracy of the imitation? No working-man talks, it was said, in such torrential Cockney, least of all with a priest, for whose sake he grooms his language, any more than schoolboys use the extraordinary jargon with which Mr. Kipling, for example, equips them in *Stalkey and Co.* That author made, as it were, a catalogue of slang, and resolved to get it all in at all costs. And once more, no one likes to feel he is 'talked down to'. Whether Fr. Vaughan did his Cockney well, I cannot be asked to judge. I have heard him talk French, Italian, American so as to keep whole roomfuls in helpless laughter for an hour, yet all these languages were spoken by him with complete inaccuracy; and as I have said, his Lancashire talk was frequently all wrong, yet gave, most certainly, the due delightful impression. (Martindale, 141–2)

Vaughan was clearly a controversial figure in his day, the subject of thousands of newspaper cuttings and about whom Joyce once wrote: 'I never see his name but I expect some enormity' (*Letters* II, 182). Conmee, too, adds his voice to this appraisal, but it would be surprising if he were mistaken about Vaughan's accent. It is reasonable to conclude, therefore, that it is not Joyce, in this instance, who is responsible for throwing a false scent, but later commentators.

Gifford and Seidman compound their error in their annotation to *Ulysses* 10:38: 'The Vaughans were a famous "good family" in Wales, but London-born Father Vaughan's connection seems to have been in name rather than heritage' (Gifford and Seidman, 261). In point of fact, Bernard Vaughan was born at the family estate at Courtfield in Herefordshire. He was the younger brother of Cardinal Vaughan and was educated by the Jesuits at Stonyhurst, a leading Catholic public school in Lancashire.[4] A different gloss is therefore called for if we are to do justice to Conmee's attitude to Vaughan. The class-conscious (and perhaps envious) Conmee takes care to distance himself from Vaughan, a Jesuit who mixed in high-class circles and had won fame as a preacher (but who also believed in social action and justice for the poor).[5] Thus, 'zealous', at the other end of the spectrum to his own 'interior' (*U* 10:36, 2), is a perfect word in this context, since it is sufficiently weighted to allow for a positive connotation, were Conmee's charitable disposition to be impugned.[6] The word also invariably carries the connotation of too much zeal. The assault on Vaughan's character is continued in the phrases 'really' and 'he said', the irony barely concealed in the repetition and in the use of the qualifier: 'Really he was. And really did great good in his way. ... He loved Ireland, he said, and he loved the Irish' (*U* 10:36–7). But perhaps Conmee's most damning phrase about his fellow-Jesuit is 'Of good family too would one think it?' (*U* 10:38) This I take to mean: 'One wouldn't think he came from a good family given the language he uses'. The series of uncharitable thoughts is sealed with a final put-down that includes a possible innuendo: 'Welsh, were they not?' (*U* 10:38) – that is, not Irish.[7]

Joyce invites us to push on beyond the contrast between the anonymity of the city and the knowable community. Dublin, we need little reminding, is, or was, a village, and, for Williams, 'a village is an epitome of direct relationships' (Williams, 203). Dublin as a knowable community is a given for Joyce. That was part of the problem. There was no escape, and too much was known about you, as can be observed in the often scurrilous comments about Bloom and Molly by Simon Dedalus and others. Interestingly, the question Joyce never really explores is: how was intimacy possible when other people knew all your intimate details? He tends not to distinguish but to elide privacy and intimacy, as if nothing more was needed for intimacy to be established than disclosure of private details. Something cognate occurs with the man in the macintosh. He is one of the few figures in Joyce's novel who remains in the shadows, and even he is transformed by the ever-active word city into Mr McIntosh in the newspaper report on Dignam's funeral – as if nothing or nobody could be allowed to remain unincorporated. In contrast, the London child, according to Ford Madox Ford in *The Soul of London* (1905), discovers sooner or later that 'the sense of impersonality, of the abstraction that London is, will become one of the most intimate factors of his daily life' (Ford, 8–9).

With the knowable community in mind, we might turn to the religious community which surrounded Joyce from childhood to adulthood. Conmee and Vaughan were members of the worldwide Jesuit community, whose Missions to China and Africa are recalled in passing by Joyce in *Ulysses*. The most powerful Order in the Roman Catholic Church, its shock-troops, attracted some remarkable individuals who valued not so much intimacy as a wider sense of community, which, ironically, was based in part on their alienation from ordinary life, from community. The English Province had jurisdiction over Ireland, and, when asked, members moved between religious houses and schools. Thus, the poet

Gerard Manley Hopkins, an English Jesuit, taught at Stonyhurst in Lancashire and at Joyce's old university – he is buried without an individual headstone in the common Jesuit plot at Glasnevin Cemetery in Dublin. The Irish Jesuit priest George Tyrrell, who converted to Catholicism in his youth and who, incidentally, lodged for a short while in the 1870s in Eccles Street in Dublin, trained in England and continental Europe. Like Joyce, Tyrrell was also interested in the politics of 'Scylla and Charybdis', in destabilizing the relation between authority and liberty, between 'the rock of tradition' and 'the whirlpool of progress' (Petre, vol. 2, 318). As we learn from his autobiography, Tyrrell's Modernist heresy stemmed in part from his belief that the Jesuit Order had become a reactionary force, a view not unlike that expressed in 'Grace'. Joyce doesn't mention the excommunicated Tyrrell or the reclusive Hopkins in his work, but Conmee and Vaughan would have known them. They, too, belonged to the same community as the Belgian Jesuit who wrote *Le Nombre des Élus*, a controversial study on the number of those who will be saved, and the sixteenth-century Jesuit martyr St Peter Claver, the subject, as we see from 'Lotus-Eaters', of a sermon by Conmee. So in the Irish context there's nothing particularly special about the idea of a knowable community, or, if there is, it is more than a matter of 'direct relationships', and it adds therefore a necessary qualification to Williams's opposition between the city and the country and makes us think again about Ford's contrast between intimacy and impersonality.

But what of the community, the company, both in the present and in the future, which is able to appreciate humour and the switching between real life and fictional portrayal? According to Martindale, 'Fr. Vaughan wanted to produce his listeners thinking aloud'; the contrast with Conmee's idea of propriety, decorum and spirituality could not be better indicated. A sermon of Vaughan's of 1907, 'Christ Before Pilate', is reproduced in his book *Society, Sin and The Saviour* (Vaughan, 123), but, by comparison with the snippet that appears in 'Wandering Rocks', it is a tame affair and does not reflect the Vaughan who obviously delighted in not mincing his words: 'Pilate! Wy don't you old back that owlin mob?' (*U* 10:35) The larger theme of 'Wandering Rocks', of Church and State, is on display in this snatch from his sermon and characteristically obscured by the language and the humour and perhaps by the suggestion that, in Conmee's eyes, Vaughan is himself a representative of the mob. Earlier in the day, an example of thinking aloud is given a more nuanced twist. Bloom recalls listening to a sermon by Vaughan where, again, the congregation is treated to the familiar Ignatian scene of Christ versus Pilate, the way of God or the way of the world. Only, this time, Bloom's response is less enthusiastic than Mrs Sheehy's: 'Christ or Pilate? Christ, but don't keep us up all night over it' (*U* 5:398–9).

## The Order of Things

Because Dublin is a word city, it is full of errors, and therefore human. This is the lesson Joyce communicates to those who come to him for urban enlightenment. *Errare est humanum*, to err is human. According to Le Corbusier, writing two years after the publication of *Ulysses*, 'The analysis of a city belongs to the realm of scientific investigation' (Le Corbusier, 72). This is not Joyce's project and his intensely observed city, the subject he tackles with the single-mindedness of a scientific inquiry, yields a different kind of insight. If you use tram routes and timetables in real life or as part of the fictional recreation of the city, make sure you check their accuracy. The most powerful experiences can't be repeated but experiments can be, so that repetition in one sense tells us all that is needed to get round the city. The same is true of the flow of a river in case you want a throwaway piece of paper to be noticed by different people at different times and locations. In novels from *The Rainbow* (1915) to *Lady Chatterley's Lover* (1928), the iron cage of bureaucracy and routine that Max Weber saw descending on modern life is rattled by Joyce's English contemporary D.H. Lawrence. As can be discerned from his famous letter to Grant Richards in May 1906 defending his stories that were to comprise *Dubliners* (*Letters* II, 134), Joyce, like his one-time mentor Ibsen, is initially attracted to the related theme of paralysis, but he then discovers another route to liberation. Imagine nothing that could not be imagined, and ensure you include errors. This, we might well conclude, constitutes Joyce's epistemological answer to a moral question.

Anyone steeped in the rule of St Benedict or educated by priests who were required at set times of the day to recite the Divine Office understood the value of obedience. In spite of his rebellious *non serviam* stance, head to one side, hands in pockets in a famous photo taken by Constantine Curran in 1902, the Irish exile is the modern writer par excellence regulated by obedience, but his obedience is not to the Church or some higher or lower authority but to language as heard and reality as constructed, to 'whatever he has seen and heard' (*Letters* II, 134). Faithfulness not to religious order but to the order of things – this he had in abundance, as if this constituted the route to salvation. He was in this sense a follower, a repeater, and he made all his readers followers, condemned, like Clive Hart, to repeat the Joycean way or to follow the black riders or letters eeling their way like the H.E.L.Y'S advertisement across the pages of his city. Whatever is known or otherwise about the City of God and the world without end, Joyce was convinced the earthly city could be accurately described.

'Wandering Rocks' is realistic to a fault. No sooner does the 'superior' step down from the presbytery steps than he is greeted by a onelegged sailor, and the reader familiar with Flaubert's novel *Madame Bovary* (1857) might recall the club-footed Hippolyte or the tramp who comes to haunt Emma on her return home from sexual adventures in Rouen. Politically, the encounter is also a reminder of the deformity of social relations in a country under the twin yoke of Rome and the Crown. Hart uses the term 'microhistory', but, unlike *Dubliners*, 'Wandering Rocks', as I have been arguing, is not 'a chapter of the moral history of my country' (*Letters* II, 134), and its political perspective is partly obscured in the labyrinth of signs. The reader delights in making connections, whether local, structural, thematic, intertextual or whatever. But, aside from the first and last sections, and the use of possibly charged images of pawnbrokers and auctionrooms, the political meaning tends not to shed light on the sections within the episode. In 'Telemachus', the theme of usurpation informs the whole episode, from 'Stately' through to the final word 'Usurper' (*U* 1:1, 744). 'Wandering Rocks' takes up the theme of the two masters enigmatically announced by Stephen in the first episode, but there is something muffled about Joyce's amplification.

According to Samuel Beckett, reality to Joyce was a sort of paradigm; he was always looking for similarities and simultaneities in words and things.[8] What is remarkable about this episode is not only the realistic texture but also Joyce's absolute control and dominance over the material at his disposal. Each detail in 'Wandering Rocks' is recorded as if it were as important as any other. Structurally, each section exists on its own, separated from the others by a series of three asterisks (in the original typescript, these asterisks were in the form of a spaced-out triangle and were therefore more prominent). Until we reach the final two sections, the episode is written throughout in short paragraphs, often of only one or two sentences in length. No signposts are given to the reader for the appearance of interpolations, and no-one accepts responsibility for the changes in narrative voice or mode. Shifts between the definite and indefinite article – or rather the absence of these – reinforce the sense of dislocation for the reader. Thus, 'a' onelegged sailor makes an appearance in the first section, but, when he appears again at the beginning of section 3, he is still 'a' rather than 'the' onelegged sailor (*U* 10:7, 228). Conversely, when connections are made by the reader – the author / narrator / Arranger is reluctant to make connections – they are sometimes quite trivial, as, for example, with Patrick Dignam junior's use of the mild 'Bloomian' expletive 'blooming' in his section: 'The blooming stud was too small for the buttonhole of the shirt, blooming end to it' (*U* 10:1155–7). Or take the word 'arch' which appears throughout the episode. A silent jet of hayjuice 'arches' from Corny Kelleher's mouth (*U* 10:221); the assistant in Thornton's bends 'archly' (*U* 10:333); on perusing *Sweets of Sin*, we read that Bloom's nostrils 'arched themselves for prey' (*U* 10:621); Ned Lambert takes his visitors among the 'flickering arches' of St Mary's Abbey (*U* 10:402). Then, too, the significance of certain details is kept deliberately in the background. It is one moment in one day in the life of Dublin but it is also a day full of significance for Joyce and Nora, the young woman who was working at Finn's hotel when Cashel Boyle O'Connor Fitzmaurice Tisdall Farrell pompously strides past it in the final section of 'Wandering Rocks' (*U* 10: 1260). Mulligan tells Haines that Stephen 'is going to write something in ten years' (*U* 10:1089–90), which would make it 1914, precisely the year Joyce embarked on the mammoth undertaking that would subsequently materialize in the book we are reading.

The Hungarian critic Georg Lukács, writing in 1909 about Thomas Mann, argues that 'the most serious regard for things is always somewhat ironic, for somewhere or other the great gulf between cause and effect, between the conjuring of fate and the fate conjured must become obvious. And the more natural the peaceful flow of things appears, the truer and deeper this irony will be' (Lukács 1964, 136–7). Joyce believed that if Dublin were ever destroyed, it could be rebuilt using his book (Budgen, 69). But Joyce has delivered, in Umberto Eco's words, 'a work that goes well beyond his poetics' (Eco, 67). Realistic detail, attention to an accurate recording of reality, how ignorance of tram or train timetables would be held against a writer – as was the case with George Moore – these are the surface features of Joyce's view of the world. But Joyce's aesthetic occupies only a portion of the territory claimed by 1930s reportage and documentary, for, in Joyce, the more the 'world-as-thing' is scrutinized, the more 'conceptual' it becomes. 'Wandering Rocks' affords a version of reality, the 'world-as-watch', but this should never be entirely confused with reality. When plaques are erected in Dublin commemorating people or events in *Ulysses*, it is worth remembering that they do Joyce both a service and a disservice, for Joyce's 'serious regard for things is always somewhat ironic'.

# 4

# Joyce, Woolf and the Metropolitan Imagination

## Barracks

'Barracks are an instrument of war', the military historian James Douet rightly concedes at the beginning of *British Barracks 1600–1914* (1998). There could be no clearer indication of this than the map he provides of the location of barracks and garrisons in Britain and Ireland in the first decade of the eighteenth century. Ireland enjoyed some seventy-eight barracks, roughly half cavalry, half infantry, and, with the exception of the mountainous regions in the north-west and west, they were scattered evenly throughout the country (Douet, 15). In contrast, England at that period maintained only twenty-eight barracks, 'North Britain' five and Wales none at all. The English barracks were mainly positioned on the coast to defend a sea empire, while in Ireland as many barracks were inland as on the coast, a reminder of the threat posed by the enemy within. A hundred and fifty years later in 1855, as if there were not enough, what is now the most famous barracks in Ireland, the one at the Curragh in County Kildare, was commissioned with accommodation for 10,000 men. *Tit-Bits* reliably informed its readers on 18 September 1886 that there were 24,000 officers and men in Ireland, of whom 3,000 were cavalry, 2,400 artillery and 14,000 infantry. As for the squat, thick-walled Martello Towers, these were erected during the Napoleonic era round the coastline of Britain and Ireland as look-out posts in the event of a French invasion. They had a swivel gun on a platform at the top of the tower and accommodation inside for a garrison of twelve 'pensioners'. By January 1884, according to a report in *Tit-Bits*, most of them had been dismantled. Twenty years later, we find them being rented out, as happened to the one at Sandycove, which became in turn the setting for the opening 'garrison' episode of *Ulysses*, an episode that recalls its historical setting on the opening page when the incorrigibly upbeat

Buck Mulligan declares to his 'messmates' while shaving: '– Back to barracks!' (*U* 1:19).

There was a long tradition, therefore, of military involvement in Irish affairs, and most of this involvement was directed at the civilian population, whether that was to do with the prevention of smuggling, the implementation of Coercion Acts – especially in the nineteenth century with the constant threat to landlords and their agents – or the suppression of local disturbances as referred to in Chapter 6. In Bartholomew's 1904 *Survey Gazetteer of the British Isles*, the year in which *Ulysses* is set, we learn that Dublin possessed 'several extensive military and constabulary barracks' and that among its principal objects of interest is the Castle, which contains 'an armoury for 80,000 men' (247). On the accompanying coloured map of Dublin, in addition to the Castle armoury, nine barracks can be identified dotted throughout the city and on both sides of the Liffey. By contrast, central London, with a population some twenty times greater than Dublin, boasted a mere six barracks or so, down from the thirteen barracks that protected central London in 1861.[1] At that time, in 1861, as in the eighteenth century, cavalry regiments were involved in policing, while infantry regiments were intended for garrison duty or colonial service. At Regent's Park and Hyde Park Barracks, there was accommodation for 390 and 369 horses respectively, while Wellington Barracks, which was positioned adjacent to Buckingham Palace, catered for 1,418 men and non-commissioned officers. Nearby, in case more support was needed, was Chelsea Barracks. Kensington Palace could call on the Hyde Park Barracks within a mile, while Horse Guards protected Downing Street and Whitehall. Regent's Park was flanked by two barracks on Regent's Canal and on Ordnance Road. As for the East End, on the 1904 map, there was a militia barracks at Dalston in Hackney, presumably for use against the civilian population, unlike the other barracks which were positioned to protect royalty and the establishment.[2]

I begin this account of Joyce, Woolf and the metropolitan imagination with reference to the history and location of British Army barracks in these islands because the work of these two Irish and British modernists affords a sustained engagement with forms of power. I have said nothing about the militia units or the 16,000 men in the London Metropolitan Police or the 1,800 men in the Dublin Metropolitan Police (DMP), who were at the forefront in the maintenance of law and order, for it is the military who reveal what is at stake here.[3] In terms of crime, Dublin at the turn of the twentieth century was no less law-abiding than Birmingham and considerably more so than Liverpool. Equally, the DMP was an overwhelmingly Catholic force, remembered by Sebastian Barry with particular affection nearly three generations after its demise in plays such as *The Steward of Christendom* (1995) and *Our Lady of Sligo* (1998). But for Joyce, his city – not 'the city' as was the subject of my last chapter – was effectively occupied, as the Earl of Dudley's procession in 'Wandering Rocks' reminds us.

For Woolf, power was at once institutionally transparent and ideologically diffuse, highly visible in terms of its gendered trappings such as wigs and uniforms, gowns and garters, and at the same time more damaging and extensive than often imagined. On the very first page of *To the Lighthouse* she takes care to describe the six-year-old boy James cutting out pictures from the Army and Navy shopping catalogue, an image of childhood and Edwardian innocence, 'fringed with joy', later transformed in adulthood by the destruction of the Great War in the clash of European armies and navies. During the staging of the Pageant of English history in *Between the Acts* (1941), Colonel Mayhew rightly asks 'What's history without the Army, eh?' (141), but the question is beautifully deflected by Woolf with the addition of the old buffer's tag 'eh?'. Woolf understood how power was attractive and, crucially, vague – 'all this' is a constant recourse by Mrs Dalloway. She also understood how there was nothing vague about the exercise of power, as *Three Guineas* (1938), the polemic she composed in the shadow of war, constantly underlines. Equally, she knew how to confront contemporary history through filters of times past. As Julia Briggs records, the middle section of *To the Lighthouse*, 'Time Passes', a section normally read in terms of the passage of time and the Great War, was actually composed during the 'gloom' and heightened political agitation of the General Strike of 1926 (Briggs, 176).

Before Big Ben strikes, Mrs Dalloway feels a 'hush ... an indescribable pause'. When royalty passes in a car on Bond Street, she senses that 'mystery had brushed them with her wing; they had heard the voice of authority; the spirit of religion was abroad with her eyes bandaged tight and her lips gaping wide' (*Mrs Dalloway*, 4, 17). In 'Wandering Rocks', an equivalent scene from *Ulysses*, the King's representative in Ireland prompts a mixture of indifference and contempt. Only the barmaids display any signs of cordial greeting and then one can't be sure if they want anything but to be seen and admired themselves:

> The viceroy was most cordially greeted on his way through the metropolis ... unsaluted by Mr Dudley White, B. L., M. A., ... stroking his nose with his forefinger, undecided whether he should arrive at Phibsborough more quickly by a triple change of tram or by hailing a car or on foot through Smithfield, Constitution hill and Broadstone terminus. ... Richie Goulding ... saw him with surprise. ... [A]n elderly female ... smiled credulously on the representative of His Majesty. From its sluice in Wood quay wall under Tom Devan's office Poddle river hung out in fealty a tongue of liquid sewage. ... Miss Kennedy's head by Miss Douce's head watched and admired. On Ormond quay Mr Simon Dedalus, steering his way from the greenhouse for the subsheriff's office, stood still in midstreet and brought his hat low. His Excellency graciously returned Mr Dedalus' greeting. (*U* 10:1182–1202)

Joyce sets up the contrast in an opening sentence which is told from the viceroy's perspective but in the style of a court report in a newspaper. For the reader, the word 'metropolis' almost immediately gives pause for thought, for what is this but the language of inflation that accompanies those in power and in their every movement – after all, the Viceroy, William Humble Ward, who in real life was given to extravagance even though his middle name suggested otherwise, was simply involved that June afternoon in fund-raising activities.[4] The use of 'unsaluted' in the next sentence carries within it a double viewpoint – saluted is a common word in Hiberno-English, meaning not so much a military salute but simply saying hello. From Dudley White's perspective, a number of possible attitudes can be identified: resentment, defiance, a republican gesture, a sense that with his standing, name and education he is above the hoi polloi or not easily impressed. On the other hand, how anyone would know White's action is 'unsaluted' is unclear, and in a court of law it would be difficult to prove that it was a gesture of protest or indeed signified anything. Dudley White, whose first name coincides with Ward's title, is preoccupied with planning his route, which is also across the metropolis, and he has his finger on his nose in a gesture that could be misinterpreted. From the Viceroy's colonial perspective, treason was potentially everywhere, so while he imagines he is processing through the streets of the metropolis and the recipient of cordial greetings, he perhaps begins to notice not so much sedition as something which is on the way to becoming an adverse marker, for he is 'unsaluted' by the natives.

The ambiguous gestures keep coming in this passage and, needless to say, we are some distance from the hush of Big Ben or the mystery on Bond Street. To smile credulously is, again, to risk misinterpretation, for 'credulously' is accompanied not by a clearly stated negative prefix such as 'un-' but by a missing or ambiguous negative 'in-'. The old woman is not smiling incredulously but credulously. The reader is unsure if this is something positive or negative or if indeed the sentence is focalized through the Viceroy. Similarly, 'with surprise': how is this to be interpreted, in positive terms or simply neutral (which is then taken by the viceroy as a sign of approval)? More familiar satire in the Irish, Swiftian, excremental mode returns in the next sentence where power meets its most majestic salute in the city's summertime effluence. Excrement, too, belongs to the imperial sphere, albeit in this case administered by the Dublin Corporation, and it is human in the tongue-like way it conveys fealty. As for Simon Dedalus, he brings his hat low perhaps, as has been suggested, because on his exiting from the greenhouse (toilet) he realizes the flies on his trousers are undone. His gesture is also misinterpreted by the Lord Lieutenant of Ireland – or perhaps his predicament across the colonial divide is indeed well-understood by him.

The Viceroy processes through the streets of Dublin oblivious of the ironic unity he creates among the people. Nothing disturbs the comfortable view of reality for those in power. Conmee, the spiritual patrolman who launches 'Wandering Rocks', believes in the providence of the Creator; the Viceroy assumes he is 'most cordially greeted on his way through the metropolis'. Christ and Caesar are both involved in philanthropic pursuits, Conmee in obtaining a place for Paddy Dignam's son at an orphan school in Artane, the Viceroy in opening the Mirus bazaar in aid of funds for Mercer's hospital. But their interest in charitable activities merely confirms positions of power, and through it all Joyce seems to be mocking, especially through the language of excess, such an attempt at hegemony in Ireland. Neither of them can see any reality other than that which is filtered through their own ideological lens. The structural unity of what is the longest paragraph in 'Wandering Rocks' is designed to reflect the Crown's view of Ireland, but its unity is constantly undercut by the less than enthusiastic responses on the part of His Majesty's loyal subjects.

This deliberate mixing of narratorial perspectives and playful misinterpretation provides not only the groundwork for humour in the passage just cited but also an insight into Joyce's metropolitan imagination. Woolf's ironizing mode issues from a sense of continuity between the outsider and the centres of power, so that even a cutting remark such as 'the spirit of religion was abroad with her eyes bandaged tight and her lips gaping wide' manages to keep Mrs Dalloway and her class within the range of our sympathy. Joyce's mode is essentially satiric and reflects the lack of connection, the gulf that is, between himself and the Crown. While Woolf is cutting, Joyce cuts or, rather, cuts out, offering no way back for His Majesty's representative, no hand of friendship, no salvation this side of colonial rule. The sheer number of soldiers constantly moving through the streets, given to patronizing the red-light area and threatening, like Private Carr, to 'wring the neck of any fucker says a word against my bleeding fucking king' (*U* 15:4644–5), the inescapable physical presence of the great pile of Dublin Castle, the network of spies (represented in *Ulysses* by Corny Kelleher), meant that any idea of a metropolitan imagination for someone brought up in Dublin was steeped in resentment or resistance. In 'Counterparts', to take a small but instructive example from the paralysed city of Joyce's youthful collection of stories, Farrington's tram 'let him down at Shelbourne Road and he steered his great body along in the shadow of the wall of the barracks' (*D* 97). So pervasive is the army's presence in the city that it's almost as if the narrator doesn't need to identify it as the Beggars Bush Barracks, a barracks which in fact was a 'semi-fortified complex' built in 1827 (Douet, 111) and located within 800 metres of the Ascendancy's town houses in Merrion Square. Little details remind us that from start to finish the narrative of *Ulysses* and the fate of its characters are permeated by the image and reality of barracks. In 'Telemachus', the 'domed' living room of the tower is described as 'gloomy' (*U* 1:323); in 'Penelope', when

Molly Bloom complains about the size of her house, it is natural for her (and for an author bent on narrative cohesion and correspondences) to have recourse to the image of a barracks: 'I dont like being alone in this big barracks of a place at night' (*U* 18:978).

Woolf's imperial background resulted in her imagining she lived on borrowed time; Joyce's colonial background brought forth its opposite, a long-term project to decolonize the mind and at the same time rid it of any religious idea of a world without end. In 1904, all of Dublin existed in the shadow of the wall of the barracks. In *Ulysses*, two barracks are mentioned by name, the Linenhall barracks, within 400 metres of Bloom's Eccles Street, and the Portobello barracks on the South Circular Road within 400 metres of Joyce's Catholic University. But, repeatedly, citizens come into direct contact with the State and everywhere there lingers the Crown's presence and its fresh engagement with the Boers, most vividly captured in Stephen's striking association of culture and politics in the Library episode: 'Khaki Hamlets don't hesitate to shoot' (*U* 9:133). By contrast, in Woolf's fiction there are no barracks (apart from a newspaper report in *Between the Acts* about the attempted rape of a woman in their barracks by troopers on guard in Whitehall), no informers, no assassins as there are in *Ulysses* with the repeated references to the murder in Phoenix Park of the Chief Secretary of Ireland in 1882, no trials as there are with Bloom's arraignment in 'Circe', and, with *Finnegans Wake* in mind and Richard Piggot's part in the London *Times*'s conspiracy against Parnell in 1887, no conspiracy or forgers.

## I Couldn't Live Without This

Dublin therefore was not a city to celebrate in quite the way London is in Woolf. In *The London Scene* (1982), the five articles she wrote in 1931–2 for publication in *Good Housekeeping*, Woolf delights in the city she constantly dramatizes in her novels: the docks and the Port of London, Oxford Street, 'Great Men's Houses', abbeys and cathedrals and the House of Commons. She was never in any doubt that London was, in the words of Elizabeth Barret Browning's spaniel Flush, 'the heart of civilisation' (*Flush*, 20), where the word 'civilisation' carries all its Victorian meanings and associations. Even the journey by express train to London, as the narrator enthuses in a memorable passage in *Night and Day* (1919), 'can still be a very pleasant and romantic adventure .... They were bound for London; they must have precedence of all traffic not similarly destined' (336). For a rare untroubled second in *The Waves* (1931), in a passage that consciously invokes Wordsworth's poem 'Lines Composed Upon Westminster Bridge' (1803), Bernard romantically thinks: 'She hums and murmurs; she awaits us' (*The Waves*, 95). The 1890s also left its mark on her imagination but, unlike Hubert Crackanthorpe, a typical writer of that decade, she could never write as he does in *Vignettes* (1896) about crowds spilling into the Strand: 'The city disgorges ... and over all things hovers the spirit of London's grim unrest' (Crackanthorpe, 55–6). Flush has a pavement view of the London season at its height, but while the pavements are cold there is no 'grim unrest', only for his master connection and humour: 'A pall of sound, a cloud of interwoven humming, fell over the city in one confluent growl' (*Flush*, 91). As Woolf informs us in one of her essays, contrast had its own attraction for her, as it does for most Londoners: 'Nothing is more fascinating than to grope and stumble in the alternate darkness and splendour of Elizabethan London' (*Common Reader Second Series*, 262).

Wherever she turns as she walks out at her favourite hour between four and five in the afternoon, Woolf notices things. On her way to the Tower she fondly recalls 'little alleys with brass bound curtains and the river smell and the old woman reading' (*A Writer's Diary*, 309). This is her London, 'my England', as she hears the city's moods and internalizes its history. 'Cockney' Woolf, as she called herself when marooned in Sussex during the Blitz (*Letters* VI, 460), must have repeatedly felt as Jinny does in *The Waves* that in the heart of London 'I am in the heart of life' (*The Waves*, 165). The two were one: life and London shared a single heart – and, the good ambassador she was, we could count on one hand the number of times in her work there is mention of the fog which hung three thousand feet thick over the metropolis on at least forty days of the year (see *Tit-Bits*, 25 March 1893). In the words of a recent commentator, London for Woolf was 'a theater of vitality and transience' (Alter, 120).

Shining through everything he wrote from 'The Dead', which he believed reflected a more generous attitude to his country, to *Ulysses*, which he fancifully imagined could be employed to rebuild Dublin as it was in 1904 if it were ever destroyed in the future, is Joyce's tribute to his native city. But Joyce was incapable of delighting in his city in the unaffected way Woolf could. Near the beginning of an early story such as 'An Encounter' he invites us to share a sense of delight even if it is couched in a boy's over-written style: 'We pleased ourselves with the spectacle of Dublin's commerce – the barges signalled from far away by their curls of woolly smoke, the brown fishing fleet beyond Ringsend, the big white sailing-vessel which was being discharged on the opposite quay' (*D* 23). The uplift, however, serves a darker purpose, for this is a boy's adventure story that goes wrong. In 'Two Gallants', after watching his friend meet up with a woman for the evening, Lenehan walks listlessly down Grafton Street and finds 'trivial all that was meant to charm him' (*D* 56), a phrase that could stand for any number of Joyce's characters. In 'After the Race', Dublin wears 'the mask of a capital', but it is a mask and another form of paralysis therefore to which the revellers contribute.

Woolf's city is also at the centre of a worldwide empire, albeit in decline. As a recent historian of 1900 London notes, 'In London's crowded streets one might hear all the accents of the empire' (Schneer, 80). Indoors, as we learn in *Night and Day*, 'There were always visitors – uncles and aunts and cousins "from India"' (34), where the inverted commas signify what the young Stephen girls perhaps thought of the trail of family members they couldn't put a name to. Soldiers and civil servants return from abroad, as with Septimus Warren and Peter Walsh in *Mrs Dalloway*, some with physical scars, others with emotional scars, but Big Ben continues to sound. With prominent obelisks to men such as Nelson and Wellington celebrating British military exploits, with street names such as Great Britain Street and Fleet Street which insisted on a British or London connection, and with pillar boxes painted red and bearing the initials of royalty and the insignia of the Crown, Joyce's city couldn't hide from the fact that it belonged to the British Empire. Even when London is compared to a 'town cut out of grey-blue cardboard', as it is by William Rodney in *Night and Day*, its reality is never in doubt for Woolf and her characters: '"I couldn't live without this" – and he waved his hand toward the City' (64). Ironically, Joyce could and did live without his city, but, even when he imagines it wearing a mask or betraying the presence of the Crown, the fascination with its reality never left him.

Bacon's 1910 *Pictorial Map of London* appeared the same year as Forster's 'London' novel *Howards End*, and in many respects it provides the best visual aid to that novel. Attractively sketched in miniature are all the Victorian entry-points to the great metropolis in the shape of the railway termini, buildings which Forster compared to modern-day cathedrals. At the hub of the rail network, London marked the point of departure and the point of arrival. Its population was growing incredibly fast, so much so that Bartholomew's *Gazetteer* recorded without any sense of anxiety that the city had no clearly defined limit and that it possibly covered some 700 square miles (Bartholomew, 516). Its centre, however, was in place and it remained somewhere to get across (by bus, tube or taxi) but not through. If *Howards End* is a London novel it is also, as the emphasis on passage through its termini reminds us, about coming to terms with London, a city which is not only 'intelligent without purpose' but which 'lies beyond everything' (102). While there is a lyrical strain in Woolf, we rarely encounter in Joyce or Woolf either a coming to terms with their native cities or a sense that their city lay beyond everything.

Each of the railway termini connected London with the provinces and the wider world beyond. *Howards End* begins in the country, with the images of a wych-elm and a meadow of newly mown hay, with the old England of the seasons and the shires, and it explores the continuity or otherwise between two sets of values embodied in two families, the hard-nosed Wilcoxes, Matthew Arnold's 'barbarians', and the sensitive and cultured Schlegels, who 'see life steadily and see it whole', Arnold's phrase that surfaces throughout the novel. As the title of *A Passage to*

*India* (1924) confirms, Forster is interested in journeys which link history, society and the cosmos. Contrast this with the journey to the lighthouse in Woolf's novel of that name. Here the journey – not a journey between London and the provinces – retains the look of a narrative device, where the physical journey stands apart from and remains to some extent unintegrated into the spiritual journeys made by the various characters. There is a moment in Pat Murphy's film *Nora* (1999) where the director imagines Joyce and Nora forced to take shelter in an empty building as a herd of cattle are driven though the streets of Dublin. The scene is striking but not particularly authentic. The country rarely surfaces in Joyce's portrayal of his city, and when it does the portrait is frequently unflattering. In *A Portrait*, Ireland is famously compared to an 'old sow that eats her farrow' (*P* 203). In *Ulysses*, the attention given to foot-and-mouth disease is presumably meant to be read not only as a specific satire on Mr Deasy, the Nestor figure who believes he has a cure for a disease that still ravages agricultural communities, but also as another Joycean take on Dublin talk. Almost entirely missing from Joyce are any garden scenes or what one commentator on Woolf has termed the 'urban pastoral' (Alter, 105). Forster, by way of contrast, roots his Edwardian novel in dual perspectives, in both the social and the personal, in both the symbolic and the economic, in the city and the country.

Forster pits the rural, feminine values of spirit, presence and continuity against the careless Wilcoxes, identified in part with masculine, London values. He doesn't have it in him to see the history of capitalism as 'the subordination of the country to the town', as Trotsky wrote in 1906 (Deutscher, 460). But, in what we might consider a critique of the metropolitan imagination, he does gesture towards the possibility of the country resisting the encroachment of London values. Such a gesture is missing from Woolf, whose novels are dominated by London even when set elsewhere. For Woolf, the countryside represents a retreat from the noise of London, a second home where holidays are spent or a place of origin as it is for the Suffragette Mary Datchet in *Night and Day*. The same moon and the same night sky are observed by people in London and in the country, trees push out their leaves in spring, and characters such as Mrs Hilbery fondly imagine that 'one would think such beautiful things if one lived in the country' (*Night and Day*, 199). When Ralph Dedham, who works in Lincoln's Inn Fields, visits Lincolnshire, where Mary's father is a Rector, he imagines writing a history of the English village. Neither the author nor her characters get beyond fairly conventional views of nature and the countryside. The countryside is a place to set up an easel and paint *en pleine aire*, as Roger Fry and Woolf's sister Vanessa were wont to do, and as Lily Briscoe does in *To the Lighthouse* (1928).

## Disturbances

The fundamental opposition or 'precipice' in Woolf is not between rural and urban, but, as the title of an early novel suggests, between night and day, between thought and action, 'between the life of solitude and the life of society' (315). Only the river and 'the fluidity out there' (*To the Lighthouse*, 132) threaten to allow nature to disturb the universe. Thus it is that the Thames Embankment is always worth noticing when it appears in her work, producing its own 'stream of thoughts' as it does for Ralph in *Night and Day* (250). The uncivilized Mrs Manresa in *Between the Acts* imagines she's 'a wild child of nature'; down from London, she removes her stays and rolls in the grass (38–9). Nature for Woolf, who as a child was a keen butterfly collector, never strays far from an ideology of subordination. Even if it does resemble an annex of civilization, variously defined with a series of clearly defined biographical, cultural and imaginative markers such as Kew, walks in the country, village pageants, trips to lighthouses or Rodmell, nature is there to be respected. When death is imminent, as in the closing moments of *The Waves*, when Bernard, sitting at table, refers to 'taking into our mouths the bodies of dead birds' (252), nature is at hand to provide a vocabulary to disturb the reader.

In *A Pageant of England's Life* (1934), an anthology dominated by London, John Drinkwater cites Blake's 'London' and then continues: 'If after reading this poem, we listen back across the centuries to John Lydgate's sprightly satire ('London Lackpenny'), we can feel something of the spiritual experiences through which a nation has passed' (Drinkwater, 146). No other modern English writer has a finer ear for listening back than Woolf, and no other modern English writer has a deeper sympathy for the spiritual experiences through which a nation has passed. I say this in spite of the famous declaration in *Three Guineas* (1938) that 'as a woman I have no country. As a woman I want no country' (*Three Guineas*, 234). For, as Mary Eagleton has rightly observed, such an assertion is undermined by the sentence which follows, how 'some obstinate emotion remains'. Indeed, according to Eagleton, Englishness for Woolf provokes 'an intellectual and political quandary' (Eagleton, M., 309), to which I would add that ambivalence in Woolf frequently, as here, combines profound scepticism, deep-rooted nostalgia and painful fear for the future. At the beginning of *Between the Acts*, the retired Indian civil servant Mr Oliver informs his audience that from an aeroplane you could still see the 'scars' on the landscape made by the Britons, the Romans, the Elizabethans when they built the manor-house and the plough which had been used to grow wheat during the Napoleonic Wars (*Between the Acts*, 3–4). The land bears wounds inflicted by each turbulent period of history, and now the country is exposed again to aerial bombardment from Europe and the south. Nothing in the opening pages to her final novel is free from premonition, and even the innocence of birds, their singing and feeding habits and migratory paths, is rendered through the lens of the coming war.

In retrospect, it seems, all roads in Woolf lead to *Between the Acts*, to an interval, a rupture, an interruption, as its title suggests. This is not the bracketed or 'long weekend' view of the inter-war years or indeed a view of history as noises offstage. The title recalls the play in her friend's novel *A Passage to India*.[5] During a performance of *Cousin Kate* at the English-only Club in Chandrapore, Mrs Moore slips out 'between the acts' to discover the *real* India, precisely the theme of Forster's tragic novel and linked here to what takes place between what might be considered the public acts of an imperial history. *Between the Acts* is also about a performance but in this case the play itself is not now abroad but at home and, more significantly, it forms part of a tragic reading of her country's fate. In *To the Lighthouse*, the empty house in the second section endures the ravages of time and war, the family, albeit depleted, reassemble, and Lily completes her painting. In *Between the Acts*, a discussion on an eighteenth-century portrait of a family ancestor leads to an evocation of the passage of time and, not to Eliot's 'Shantih, shantih, shantih', but to an insistent series of hollow adjectives: 'Empty, empty, empty; silent, silent, silent'. The mood is then deepened by Woolf with an image of annihilation that links a national history with modern warfare: 'The room was a shell singing of what was before time was' (33), where 'shell' reverberates in the mind until it loses all sense of a covering or protection. When she writes, 'The audience was assembling' (68), there is a suggestion that the Pageant constitutes a final roll-call for the English before the act of dispersal with the coming of war. 'Dispersed are we' the gramophone blares out, alternately in empty triumph and by way of an accompanying lament as the audience do indeed disperse.

As indicated in my Introduction, there is little by way of premonition in Joyce and, although we hear a powerful protest against war in the Willingdone Museum passage and elsewhere in *Finnegans Wake*, there is never a threat of war as there is in Woolf. On the other hand, the colonial encounter destroyed any easy recuperation either of the self or of Irish experience per se. It's not for nothing that his most famous novel begins in a disused army garrison with the dispossessed son in struggle in an episode whose final word is 'Usurper' and which carries the uncompromising image of Irish art as 'the cracked lookingglass of a servant' (*U* 1:146). Woolf's evocation – distillation is a better word – of English history, especially Elizabethan England, is everywhere on display in her writing. A product of the nineteenth century, what she sought was a culture which incorporated Ruskin and Arnold, not one which had been artificially divided by the pattern-seeking Forster. Because she was brought up in a household that was at the centre of London intellectual life, she needed no tutor such as Thomas Arnold or George Saintsbury to mark out the tradition or tell her what to think or what to oppose. If in the 1880s and 1890s John Joyce had invited home to dinner the leading Irish writers and intellectuals of the time such as George Moore, Emily Lawless, J.P. Mahaffy, Douglas Hyde, George Bernard Shaw, Oscar Wilde or W.B. Yeats, the character of his son's contribution to modern Irish writing would almost certainly have been different. Joyce's unerring ear is for the sounds in the language and he believed he could do anything with words. The more inward Woolf is a listener for sounds in the culture which give us a history and which at the same time cannot be so readily articulated. The nearest Joyce gets to this is in the closing moments of 'The Dead' when the snow begins to fall over Ireland, and the West – home of Nora and her former lover Michael Bodkin, and a region beyond the Pale, which the English had difficulty settling – suddenly comes into view across 'the dark mutinous Shannon waves' (*D* 223).

The lyrical passage in 'The Dead' issues in part from Joyce's unease in his relationship with Nora. Ironically, the writer given to confronting the 'demons' which assail her in the passage from conception to work (*To the Lighthouse*, 28) bore a sense of ease missing from Joyce. Ease is a defining quality in this regard, ease which surfaces throughout Woolf's fiction, as when a whole person's life is summed up in a conversational phrase such as 'this led to that' (*Between the Acts*, 22) or in Rodney's gesture to the City of London cited above or the way Mrs Ramsay confronts life again with the one word followed by a colon: 'Life:' (*To the Lighthouse*, 81). Ease also dominates her critical writing so that even a portentous subject such as 'Modern Fiction' is handled with a lightness of touch whose provisional insights need no grounding in some abstract theory: 'Look within and life, it seems, is very far from being "like this"' (*The Common Reader*, 148). Such ease, we can observe in passing, is not to be confused with being casual, the tone we find for example at the beginning of *Howards End*, where 'One may as well begin with Helen's letters to her sister'. Woolf's judgements, her surveys, are not casual and at the same time betray little sign of anxiety. Typically, we hear her arguing through something as if the line was both grounded and also in the process of being defined as she went along. In spite of her father's domineering presence, the ease stems in large measure from an upper-middle-class background, which in adulthood imparted to her a confident 'family' view of English Literature. Wherever you start, you end in connection. This family was related to that family, this author to that author, and the more distinguished ones were mentioned in the Domesday Book or in her father's *Dictionary of National Biography* (1885), or they had been personally introduced to her at the family home in Hyde Park Gate. Joyce's father bequeathed him wonderful stories, sayings and characters, but it was a family in decline and constantly on the move, a family which never knew ease, a family which, if it looked within, discovered life was precisely like this. It can never be forgotten that without the huge sums of money he received from his communist patron Harriet Shaw Weaver – by July

1923 she had parted with £21,000 or a million US dollars in today's money (Norburn, 199) – Joyce would have struggled more than he did to complete *Ulysses* or embark on his next big project *Finnegans Wake*.

## The Outsider

One can understand why Joyce was drawn to creating an outsider in the character of Leopold Bloom. The more intriguing question is why Woolf looked beyond her class horizons. She is in this sense a more complex figure than Forster or, indeed, other members of the Bloomsbury group, a point worth dwelling on. Jonathan Rose in *The Intellectual Life of the British Working Classes* (2002) rightly insists in his chapter entitled 'What Was Leonard Bast Really Like' that the self-taught lower middle class and the working class at this period were brighter and more intelligent than they have been portrayed, but what he overlooks is that Leonard Bast is as he is because of the limitations of Forster's class horizons (which is not something that could be said of Joyce and Bloom or Joyce and the character who comes closest to Bast, namely Mr Duffy from 'A Painful Case'). This is not to defend or absolve Forster but to suggest that we need a more sophisticated account than one which is restricted to representative types and the accuracy or otherwise of their representation. Not for nothing does Forster characteristically risk the collapse of his analysis when, self-deprecatingly, he wonders in *A Passage to India* if his discourse is closer to muddle than mystery, a move which simultaneously betrays a half-awareness of precisely his horizons and also how they might be shored up.

At the same time we might also notice that Forster is more radical or more accommodating than he sometimes appears, as in his use of phrases such as 'the Schlegel fetishes' (*Howards End*, 24) (a deliberately ironic comment on their commitment to Votes for Women etc.) and 'superstructures of wealth' (44), where 'fetishes' and 'superstructures' carried in 1910 an anthropological or Marxist inflection rather than, as with fetish today, a Freudian one. It is also in keeping that he refuses to maintain the clear-cut oppositions he sets up, as if he wasn't quite sure where his politics were taking him. When he compares the (former) great arches at Kings Cross to 'fit portals for some eternal adventure' (13), he deploys material symbols to invoke a spiritual world. Conversely, Miss Munt, the aunt ever-anxious to protect her cultured nieces, invests in safe railway shares; Margaret admits her own values are based on financial security; Helen in the novel comes to identify with the lower-middle-class outsider Leonard. Not all the scales are loaded against the Wilcoxes for, as Forster indicates in a paragraph offering what I take to be a critique of the emerging Bloomsbury group, 'the world would be a grey bloodless place were it entirely composed of Miss Schlegels' (28). If

Forster is guilty of anything it is, as Woolf suggests, feeling 'responsible for his characters' behaviour' and wanting to 'solve the problem of the universe' (Woolf 1943, 111).

Outsiders in Woolf's work abound – Miss Kilman, Peter Walsh, Septimus Warren, to name a few from *Mrs Dalloway*. Indeed, we would be hard-pressed to say there are any 'insiders' in her writings. They are not outsiders in the sense that Franz Biberkopf is. Or, for an example closer to home, we might take Carinthia Leicester from Coyle's novel *Piccadilly*. This begins with a newspaper hoarding announcing 'Unemployed Agitation'. The unemployed shorthand typist Carinthia understands only too well her predicament, the causes of her own sense of isolation, and the fate that might await her. When she passes bootblacks and organ-grinders in the street, she imagines what it would be like to sink so far in the labour market. She also suffers constant irritation when she sees the middle class at leisure, sitting in the new Pullman buses 'as if on shelves in a glass case with comic masks of destinations upon their expressions'. Not surprisingly, when she glanced up New Bond Street she 'flamed again with envy and the pain of an additional exclusion' (Coyle, 22–3). This is exclusion of a different order, one which puts Mrs Dalloway in her place, and Coyle does so in a novel which also explores 'discoverable depths of being' and the turn inward (11).

Even in a whimsical text such as *Flush* (1933), Woolf can't stop herself dividing the world into two, in this case outcast London, in the guise of Whitechapel, contrasted with the image of Elizabeth Barret Browning reclining on a sofa in Wimpole Street. *To the Lighthouse* is no less sharp but here the contrast is seen from within, and within the same social class. In the heart of the family round the dinner table, Mrs Ramsay plays host, ensuring everyone is at ease, but as she ladles the soup she feels 'out of everything', her mind struck by the discrepancy between what she was doing and what she was thinking (*To the Lighthouse*, 112–13). Forster doesn't have the scepticism to broach the possibility of the 'inadequacy of human relationships' (*To the Lighthouse*, 55). 'No, not yet' marks the closing moment of *A Passage to India*, a recognition that across the colonial divide personal relationships proved impossible in a country, not unlike Joyce's Ireland, where there was an 'Army of Occupation' (26–7) – a blunt phrase which Joyce, who was not given to politeness or reticence, never in fact resorts to. The more philosophical Woolf presses on to the end and has Mrs Ramsay notice how the light from the lighthouse is steady, pitiless and remorseless (88). In Dorothy Richardson's *Dawn's Left Hand* (1931), Miriam comments that 'The torment of all novels is what is left out' (Richardson, vol. 4, 239). Woolf's abiding interest lies precisely in what is left out, not the lack of knowledge of which Miriam accuses Henry James nor Conrad's 'know-all condescendingness' but what remains after the guests have departed, or indeed when the guests are still there to be entertained across the table.

In *Mrs Dalloway*, the fates of Mrs Dalloway and Warren are not pitted against each other, as they might be in a novel by Forster, but are deliberately yoked together, as if what they shared was not only greater than what separated them but pointed to a temporal sequence not defined by Monday and Tuesday, to a realm outside British empiricism, and to a space somewhere between 'To' and 'Between'. In some respects such attention to a common ground is only convincing because we accept that the novel provides a critique of an upper-middle-class view of the world, for, clearly, the cards in life have been stacked against Warren in a way they haven't been against Mrs Dalloway. And yet, Woolf manages to engage our sympathies for the wife of an MP not because she is linked with Warren but because Clarissa remains unaware of the significance of her links with him. If the novel was a Greek tragedy – and narrators in Woolf's experimental fiction have the look of a Greek Chorus – Mrs Dalloway might well have contributed to her fate by walking on ground reserved for the gods or some other form of hubris, but this is not a novel about retribution or sin, and if there are any recognition scenes these tend to be available to others or captured only fleetingly in memories from the past.

In October 1886, *Tit-Bits* printed an article entitled 'Where Do We Women Eat?'. While eating a tea-cake in a coffee-shop off Holborn in London, the thought comes to the (male) author about where exactly the thousands of female workers, who would not be provided with meals at work, eat. He undertakes a quick survey of cheap eating-houses but discovers only men, and the conclusion he comes to is that he is 'content to inscribe amongst the great social problems of the day, this of where do women eat?' The supercilious tone is irritating but it is in keeping with the period. In Ward Lock's 1904 *Guide to London*, for example, the informative tone slips a gear on only two occasions that I have found, once in reference to 'our country cousins' (31) visiting the metropolis, the other to women and shopping in Regent Street, a street which is 'perhaps, to ladies, the most attractive of London's arteries' (134).

A concern with exclusion drives Woolf's politics, exclusion that is often best expressed by what isn't said or by the books on the shelves that women didn't write. If she had written *Ulysses*, no doubt she would have focused on Dilly Dedalus rather than on her brother Stephen. As it happened, as Carinthia Leicester reminds us when she accompanies a Russian émigré to a reasonably priced, third-floor restaurant overlooking Leicester Square with a table d'hôte menu, by the 1920s coffee-shops and restaurants were opening up to working women. But in general, Woolf's politics cannot be assuaged by meliorism, market adjustments or targets. 'Meliorism in massquantities' (*FW* 447:2–3) was fine for Jaun (the upright 'dogmestic' Shaun in sleepy mood) in his campaign for civic improvement, but not for Woolf or for Shem, the Joyce figure who was so low 'he preferred Gibsen's teatime salmon tinned, as inexpensive as pleasing, to the plumpest roeheavy lax ... that ever was gaffed between Leixlip and Island Bridge' (*FW* 170:26–9). To risk an oversimplification, people who espouse the politics of improvement get off the train far too early and then accuse those who remain of utopianism or of abandoning politics. What they forget, or what they also forget, is that, in the phrase that Leonard Woolf selected for the autobiography of his years after his wife's death, it is the journey not the arrival that matters. Like Joyce, Virginia never got off the train and hence she remains an intriguing figure for those who can't buy into the politics of the present or those who never stop looking to the future.

## Concluding Remarks

Joyce and Woolf founded no political parties and initiated no political movements, but their work betrays the close alignment between conscience and consciousness. Temperamentally, Joyce, who understood 'overdetermination' long before its appearance in contemporary critical theory, couldn't stop toying with positions, whether personal or political. So the attempt to pin him down will always prove inviting but elusive. At one moment he resembles an anarchist, 'anarchistically respectsful of the liberties of the noninvasive individual' (*FW* 72:16–7), at another moment someone on the Left, 'a plain pink joint reformee in private life' (*FW* 59:27–8). Not unlike Nelson Mandela, he believed in 'everyman his own goaldkeeper and in Africa for the fullblacks' (*FW* 129:31–2). In regard to modern life and art, he connected both with a price: 'It was life but was it fair? It was free but was it art?' (*FW* 94:9–10). When, at the end of *To the Lighthouse*, James reflects on the meaning of the lighthouse, Woolf could be describing her own position vis-à-vis gender, art and politics: 'For nothing was simply one thing' (*To the Lighthouse*, 251). In their stress on states of mind, Joyce and Woolf rearrange the furniture of the known world and also remind us that, indeed, nothing is simply one thing.

That they emerged at the same moment in history is evidence that the culture needed to reconnect with the life and freedom of the mind. That they continue to hold sway is evidence that they still have work to do. Woolf considered Joyce an outsider and was uncomplimentary about *Ulysses*, although she and Leonard at one stage gave some consideration to publishing it. The novel was, she confided in her diary on 6 September 1922, drawing on years of unreconstructed class prejudice, 'underbred, not only in the obvious sense, but in the literary sense' (*A Writer's Diary*, 56). There was no meeting of minds, at least here. But inside the colonial city of Dublin and the imperial city of London, what energized them both was freedom, freedom from the nets of 'nationality, language, religion' (*P* 203) and from the circumscribing of consciousness to 'gig lamps symmetrically arranged' (*Common Reader*, 149).

Woolf fills her canvas with texture and colour, with tone, that is, rather than sharp outlines. If she disturbs us it is not because she chimes with our experience of things but because her sense of displacement is so acute that it unnerves us. Joyce's disturbances tend to be local in effect, as I argue in Chapter 6, but they also tend to accumulate, as I argue throughout the pages of this book. But there is nothing in Joyce's depiction of Dublin to compare with the return to an empty landscape that Woolf envisages for the city where once mammoths roamed in Piccadilly and rhododendrons bloomed in the Strand. In the closing, thickly significant, moments of *Between the Acts*, Lucy has lost the page of the book she is reading, H.G. Wells's *Outline of History*. We see her turning the pages and 'looking at pictures – mammoths, mastodons, prehistoric birds' (*Between the Acts*, 196), and the narrator then ominously adds, Kurtz-like: 'The darkness increased'. *Finnegans Wake* ends with a local disturbance, not with a dash or blank space as was the case with Sterne's *A Sentimental Journey* but with a keyboard return, with the image of the river, the banks of Joyce's Anna Livia and the idea of recirculation, with the reader returning to the beginning of the text where the sentence is for the time being completed with 'riverrun, past Eve and Adam's, from swerve of shore to bend of bay, brings us by a commodius vicus of recirculation back to Howth Castle and Environs'.

# Part III

## Joyce and Language

# 5

# The Issue of Translation

## Stately and Serene

Simony, rheumatic wheels, wonderful vocables, moocow, pick pack pock puck, tundish, stately, introibo ad altare dei, metempsychosis, the word known to all men, ephebe, ineluctable, sonnez la cloche, riverrun, foenix culprit, hesitency. If Joyce tells us anything about translation it is that language, especially in its written form, is always in some sense already part of translation. Take the use of 'serene' in the clause that appears at the end of 'Penelope': 'the night we missed the boat at Algeciras the watchman going about serene with his lamp' (U 18:1596–7). This is an unusual word on Molly's lips and one that we might miss right at the end of *Ulysses*. We sense that she does not intend a poetic use of language for the word seems to betray an unconscious conflation on her part of English and Spanish. If this is right, the word is not so much 'serene', therefore, as a commonly heard word in Spanish 'sereno'. Bloom imagines Molly has '[f]orgotten any little Spanish she knew' (U 4:60–1), but perhaps she still retains enough for it to linger in her mind and confuse her. What she recollects is perhaps a watchman's expression such as 'todo sereno', all quiet, or perhaps she has somewhere in her mind the Spanish word for watchman 'el sereno'.

It is not only words that Molly conflates but also syntax, for 'serene' is an adjective but carries within it a noun and perhaps an adverb – presumably the watchman is going about not so much serene as serenely. As Lindley Murray noticed in his early nineteenth-century study of grammar,

> Young persons who study grammar find it difficult to decide, in particular constructions, whether an adjective or adverb should be used. ... They should carefully attend to the definitions of the adjective and adverb, and consider whether ... quality, or manner, is indicated. In the former case, an adjective is proper; in the latter, an adverb. (Murray, 163)

The issue is a large one not only for the grammarian but also for the student and the translator. Murray is actually named by Joyce in the 'Eumaeus' episode in a delightfully unEnglish sentence which is designed to poke fun at Murray's prescriptive and rule-governed account of English grammar:

> I looked for the lamp which she told me came into his mind but merely as a passing fancy of his because he then recollected the morning littered bed etcetera and the book about Ruby with met him pike hoses (*sic*) in it which must have fell down sufficiently appropriately beside the domestic chamberpot with apologies to Lindley Murray. (*U* 16:1470–5)

Molly that morning had used the ungrammatical phrase 'fell down' and Bloom repeats it here. Even though the narrator inserts '(*sic*)', that morning when she is inquiring for the meaning of the word metempsychosis in a novel she is reading, she does not actually say 'met him pike hoses'. In 'Calypso', it is Bloom who remarks 'Met him what?' (*U* 4:336). So the *sic* is either a further example of memory playing tricks with Bloom (or the reader) or perhaps it is the case that Molly did indeed say it but the text, which too forms part of the metempsychosis theme, didn't report it at the time. Needless to say, it is not Bloom but someone else, possibly the Arranger in the guise of a narrator or the English language, who is apologizing to Murray.

*Ulysses* also begins with a word that hovers between an adjective and an adverb: 'Stately, plump Buck Mulligan came from the stairhead, bearing a bowl of lather on which a mirror and a razor lay crossed.' Is it, to use Murray's distinction, quality or manner which is indicated by 'Stately'? Is it that Mulligan is himself stately or is this how he moves? They raise different issues, but the two words 'serene' and 'Stately' have an illustrative function for the translator and critic alike. They serve to remind us that *Ulysses*, from start to finish, is a pedagogic novel instructing us not only about language, its grammar and vocabulary, but also about the issue of translation, including the 'translation' involved in parts of speech. To be slightly pedantic, in the first episode alone there are some 113 words which end in –ly. Roughly sixty-six of these are adverbs of manner ('coarsely', 'sternly', 'neatly', 'impatiently'), sixteen are adverbs of time ('suddenly', 'hastily', 'briskly', 'smartly'), twelve are adjectives ('lovely', 'shapely', 'ghostly', 'friendly'), six are adjuncts (as in 'only'), four are intensifiers (as in 'simply'), four are what we might define as attitudinal disjuncts (as in 'surely', 'personally') and there is one noun ('tilly'). In terms of parts of speech, 'Telemachus' is an overwhelmingly adverbial episode, given as much to manner as quality, and therefore as much about *how* as *is*, about attitudes towards the world as about the world itself. As if in support of the embattled warrior son looking for his enemies, the episode begins with an adjective which resembles an adverb and ends with a noun acting as a sentence: 'Usurper.' Eventually, we might conclude, Stephen gets there. In between we have Mulligan and a string of mocking adverbs which include solemnly, gravely, sternly, gaily, contentedly, earnestly, casually, entirely, blandly, tragically, piously, tritely and solemnly again. Stephen attracts his own measure of adverbs of manner: wearily, gloomily, coldly, thirstily, gravely, listlessly, drily and discreetly. Haines, too, is not neglected: confidently, guardedly, calmly and unfairly. The adverb 'gravely' appears on four occasions, 'silently' three times.

How translators handle words ending in -ly is invariably interesting for those whose first language is English, especially since it is rare to find equivalents or overlaps in European languages in this area. Prefixes, too, present problems in this first episode and, if a fuller treatment were required, we might also want to include a consideration of words beginning with un- such as 'ungirdled', 'untonsured', 'uncombed', 'unsteady', 'uneager', 'unclean', 'unbind', 'unclipped' and 'unlace'. The first word of *Ulysses* is frequently converted without hesitation into an adjective, a move for which there is some support. In the newspaper episode of *Ulysses*, as if to remind us that 'stately' is to be distinguished from an adverb, Joyce gives us 'statelily' when 'a stately Figure' enters the newspaper office and 'passed statelily up the staircase' (*U* 7:42–5). But in a sense Joyce is calling attention to how what is formally correct in terms of grammar can sound stilted when used in practice. The German translation by Hans Wollschläger has a similar word with a suffix close to English 'Statllich und feist' (Wollschläger, 7), stately and plump. The French translation by Auguste Morel, who was assisted by one of Joyce's tried associates Stuart Gilbert, converts 'Stately' into 'Majestueux' in a phrase that expresses no doubt: 'Majestueux et dodu' (Morel, 9), majestic and plump. In his 2003 Spanish translation, Francisco García Tortosa is slightly more cautious by allowing for the comma to come into play but then conveys an attitude which might or might not be implied by 'plump': 'Majestuoso, el orondo Buck Mulligan' (Tortosa, 3), majestic, the self-satisfied or puffed-up Buck Mulligan. In his 1975 Spanish translation José María Valverde starts *Ulysses* with 'Solemne, el gordo Buck Mulligan' (Valverde, 71), solemn, the fat man Buck Mulligan. The Argentine translator J. Salas Subirat has 'Imponente, el rollizo Buck Mulligan' (Subirat, 35), where 'rollizo' or plump has, for English ears, all the swagger we might associate later with Mulligan. 'Stately' can imply majestic and solemn but implication is not equivalence. 'Imponente' in Spanish is impressive or imposing (especially of a building), while 'Majestueux' is close in French to imposing, but Joyce's opening would take on a different character if begun 'Imposing, plump Buck Mulligan'.

Joyce launches his epic with a sentence which is not particularly inviting and with a word whose oddness is compounded in part because it ends in -ly. The juxtaposition of 'Stately' and 'plump' is also unusual, as if the eye of the satirist was already at work. Ironing out such strangeness or coldness or insisting on the character of the opening character is a translator's prerogative but, as is apparent, the view we have of *Ulysses* is coloured from the outset by whatever choices are made. Robert Frost famously remarked that poetry is what gets lost in translation. With *Ulysses* in mind we might want to revise this and aver that it is not the intensity of poetry but the extraordinary hinterland of Joyce's prose that gets lost in translation. Joyce's ear was so precise that, whatever we decide about his translators, we rarely catch him out with regard to tone or pitch or indeed telling us things we don't need to know. Yeats felt that, when he first met the old Fenian John O'Leary on his return to Dublin, he was in the presence of his theme as a poet. Something similar can be said about Joyce, only now it is language that is his theme. Joyce repeatedly shows how words themselves carry themes, how 'Stately' for example returns us to the issue of style and conventions of writing, how it belongs with a discussion not just about character but also about stately prose, which we touched on in Chapter 2. Some commentators have ingeniously deciphered the word 'yes' in 'Stately'. Whatever the case, there is merit in appreciating that the 'Tower' episode ends with 'Usurper' as if to recall the fate of Telemachus surrounded by his mother's suitors and to underline the issue of the succession of Odysseus' *state* therefore.

To return to how 'serene' at the end of *Ulysses* is translated in Spanish. In the Argentinian edition the clause is rendered as 'el guardia haciendo su ronda de sereno con su linterna' (Subirat, 728), 'the guard making his watchman's round with his lantern'. This not only misses out on the different connotations of serene but turns the watchman into a guard. Tortosa opts for a noun and playfully repeats the word: 'el sereno de un sitio para otro sereno con su farol', which translates as 'the night watchman going about with his lamp with composure / coolly' (Tortosa, 908). Valverde italicizes the word *sereno* to remind his Spanish readers that the word is closer to Spanish than English (he does the same with *posadas* a few lines earlier) (Valverde, 788). For different reasons, neither of these last two translations is quite accurate, for both fail to capture Joyce's peculiar use of 'serene', a word which in this case, unlike 'Stately', is forever in play between English and Spanish.

## Language and Identity

Translation is ever-present in Joyce, nowhere more so than in the biography of his driven early years. Like Ibsen, he took things to heart, identifying with the language of the minority, for as he puts it in *Finnegans Wake*: 'no mouth has the might to set a mearbound to the march of a landsmaul' (*FW* 292:26–7). Just as 'no man has the right to fix the boundary to the march of a nation' – which was Parnell's famous slogan in regard to Irish nationalism – so no-one should be able to set a limit to the march of a rural dialect such as Landsmaal, which some Norwegians in the nineteenth century hoped would become the standard language of Norway. Joyce's humour shines through this but it shouldn't be allowed to detract from his feelings in this regard. Ireland is a 'landsmaul', a small land, but it still has rights to self-determination, just as Norway does vis-à-vis its Swedish and European neighbours.

Joyce, however, took care to distance himself from what he considered the narrow ground on which the debate about language and nationalism was being conducted in his own country. In 'The Necessity for De-Anglicising Ireland' (1892), Douglas Hyde famously attacked the whole concept of hybridity:

> I have no hesitation at all in saying that every Irish-feeling Irishman, who hates the reproach of West-Britonism, should set himself to encourage the efforts which are being made to keep alive our once great national tongue. ... In order to de-Anglicise ourselves we must at once arrest the decay of the language. ... We must arouse some spark of patriotic inspiration among the peasantry who still use the language and put an end to the shameful state of feeling... which makes young men and women blush and hang their heads when overheard speaking their own language. (Hyde, 136–7)

As can be gleaned from his unsympathetic portrait of Miss Ivors in 'The Dead', written in Trieste in 1907, this was not Joyce's view of language or indeed of translation. Political independence, yes; independence for 'our once great national tongue', no if that meant the exclusion of English. When tackled by Miss Ivors as to why he holidays abroad in France or Belgium or Germany, 'Well,' said Gabriel, 'it's partly to keep in touch with the languages and partly for a change' (*D* 189). Joyce too was someone who kept in touch with the languages of Europe, ever conscious that language belonged to a discourse on freedom and the exploration of identity, both of which he saw largely in terms of difference and coincidence. Significantly, when he left Ireland he 'caught the europicolas and went into the society of jewses' (*FW* 423:35–6), that is he caught the *piccolo velocità*, the goods or slow train to Europe (where he would write articles for *Il Piccolo della Sera*, the Italian daily newspaper), catching in the process not so much erysipelas, a kind of skin disease, but the itch to live in Europe. As can be discerned in the phrase with its New Testament associations how he 'went into the society of jewses', his journey was not only linguistic but also religious and cultural. This was the alpha to omega of Joyce's life – from the Society of Jesus, from his schooling at the hands of the Jesuits, to the society of Jews, that is from Catholic Ireland to multicultural Europe.

From the other side of the Alps, the issue of language and identity in Joyce takes on a different complexion. With an edition of Joyce's Italian writings in front of him, mostly written in Trieste between 1907 and 1912, Giorgio Melchiori claimed that Joyce was 'scrittore italiano', an Italian writer: 'Joyce scrittore italiano'. For Melchiori, 'non soltanto il Joyce privato e domestico, ma il Joyce gionalista, il Joyce saggista letterario, il Joyce politico è scrittore italiano' (Corsini and Melchiori, 15). That is 'not only the private, domestic Joyce, but the journalistic Joyce, the literary essayist Joyce, the political Joyce is an Italian writer' (Bosinelli, 321). Between the ages of twenty-five and thirty, as Rosa Maria Bosinelli takes care to emphasize, Joyce used Italian and only Italian as 'the language in the sociological, historical and political field; the language of his production in the field of literary criticism; and as the language of everyday, familiar life'. Trieste, 'ah trieste' as he affectionately called it in *Finnegans Wake*, may have been where 'ate I my liver' (*FW* 301:16), but it was also where the Irish family man insisted on his Italian identity, naming his children Giorgio and Lucia. As soon as he descended from his flat onto the streets of Trieste, a city that was 'my second country' as he reportedly told one of his Triestine friends Francini Bruni (McCourt, 252), Joyce was in the presence of Europe and its various tongues and competing nationalities: Italian, Slav, German, Austro-Hungarian and what Melchiori decribes as 'levantini', that is Jews and other people from the Middle East, the Levant being historically defined as the Mediterranean lands east of Italy. But the *lingua franca* was not that of the occupying Austro-Hungarian power but the rich and unpretentious Triestine dialect.

Joyce's other Italian city was Rome. He arrived there with Nora and Giorgio in July 1906 to take up a post in the private bank of Nast-Kolb and Schumacher and stayed for seven months and seven days. It was not a happy time for him. 'Rome', he remarked to his brother Stanislaus, 'reminds me of a man who lives by exhibiting to travellers his grand-mother's corpse' (*Letters* II, 165). But for Melchiori writing in a collection entitled *Joyce in Rome* (1984), Rome provided not only the genesis of Joyce's great novel *Ulysses* but also, in the words of his co-editors, 'the most fruitful [period] in the whole of his intellectual life' (Melchiori, 12). Melchiori notes that, in correspondence written during his stay in Rome, Joyce referred to the idea and the title of *Ulysses* (see letters dated 30 September and 13 November 1906 respectively). He continues by citing the information (or lack of it) about Alfred J. Hunter in Ellmann's biography, and how Joyce thought of writing another story for *Dubliners* to be called 'Ulysses', which would focus on a real-life Dubliner and his wife, who was rumoured to be unfaithful. The crucial question for Melchiori is why Joyce chose at this particular time a Jew for his central character, and the answer, which returns us to the 'europicolas' quotation above, is that Jews were then a focus of attention not only in Roman politics but also in the influential political writings of Guglielmo Ferrero, who was much admired by Joyce. In addition, in contrast with the multiculturalism of Trieste, Rome was at the centre of Christianity where the Jew was still an alien. Joyce's choice of Bloom as his central character in *Ulysses* was at once, therefore, political, telling and Roman in origin.

Distance enabled Joyce to write about his native city, but it wasn't always, as he himself revealed in a letter to his brother Stanislaus during his stay in Rome, an accurate picture he painted – it was sometimes 'unnecessarily harsh' (*Letters* II, 166). Melchiori places perhaps too much weight on identity and not enough on Joyce's sense of displacement or on his characteristic recourse to 'double exposures', on the way his mind, in the words of Carola Gideon-Welcker, was constantly taking 'double exposures' (Gideon-Welcker, 210). The quotation from *To The Lighthouse* used in the last chapter can be reused here: 'For nothing was simply one thing'. Elsewhere, Melchiori writes that Joyce's experience as an Italian writer 'taught him the mechanics and the secret alchemies of a language which could be studied with scientific detachment precisely because it was not his own native language' (cited in Pugliatti, 140). Again, this too needs a counter-weight, for Joyce, who read modern languages as an undergraduate in Dublin, underwent an early training in linguistic detachment, a training that had indeed commenced much earlier if *A Portrait* is to be believed, for, from a very early age, his consciousness had been impressed with the way God has a name and this name is different in different languages. Joyce invites such claims to ownership and Melchiori's emphasis is a valuable reminder to those who still assume Joyce is nothing but an Irish writer, but to my mind Joyce moves back and forth across and between walls and sides. In the encounter in *A Portrait* between Stephen and the Prefect of Studies over the word 'tundish', we can sense the autobiographical undertow but Joyce is only temporarily delayed by the thought that his speech is 'acquired'.

Arguably, Zurich has a stronger claim on Joyce. 'What a city!' he exclaimed to Gideon-Welcker about Zurich, no doubt with his native city also in mind. 'A lake, a mountain and two rivers are its treasures' (Gideon-Welcker, 210). With its plentiful supply of the 'electric' Swiss white wine, 'Fendant de Sion', it was more than enough to make Joyce feel at home. One of Joyce's four European cities, Zurich was twice a sanctuary for him from two World Wars and, fittingly for a city that resembles *zurück* (the German word for 'back'), it became his final resting-place. Zurich, or 'Turricum' (*FW* 228:22) in Latin, the city of steeples or towers, is where Joyce, 'the same zurrichschicken' ('send back') 'swobbing broguen eerish myth brockendootsch' (swapping broken Irish for broken German) (*FW* 70:8 and 4), 'collapsed carefully under a bedtick from Schwitzer's, his face enveloped into a dead warrior's telemac' (*FW* 176:34–6), and wrote *Ulysses*. Collapsing under a bed from Switzers, the department store in Dublin, he wrapped himself under an overcoat to write 'telemac', that is 'Telemachus', the first episode of *Ulysses*. Interestingly, the word 'enveloped' might be an unconscious reference on Joyce's part to Arnold's description of Tennyson's 'Ulysses' where, as we saw in Chapter 2, the epic hero is 'enveloped in antique heroic dignity'. Zurich is both / and: both apart from (and therefore a protection for Joyce) and a part of the course of European history. It is more; for while it is the city of SS. Felix and Regula (prosperity and order), it was also the cradle of Dada, the 'white in black arpists' (*FW* 8:33) who anticipated Joyce's own 'warping process' (*FW* 497:3) in 'Work in Progress', the city that also sheltered Lenin before he caught his own sealed train back to Russia to lead the 1917 Revolution. If such were possible, Zurich brought out even more of the subversive in Joyce. When he arrived from Trieste in 1915 he commented, '*Zurich ist so sauber*' ('clean', but also 'sober' to English ears); at his last Christmas in 1940, he turned to Gideon-Welcker and remarked (uncannily, as it turned out), 'You have no idea how wonderful dirt is' (Ellmann 1982, 740).

In the crucial period of Joyce's stay in Zurich during the years 1915–20, most of *Ulysses* was composed. A commemorative tablet on a house in Via Frattina in Rome proclaims *evoko la storia di Ulisse*, that in Rome in 1906 *Ulysses* was 'evoked'. Melchiori's argument is that from its very inception *Ulysses* is a political novel, which he links with Joyce's discovery in 1906 of politics as ideology. There is merit in tracing an intellectual idea back to its origins so long as it is also understood that Joyce's ideas changed fundamentally during the writing of the novel. The post-1920 *Ulysses* is almost a different book from when the 'idea' was first planted and when he actually began its composition in 1914. In that sense Zurich is his defining city, the place where in the process of composition he refined – and the two went hand in hand for Joyce – the conception of his work and the art of writing.

There is ample evidence in the illustrations in Thomas Faerber and Markus Luchsinger's *Joyce in Zürich* (1988) to indicate the importance of the German-speaking 'lyonine city' (*FW* 155:6) to Joyce. The list of photographs includes the Hotel Pfauen, the Augustiner Restaurant, which is humorously described as *der Kirche der Altkatholiken*, the Old Catholic Church or the church of old or ex-catholics, and the Kronenhalle, the restaurant where Joyce was taken ill on 10 January 1941 when celebrating Paul Ruggiero's birthday. Then, too, there are the various Joyce houses, Joyce's many friends, examples of poems and letters in Joyce's handwriting, a reproduction of the cover to issue number 2 of *Der Dada,* drawings by his close friend the English artist Frank Budgen and the striking sketch of Joyce by Wyndham Lewis, as well as the game of *Labyrinthspiel* which Joyce played with Lucia and which perhaps, as we saw in Chapter 3, contributed to his handling of his native city in the 'Wandering Rocks' episode of *Ulysses*. In the accompanying text the discussion ranges equally widely: 'Dadaland Zürich', Joyce's financial position while in Zurich, Georges Borach on Joyce's singing (in the 1918 *Who's Who* for Zurich Joyce lists singing as his recreation), the Martha Fleischmann episode (together with Budgen's illustration for 'Nausicaa'), Joyce's direction of the English Players at the Pfauen Theatre in June 1918 and the subsequent dispute with Henry Carr over the latter's fee for playing Algernon in Wilde's *The Importance of Being Earnest*. The book also includes a moving photograph of Ezra Pound at the end of his life looking at Milton Hebald's statue of Joyce in the Fluntern Cemetery looking at him, a farewell in its own way to modernism and to the great generation of modernists.

Unlike Rome, Zurich was a city Joyce kept returning to. In 1930, he was operated on by the eye surgeon Alfred Vogl; in 1934, he accompanied his mentally ill daughter Lucia to see C.G. Jung; in 1935 he was with Nora and friends in Lucerne; in other years in the 1930s he was in Berne, Basel, Feldkirch, Lausanne and Montreux. *Finnegans Wake* is full of references to Zurich: the burning of the winter-demon Böögg ('Mister Begge', *FW* 58:16) during *Sechseleuten*, the spring festival ('Sexaloitez', 'saxy luters', 'silks alustre' are variations on this tune in *Finnegans Wake*); Zurich's ugliest building, the Sihlpost or main post office, becomes in the lyrical prose of 'Anna Livia Plurabelle' the 'sillypost' (*FW* 200:22); and we can't forget the question I posed in the Introduction: 'Yssel that the limmat?' (*FW* 198:13). His favourite portrait was taken at the Platspitz where the Sihl and the Limmat meet. True to type, he has his back to the camera, hands on hips, cane in right hand, hat to one side, railing in front decorated with bird-droppings. He returned to the city in December 1940 effectively as a refugee from Saint-Gerard-le-Puy in Vichy France and he died there in January 1941. Ironically, given his importance now to the city, in late 1940 it took considerable effort and money on the part of Joyce's Zurich friends (most notably Carola Gideon-Welcker) to get him across the border.

The identity of Joyce has as many claimants as the countries he visited or the languages he spoke. With Bloom's Hungarian background, the reference to Arthur Griffith, whose study *The Resurrection of Hungary: A Parallel for Ireland* was published in the hallowed year of 1904, and Bloom's imagined part in Griffith's idea of Sinn Fein, there is much to be said for thinking of *Ulysses* as a Central European text. It comes as a shock to recollect that when Joyce left for Zurich in 1915 he had spent a third of his life under the Austro-Hungarian Empire. In a closely argued historical account entitled *Joyce's 'Ulysses' as National Epic: Epic Mimesis and the Political History of the Nation State* (2002), which is primarily concerned with how to connect the date on which the Irish epic *Ulysses* is set with the year when the Irish Free State came into existence, Andras Ungar has suggested that from Lipoti to Rudolf to Rudy, from grandfather to father to son, Bloom's vulnerable sense of continuity connects with what happened to the Hapsburg dynasty with the death of Maximilian in front of a Mexican firing-squad and the mysterious death of the imperial heir Crown Prince Rudolf in 1889. It would be difficult to top that, and yet, as we saw with Melchiori, Joyce invites such moves to appropriate him and claim ownership. And we have said nothing about the French Joyce, the German Joyce, the Russian Joyce, Joyce and the Chinese, Joyce and the

Norwegians, Joyce and the Danes or Joyce and the Scandinavian origins behind Humphrey Chimpden Earwicker, the HCE figure in *Finnegans Wake*. As for the Dutch Joyce, Erik Bindervoet and Robbert-Jan Henkes's remarkable bilingual edition of *Finnegans Wake*, in which they set out to adapt the Dutch language to the language of the *Wake* rather than the other way round, is a further reminder not only of the close proximity of English and Dutch but also of Joyce's Dutch credentials.

Translating Joyce involves us in taking sides, and yet we would do well to retain a sense of the fundamentally overdetermined nature of Joyce's enterprise. Rome and Zurich, Paris and Dublin give us *Ulysses*. At home in Trieste, the Irishman, whose first language was English, who travelled under a British passport and who was in receipt of a grant from the Royal Literary Fund, spoke Italian. In his native Dublin, the Norsemen, who founded the city in the ninth century, managed to hang onto placenames into the modern period. In 'The Ballad of Persse O'Reilly', Joyce consigns 'the deaf and dumb Danes' (*FW* 27:26), the men from the east, to Oxmanstown, but we shouldn't forget that in the area now underlying Islandbridge and Kilmainham there is the largest Viking burial ground outside of Scandinavia. If there is a modern European imaginative text par excellence, written with Europe in mind, it would be *Finnegans Wake*, but I doubt if too many members of the Council of Europe have read it and, if they have, it would be interesting to know which language they have read it in (for in one sense, as the Dutch translators remind us, we all read this text in our own language). It's pretty certain that there never will be a time when *Finnegans Wake* could be understood in the same way by people speaking different languages. The text is rooted in difference, taking up into it all these different European and other languages, but it goes without saying that it refuses any suggestion that they can be melded together into a new language or one thing. In a similar way, virtually no neologisms, no 'fire-new' words, have come into English, or any other language I suspect, from *Finnegans Wake*, and yet there are many that deserve to, such as 'bisexycle' for bicycle, or 'moanday' for Monday, or 'shatterday' for Saturday, or 'dumbestic husbandry' for domestic husbandry / dumb beast husband dry, or 'eatupus complex', a humorous way of thinking about Freud's Oedipus Complex.

From the scrupulous meanness of *Dubliners* to the feast or 'lashons of languages' (*FW* 29:32) that characterizes *Finnegans Wake*, Joyce's writing deliberately calls attention to its angularity and its quality of resistance. Where Shakespeare in *Love's Labours Lost* enjoys poking fun at cultural difference, at national stereotypes such as the Spanish object of ridicule, the 'fantastical' Don Armado, Joyce's interest lies elsewhere. And this is true even if we admit to the English and Jewish stereotypes in the characters of Haines and Bloom. The feast Joyce invites us to share is situated closer to the classroom than to the idle gossip of the stage or the playing fields of Eton. Triumphs are hard won and more often than not are and are not local in effect. As John Florio's *Queen Anna's new World of Words; or, Dictionarie of the Italian and English tongues* (1611) confirms, Shakespeare had the benefit of 'fire-new' words, for this was a period when English expanded hugely. Joyce, by contrast, came upon a vocabulary already well established and, partly through a warping process, partly through the use of portmanteau words, partly through the idea of acquired speech, embarked on a project to extend our consciousness and understanding of how language works and what implications this has for identity.

## The Issue is Translation

In any encounter there are two sides. The colonial encounter between Britain and Ireland encouraged Joyce to catch not the boat train to London Euston – as Shaw, Wilde and Yeats had done a generation earlier – but the 'europicolas' to continental Europe. That encounter no doubt encouraged him, when he came to embark on *Finnegans Wake*, to 'murder all the English he knew' (*FW* 93:2). Surrounded by translation he was always attuned not only to the oppositional but also to the multiple viewpoint, and he took particular delight in registering and then crisscrossing the walls that divide linguistic communities. He would have been familiar with one of the common derivations of the Latin word 'translation', namely *transfero / translatum*, to carry across from one side to another. In Greek, the idea of sides is present in μεταφέρω, metaphero, from which our word metaphor derives. Metaphor, too, is associated in Greek with translation, as in transferring a word to a new sense, or changing a meaning from literal to figurative. The word μεταφέρω is also used in transferring money. Once a sum of money has been transferred the deed is done, but this is rarely the case with the 'transfer' of words in Joyce, for repeatedly the reader is forced to check on things, how the word was used before, both within the text itself and outside, whether its meaning has a wider distribution and more complex hinterland.

In 'Book of Many Turns' (1972), Fritz Senn praised the flexibility of English, how the title of 'The Dead' could refer to an individual or more than one individual. This is one of Senn's rare mistakes, for 'the dead' has to be a collective noun or refer to more than one individual. Thus it's not possible to say of a body in a room laid out for burial, 'The dead's inside the room.' Or of Michael Furey that he is 'the dead' in this story. Unlike the expression 'the deceased' or 'the dearly departed', it would have to be the dead person or something similar. So English isn't that flexible and constant checking is required. This serves as a reminder that another Greek word for translation is μεταγράφω, metagrapho, to write differently, to alter or correct, to interpolate or falsify. If translation studies went under a name such as metagraphic studies we might never step outside the realm of negotiation or be pressured to find equivalents between languages or come down on one side or the other. Writing differently is what Joyce does or what Joyce does best, a writer – and here one can concur with Melchiori – who needed contact with different linguistic communities to realize or confirm the shocking truth that God is *Dieu* in French, that speech is always acquired.

In the context of Senn and translation, let me pick up on two other remarks from an article he wrote forty years ago in the *James Joyce Quarterly* entitled 'He Was Too Scrupulous Always: Joyce's "The Sisters"'. The article carried eleven footnotes, five of them concerned with translation, Senn's trademark pattern. The first phrase is 'the essential flawedness of all things in this world', and the second is 'traits of affirmation that work through indirection' (Senn 1966, 66–72). 'Flawedness', a word that is not quite English (and Senn knows this even as he lets it appear without quotation marks), is Senn's way of saying don't let's get too pretentious. The point is made with a directness only someone who appreciates indirection could make. Against the tide of idealism that characterized and still characterizes much of Joyce studies – how Joyce was in the vanguard of liberty or in the rearguard of unreconstructed chauvinism – Senn, his dictionaries and Homer beside him, has always insisted on looking at the words on the page and noticing all those black riders, white spaces, and printer's bitches. How could the translator and non-native speaker not be forced to delay in the face of a malapropism such as 'rheumatic wheels' or a misunderstood word such as 'met him pike hoses' or the sentence that is a litmus-test for all translators 'And going forth he met Butterly' (*U* 1:527)? Before the rush to judgement – Joyce is x or this means that – dwell on the pause and, when you've done that, pause again.

As for Senn's affirmation by indirection, the second statement I've pulled out, this too is the product of years of careful translation, a process of retrieval from the mound that constitutes part of Joyce's legacy. Joyce does affirm, though not in the way Conrad does or Beckett, and Senn is careful to avoid telling us what that affirmation consists of, but it isn't to be confused with high-mindedness or pomposity or indeed waywardness. And even if the words are foregrounded as objects, they ironically lend support to the sense of 'indirection' that Senn notices. 'Pick pack pock puck' – what exactly is that run of words if not a linguistically precise sequence whose meaning has been delayed, an exercise in phonology from a Berlitz classroom, wonderful vocables which hint at something other than the sound of leather on willow?

Throughout the pages of the *James Joyce Quarterly*, the issue of translation recurs, or as Senn put it in the Spring 1967 issue 'The Issue is Translation'. At the James Joyce International Symposium in Trieste in 1971 there was a *Finnegans Wake* translation panel with Rosa Maria Bosinelli joining others in a 'pessimistic assessment as regards the possibility of a satisfactory "literary translation" '.[1] However, as if to confound the sceptics and the pessimists, translations of Joyce's writings have never stopped appearing. 'The issue is translation'. What exactly, though, is the issue? Cultural identity, cultural difference, cultural chauvinism, scepticism, pessimism, the outsider in language? What exactly is the subject or focus? The English language? Or some other language? 'Are we speaching d'anglas landadge or are you sprakin sea Djoytsch? (*FW* 485:12–13) Or is it the lack of equivalence, of transfer values, between languages after the collapse of the Tower of Babel, what gets lost in translation? Or is it something to do with the appropriation of Joyce? Was Bernard Benstock right when he impishly suggested in 1972 that *Ulysses* is no more (but no less) about Ireland than *Moby Dick* is about a whale, a remark that also has relevance here (Benstock 1972, 100–1)? I raise all these issues here without resolving them but as my remarks above suggest I am clearer in my own mind how I would go about resolving them. It goes without saying, however, that some of the best readers of Joyce are non-native speakers, non-native English speakers that is, who find themselves hesitating at precisely the points where for others there is nothing to report.

# 6

# Joyce's Use of Language in 'Sirens'

From the 'pok!' in 'Ivy Day in the Committee Room' and the 'pick, pack, pock, puck' sequence of sounds in *A Portrait of the Artist as a Young Man* to the constant play on sounds throughout *Ulysses* and *Finnegans Wake*, Joyce reveals he is a sound writer. While in the earlier texts the sounds can be quickly identified and eventually slotted into the narrative or characterization or theme, in *Ulysses* this is often less possible, as if something else is at work. My focus in this chapter is 'Sirens', for this is the episode where a peculiar kind of tension can be most keenly felt. The tension I have in mind concerns not so much the figure of the Arranger or linguistic contamination as what we might term the 'local disturbances' that surround particular passages or sentences. 'Sirens' begins enigmatically with 'Bronze by gold heard the hoofirons, steelyringing' (*U* 11:1). Glossing this requires something more than tying it to the consciousness of the two barmaids or indeed to the wider theme of the episode. With the help of some such awkward sentences and phrases taken for the most part from the Overture or Prelude to 'Sirens', I want to consider the processes at work here and especially how they might connect with politics and the colonial encounter.

Whether in terms of syntax or phonology, symbols or themes, character development or narrative unfolding, the Overture is frequently read as a forerunner for the music episode which follows. John Gordon, in keeping with his stress on 'reality', adopts a more agnostic view. The Overture he describes as a 'cacophony' which resembles 'simply, the random plonks, toots, and sawings of an orchestra tuning up, waiting for the conductor to begin' (Gordon, 75). But music still exerts an influence over Gordon's view: a 'cacophony' is a collection of sounds, the conductor is tapping on his baton, and the orchestra is preparing to play. My own preoccupation in this chapter is not primarily with the way sounds connect with meaning (whether that is understood in metaphoric or literal terms), but with the putative separation of sounds and meaning. At times the phonological and semantic fields overlap; at other times there is no overlap and all we are left with is sound sense. At times a translator – and translation gives us the sharpest insight into what's at stake here – may emphasize sounds independent of meaning; at other times the translator may resort to a semantic equivalent independent of the original sound. A focus on the separation of sounds and meaning, or an initial acceptance of that separation, can help to reduce the pressure to read the episode in the light of the Overture, and at the same time it frees up the possibility of interpreting 'Sirens' in terms of 'local disturbances' or of establishing an analogy or parallel between language and politics.

As if to thwart a smooth or Conmee-like reading, the language of 'Sirens' is surrounded by 'local disturbances'. We are constantly delayed in this episode and frequently have recourse to micro readings which yield a peculiar kind of local satisfaction. 'Bronze by gold' is often read in terms of the previous episode and the colour of the barmaids' hair. After the Viceregal cavalcade comes the female reply to the metallic sound of the horses and their tackle. As with other opening sentences to episodes in *Ulysses*, 'Sirens' begins in search of meaning, in this case with metonymy, with parts for the whole, with coins of the realm, with a commodity, with barmaids and service and commodification. My purpose in deploying the phrase 'local disturbances' is to give shape to something that might otherwise go unnoticed. The phrase itself I have borrowed from George Cornewall Lewis's *On Local Disturbances in Ireland and On the Irish Church Question* (1836), and the direction of my argument is towards establishing not so much a connection as a parallel between local disturbances in language and local disturbances in Irish history.

Lewis's study begins: 'For the last seventy years Ireland has been the scene of constantly recurring disturbances; sometimes consisting only of the murder of a few persons, or the burning of a few houses, and sometimes rising to general insurrection' (Lewis, 1). The disturbances Lewis has in mind date from 1761 with the appearance in Munster of the Whiteboys, an agrarian association which was formed initially to resist the payment of tithes to Protestant clergymen but which later broadened out to agitate on behalf of the peasantry and tenant farmer against landlords and their agents. The 1780s witnessed the rise of militancy in the north of Ireland with the establishment of the Peep- or Break-of-day-Boys, a sectarian militia who took to searching for arms among the homes of their Catholic neighbours; Catholics responded by forming their own association, the Defenders. Then in the 1790s the temperature increased significantly when the Peep-of-day-Boys founded the Orange Order and the Defenders merged their interests with Wolfe Tone's United Irishmen. The reference by Lewis to 'general insurrection' is to the 1798 Rising ('rebellion' according to Lewis), which sought by a series of military risings largely centred on the South East, the Midlands, and the North of Ireland, to break the connection with Britain and establish an independent republic. All these are considered 'local disturbances' by the Whig commentator Lewis, but, inadvertently, in summarizing all these in a single sentence, he provides us with a way of connecting the local with the national, the land question with the nationalist issue, history and politics. In 'Wandering Rocks', the Lord Lieutenant of Ireland smiles benevolently on the King's subjects, but in 'Sirens', away from the gaze of the Crown, the colonized are impertinent, mock the conquering hero and sing rebel songs about the croppies who cropped their hair as a sign of sympathy with the French Revolution. According to Lewis, 'every Irish Catholic was presumed to be disaffected to the State, and was treated as an open or concealed rebel' (Lewis, 46–7). 'Sirens' is not a revolutionary tract, but its local disturbances suggest it can be read in rebellious terms and this is what I attempt to do here.

## Imperthnthn thnthnthn

Anyone approaching the Overture to 'Sirens' with meaning in mind is in for a bit of a shock. Simply filtering the sounds that jostle in the ear is enough for many readers. 'Imperthnthn thnthnthn', to take one example, will challenge anyone not advanced in elocution. Eleven letters in one word and nine in the other with only two vowels and those in the first word. Im-per-thn-thn – four syllables in the first word; thn-thn-thn – three in the second. To make sense of the pronunciation is to pronounce the words, or, vice versa, to pronounce the words is a sign that they have been understood: that seems to be the challenge. The individual sounds can be broken down into phonemes, or gathered together into syllables, into morphemes, but, whichever approach is adopted, top-down or history-from-below as it were, the aim is to produce a sound for the whole word. Reducing the word to, say, I-m-p-e-r-t-h-n-t-h-n wouldn't be right – more like a not very good English lesson, one that would certainly have been avoided by a good teacher at the Berlitz School in Pola or Trieste. The pressure lies in achieving a sound for the whole word.

The sound in this case seems suspended until some other clue comes along. Im- indicates a negative, as in the English words 'imprecise' or 'implausible'. Imper- suggests the beginning of a number of English words such as 'impermanent', 'impermissible' or 'impersonal'. Add the 'thn' and you almost have 'impertinent'. In *Tit-Bits Monster English Dictionary* (1899), 'impertinent' is glossed as 'irrelevant; meddling; rude'. Today, we would rarely hear in conversation 'impertinent' meaning 'not pertinent' or irrelevant (and this is not the primary meaning in this episode, though it might become so if we thought the bar staff in the Ormond Hotel were irrelevant to Church–State matters). In this the word is unlike 'impermissible', which is 'not permissible', or 'impermanent', which is 'not permanent'. The word then is odd, and so too is the other word used later by Miss Douce 'insolence', which again is not

'not solence'. When we return to the sound, we find that deciphering the sound is dependent on meaning, on there being a word to link with the sound. But at this point in 'Sirens' there isn't a word. We have to wait for 'bootssnout', the general helper, to set down the tea for Misses Douce and Kennedy before we can connect sound and meaning:

> —There's your teas, he said.
> Miss Kennedy with manners transposed the teatray down to an upturned lithia crate, safe from eyes, low.
> —What is it? loud boots unmannerly asked.
> —Find out, miss Douce retorted, leaving her spyingpoint.
> —Your beau, is it?
> A haughty bronze replied:
> —I'll complain to Mrs de Massey on you if I hear any more of your imper-tinent insolence.
> —Imperthnthn thnthnthn, bootssnout sniffed rudely, as he retreated as she threatened as he had come. (*U* 11:91–101)

It becomes apparent that you can only translate or read this phrase in the Overture in the light of what's to come in the episode, so delay and re-reading, as Fritz Senn has rightly suggested, are part of the reading experience. In general comments on Joyce's language, Margaret Schlauch makes the point that 'the most audacious coiners of verbal currency are limited to units capable of conveying sense – and therefore meaningful because they are to some degree familiar' (Schlauch, 235). 'Imperthnthn' is a negative, and close to negation, to parody. It offers itself as a parody of subservience, a parody of female dominance, a parody of sounds in search of meaning and perhaps also a parody of those who imagine difficulty belongs to major protagonists, for what is this but a minor spat among the junior staff in the Ormond Hotel. As it happens, the discourse on class repeatedly surfaces in this episode, often linked with gender inequality, as if Joyce's aim is to suggest that, even if they are unfocused, the local disturbances have a political import. Miss Douce shares a joke with her fellow barmaid Miss Kennedy about a 'snuffy fogey' with a 'goggle' eye they encountered at the Antient Concert Hall. The narrator informs us that Miss Douce 'snorted down her nostrils that quivered imperthnthn like a snout in quest'. Here the nose is in quest of haughty imitation, but haughtiness evades her as the sound she makes is compared to snorting like a pig, the snout an echo of 'bootssnout', close that is to parody or merely answering back, a rebel without a cause.

What does the company of Joyce's translators make of 'Imperthnthn'? How in other words do they tackle the issue of sounds raised in this episode? Unlike 'Rrrpr. Kraa. Kraandl.', the farting sound at the end of the Overture, 'Imperthnthn' is more than just a physical sound for it also exhibits a semantic possibility. The French translation by Morel has 'Impertnent' followed by 'tnentnent' (Morel, 392). This is closer to meaning than sound, but, ironically, to English ears this could suggest the letter 'i' is missing or that someone has a speech impairment, given to slurs in speech. 'Impertintín' followed by 'tntntn' is how it is rendered in Spanish by Valverde (Valverde, 229). Valverde provides a surer reflection of the original effect where a gulf divides sounds from meaning. 'Impertinente' is impertinent with an e. 'Tntntn' is nasal, the sound reverberating round the nose, the after-effect. In this translation the first word is close to meaning, the second to pure sound. Giulio de Angelis' 1960s Italian translation has: 'Impertnt tntntn' (de Angelis, 345). These different versions, then, each have their own effect, but all these translators are keen to allow the sounds to stand as sounds. The Argentine translator Subirat mixes things. In the Overture he has 'Impertnent tnentnent', two pages later 'Impertntn tntntn' (Subirat, 285, 287). In the most recent Spanish translation, Francisco García Tortosa reads the phrase in the light of what's to come, placing more weight thereby on meaning than on sound, in the process inadvertently collapsing Miss Douce and the insolent boy into the one figure: 'Impertintnt insolentnt' (Tortosa, 293:2). In this regard, Senn makes the valuable point, sometimes missed by translators as here by Tortosa, that once we learn 'Imperthnthn thnthnthn' means impertinent insolence 'we are likely to think [it] actually *means* "impertinent insolence", but it only does so by proleptic and unwarranted foresight' (Senn 1995, 84). But then, looking back on history sometimes allows us to discern that what appear at the time merely spats or 'impertinences', such as the Whiteboy disturbances, are in fact part of a larger struggle for articulation.

## A husky fifenote blew.

## Blew. Blue bloom is on the.

These lines, which provide another example of sound sense, present a different challenge, for the focus is in part on homophones, on words with the same sounds but different spellings. We can begin, however, with grammar and history. 'Blew', the past tense of the verb to blow, requires a subject and it is only later in the episode that we learn that the reference is to Simon Dedalus blowing into his pipe and transforming it into a musical instrument, producing the sound of a fife. Fife in turn recalls drums and the military and the period of the croppy boys and the local disturbances throughout Ireland in 1798, the Year of the French. The word 'husky' recalls the 'fury hoarse' of the yeoman captain in 'The Croppy Boy' as he casts off his priestly robes to reveal his true identity (see Appendix 1 for the song's lyrics). The phrase 'husky fifenote' is not meant, therefore, to be lyrical. Deception or 'decoy' is one of the themes of this chapter, a view also in evidence in the series 'blew Blew Blue', which suggests frustration rather than flow. Morel, we might notice in passing, possibly on account of the 'Soft word' which follows or of Lenehan's lisping to Miss Kennedy a 'low whistle of decoy' (*U* 11:328), mistranslates 'decoy' as 'séduction', and Subirat, Hans Wollschläger and de Angelis follow in his wake with 'Seducción', 'Verlocken' (to entice) and 'lusinga' (flattery). Lenehan would like his decoy to be part of a seductive encounter, but that is another matter. In answer to Stephen's expression of desire in 'Proteus' – 'Touch me. Soft eyes.' (*U* 3:434–6) – 'Sirens' replies 'Decoy. Soft word.'

'Blew', another 'Sirens' word, is continued in the next line. 'Blew. Blue bloom is on the.' The alliteration is nicely captured in the German translation: 'Blus. Blau Bloomelein im' (Wollschläger, 355). A characteristic procedure in this episode is the switching from one consciousness to another via the same word or sound. Normally it marks a shift to Bloom, who doesn't arrive at the Ormond until much later in the episode. At this point there is a switch from Simon Dedalus and his pipe blowing to blue Bloom. In the song 'The Bloom is on the Rye' it is late spring, summer is coming, and the bloom is on the rye (rye does have a blue colour when in bloom). We might also discern another aspect to this switch from Simon to Bloom, from biography to fiction, from sound to association, history to the present, for Joyce's father sang this particular song to May Joyce. The song is upbeat, Bloom, on the other hand, is blue. 'Blew. Blue bloom is on the.'

The Spanish translation by Valverde is 'Sopló. *Bloom* (italicized), flor azul hay en el.' The translator makes no attempt to reproduce the assonance of bl bl bl or ew ue oom. As for Bloom, he is described as 'flor azul', a blue flower. This is not without merit, especially the lower case 'bloom', which allows scope for the song to be heard first. But it is not so much a translation as a paraphrase, a paraphrase which makes no attempt at a phonological equivalence either. We know the reference is to Bloom; indeed, in the Rosenbach manuscript Joyce writes it in upper case. The English is not 'Bloom, blue flower' but the more enigmatic 'Blue bloom'. A little later in the episode, 'en el' is completed by 'centeno' or rye, but this would only work if there was a song or phrase such as 'flor azul hay en el centeno'. Otherwise the missing word is entirely dependent on the unfolding text. Tortosa invites a different reading when he suggests an alternative meaning to 'Blue', not the colour but blue, the substance once widely used in washing clothes: 'Sopló. Brotebloom añil en el' (Tortosa, 293:8). 'Brotebloom' brings together Bloom's name and a word which contains several meanings: to sprout or appear as in plants; to rise as in the morning; an outbreak (of violence) or rash. In translating this back into English, the literal reading – 'He blew. Sprouting Bloom blue in the' – conveys the idea of something that is forced or being forced. Other translations produce a slightly different effect: 'Bloom appears blue in the' or 'Bloom rises blue in the'. Less dramatically, the sentence is later completed, like Valverde, with 'centeno' or rye, but then the blue in washing looks even more out of place. Subirat's translation also departs from the original and insists on closure at this point: 'Floreció. La azul floración está sobre los cabellos coronados de oro' (Subirat, 285). Literally: 'He bloomed. The blue flowering is on the crowned gold hair.' Here 'blew' has been changed into bloom and 'rye' has been rendered metaphorically and painted a different colour.

Contrary to what one might think given Joyce's choice of blue and white (the Greek flag) for the cover of the Shakespeare and Company edition of *Ulysses*, the Greek translation amends blue to milky white. Again, this provides an interesting modification especially in the light of the reference to the Milky Way in 'Hades' or when we recall the derivation of the English word galaxy: 'Galaxios anthos pano ste' (Kapsaskis, 304). A milky white flower is in bloom. Here Bloom is 'anthos', a flower, and linked therefore with the word anthology, his identity composed of little refrains, flowers that adorn an anthology. 'Sirens' repeatedly anticipates the language of *Finnegans Wake*, and in retrospect we can discern how in the character of Bloom Joyce is learning to exploit the 'paradigmatic ear', which is one of the distinctive features of the *Wake*. In the Greek translation Bloom's name is Mploum, the sound made on diving into the sea; sometimes it means the dive itself as in the phrase 'let's go for a mploum' (mp constitutes the equivalent of b in modern Greek). In the Greek translation there is a descant of sorts on Bloom's name and flowers. The French translation, which elsewhere plays ingeniously on 'florit', 'fleury' and 'fleuri', has Bloom 'aux champs' or in the fields as if he were in some physical location. Bleuet is cornflower; French Canadians use bleuet for blueberry. 'Bluet Bloom est aux.' There is little suggestion here of melancholy unless the bleu in bluet can carry that inflection. De Angelis' 'Bloom blu è la patina sul' brings together 'blu' and 'sul', blue and on, a colour adjective and a preposition without an object. 'Patina', for 'bloom', sets up a different set of associations, not yet a flower but a glaze or varnish. Later, the sentence is completed with 'fior de segale', flower of rye (de Angelis, 353). In German, blue little Bloom is blooming in a cornfield: 'Blau Bloomelein im Kornfeld blüht' (Wollschläger, 363). Few translations give us anything of blue's range of meanings in English (blue as in melancholy, blue as in blue joke, blue as in the blues, blue as in bolt from the blue) or of its recurring interest both for the author of the 'Blue Book of Eccles' (*FW* 179:26) and for critics from John Addington Symonds's *In the Key of Blue And Other Prose Essays* (1893) to William H. Gass's *On Being Blue: A Philosophical Inquiry* (1975).

## Idolores

'Trilling, trilling: Idolores.' In the song 'The Shade of the Palm' the line goes 'O my Dolores, Queen of the Eastern Sea'. In Miss Douce's rendition she alters 'my Dolores' to 'Idolores'. Lydia becomes the object of worship; she is I, and idol. This is a nice touch by Joyce. Miss Douce identifies with what she hears or thinks she hears. Trilling, trillante, trinando, trillernd, fredonne in English, Italian, Spanish, German and Italian. In whichever language, she is like a bird: Idolores. Like a bird, she also wants to be noticed. Look at me, she says, sensuous barmaid, recently returned from my holidays down the country with my body suitably tanned, or hopefully giving the impression of being tanned. In the one word, Joyce combines an array of associations: I, idol, Dolores, dolours, sorrows. The word also allows Joyce scope later in the episode to substitute the 'I' for 'he' when Bloom, listening to Ben Dollard's rendition of 'The Croppy Boy', expresses a confusion as to the identity of 'he': 'At Geneva barrack that young man died. At Passage was his body laid. Dolor! O, he dolores!' (*U* 11:1131–2). The French translation of the original is more narrowly conceived. 'Adolores' (Morel, 392) is an acceptance that there is no idol here. In Subirat's and Valverde's Spanish translations 'Aydolores' carries 'ay', perhaps an expression of (Greek-like) pain. Even if it remains outside the category we might assign to an insight, it is worth noting that the initial syllable in 'Idolores' can also be spelt 'eyed', precisely the word that the narrator deploys in connection with Boylan's male gaze on hearing Miss Douce's garter smack against her thigh: 'Boylan, eyed, eyed' (*U* 11:419). Here the comma separating the subject from the verb reminds us of the constant recourse to metonymy throughout this episode; it also highlights the rush of blood and the idea of an action not symbolizing but enveloping the person, for Boylan is all eyes. Boylan is also being eyed by Miss Douce; hence the repetition 'eyed, eyed'. In Valverde's translation the original is reproduced as 'Boylan observaba, observaba' (Valverde, 340), in Subirat as 'miró, miró' (Subirat, 296), but observing and eyeing are not the same thing. Tortosa, in contrast, reminds us that Spanish, too, has a similar way of indicating what is at stake here: 'Boylan, ojeaba, ojeaba' (Tortosa, 306:526). 'Boylan la fixe, fixe' (Morel, 409) is the French translation, which picks up on one aspect of the original for, while Miss Douce is gliding, the male gaze fixes her, fixes.

Later in the episode, we learn that the mare carrying Boylan for his rendezvous with Molly is too slow for the carriage's occupant: 'Too slow for Boylan, blazes Boylan, impatience Boylan, joggled the mare' (*U* 11: 765–6). Uncharacteristically, at this point Valverde decides to throw caution to the wind and produce a translation for 'blazes Boylan' that potentially links him with every playboy of the western world including Synge's playboy Christy Mahon: 'playboylan' (Valverde, 350). Nowhere in

*Ulysses* is Joyce tempted to make such a comparison, or even call Boylan a 'boyo', yet, in spite of confining his day to 1904, he might have done so by a form of 'retrospective arrangement'. Not to be outdone, Tortosa in the next phrase plays on Boylan's name: 'Boylando de impaciencia' (Tortosa, 317:979–80), where, alongside the Spanish 'bailando' or dancing, the English 'boiling' can also be heard in the gerund construction, boiling with impatience – in contrast with the patience of the modern Odysseus or indeed Molly's 'penelopean patience' (*FW* 123:4–5). De Angelis also plays on Boylan's name as here with 'impazienza Boylante' (373), a collocation he had anticipated when he translates 'With patience Lenehan waited for Boylan with impatience, for jinglejaunty blazes boy' by making use of the phrase 'Boylan boylente d'impazienza' (355). Wollschläger, too, enjoys this combination 'die boylende Ungeduld', where 'boylende' perhaps carries the idea of a bruise or swelling, and perhaps also a page boy plus loin, a loin boy.

### Peep! Who's in the … peepofgold?

The preceding line in the Overture begins 'Trilling, trilling', and one can see why some translators have felt the pressure to continue with the sound of a bird such as a cuckoo. This is how Valverde and Morel render 'Peep', complete with flying exclamation marks: '¡Cu-cú!' and 'Coucou!' Presumably the intention is to suggest an analogy between the bird which steals nests and Boylan stealing Bloom's bed and thereby cuckolding him. Tortosa imagines 'Peep' is simply a bird sound, a tweet, 'pio' in Spanish. The problem with this line of interpretation is what to do with the 'peepofgold', for, unless it's the fleck or markings in flight, there's little that is bird-like in 'peepofgold'. Valverde, following Morel and de Angelis, is inventive and coins a word 'cucudeoro' ('coucoudor' in French, 'cucudoro' in Italian), a golden cuckoo, but that seems strained: 'Who's in the golden cuckoo?' Tortosa, who is equally astray at this point, takes his cue from Subirat's 'piodeoro', shortening it to 'piodoro', a golden tweet or peep. Unfortunately, the confusion is compounded by Morel: 'Coucou. Ah la voilà!' (Morel, 402) 'Cuckoo. Ah here it is!' Ironically, these versions pay too much attention to sound, too little to meaning. 'Peep! Who's in the corner?' (11:242), not 'Who's in the peepofgold?', is how the sentence later appears in 'Sirens', where 'peep' refers not so much to a bird sound as concealment, a meaning incidentally available to both the French and Spanish translators in their own languages. This is its primary meaning here, a switch, therefore, from sound to meaning, a move which is confirmed by the odd joined-up phrase 'peepofgold' and by the later reference to 'corner'. 'Kiek mal an', the German translation for 'peep', is a dialect expression used in Berlin and northern Germany, but it is more straightforward, free of ornithology or sexual association, restricting itself to the idea of being curious, perhaps with cheek added on.

There are two other ways of interpreting this phrase, one of which emphasizes the idea of a peepshow, of the part for the whole. The 'gold' in 'peepofgold', we might agree, is a reference to 'goldgirl' Miss Kennedy. Miss Douce sings 'Idolores', shows off her figure, and smacks her thigh with her garter. Miss Kennedy shrieks and stops her ears but, as 'gold flushed more' suggests, she is more reserved than her colleague. She also has something to show, but not to Lenehan. At this juncture in 'Sirens' she is reading, her head is down, and her face is concealed by her golden hair. 'Who's in the peepofgold' seems to concern the printed matter Miss Kennedy is reading. 'Did she fall or was she pushed?' (*U* 11:333) Lenehan enquires, only to be rebuffed. Who or what in other words is absorbing her attention? And what is she reading? Could it be a salacious novel such as *Sweets of Sin*, the novel which Bloom has bought for Molly and which carries in its title a pun on the English name of her rival Miss Douce? Joyce leaves it open, in line therefore with the enigma of the phrase itself. We might also, though, discern a link with the confession scene in 'The Croppy Boy', where in the phrase 'Who's in the corner?' can possibly be heard 'Who's in the confessional?'

This brings me to a second line of interpretation, one which is essentially historical and political, and which seeks to anchor the phrase in the period of 'The Croppy Boy'. Behind the phrase 'peepofgold' I hear 'Peep-of-day-Boys'. In contrast with the Whiteboys, who would attack the landowning classes and their agents at night wearing white sheets, the 'peep of day' boys would attack their Catholic enemies at break of day, an historical reference continued four lines later in the Overture in 'The morn is breaking'. We might also recall at this juncture that at the Christmas Dinner in *A Portrait of the Artist as a Young Man*, Simon Dedalus points to a portrait of his grandfather to remind his family that he was condemned to death as a Whiteboy. So 'peepofgold', which has a specific sectarian origin, seems to invoke a wider context which links eighteenth-century agrarian agitation with the emergence of Irish nationalism and Joyce's own family history.

Beneath the robes of the yeoman captain who's impersonating Father Green, the croppy boy catches sight of the soldier's scarlet:

> The priest said nought, but a rustling noise
> Made the youth look above in wild surprise;
> The robes were off, and in scarlet there
> Sat a yeoman captain with fiery glare.

'Peep' carries an echo of that period when the Irish were cornered by various decoys and betrayals and suffered defeat at the hands of the Crown. Many of the exclamation marks in the Overture – not all, as references to Verdi's *Otello*, Bellini's *La Sonnambula*, Flotow's *Martha* remind us – capture a sense of loss and alarm associated with that period in Irish history. The episode also marks Bloom's closest identification with Irish nationalism, perhaps providing a backdrop to the 'Cyclops' episode which follows. The last reference in the Overture, which is also the most scurrilous, is to Robert Emmet's Speech from the Dock in 1803: 'When my country takes her place among the nations of the earth then and not till then, let my epitaph be written. I have done.' But Joyce is not out to destroy but to enforce the connection. After all, in 'Nestor', Odysseus's son, in conversation with his paymaster Mr Deasy, feels the full force of not only 'the black north' and the 'true blue bible' but also the Orange taunt 'Croppies lie down' (*U* 2:276). We might also make something of the way 'Sirens' begins with 'Bronze by gold', a phrase normally interpreted as the colour of the colour co-ordinated barmaids' hair or, following Gifford and Seidman (1989), as connected with 'the principal metals in the Homeric world'. But the phrase also lends itself to a reading in terms of the scarlet and the green, the harp and the crown. Bronze and gold are traditional colours of merit and of regiments in the British Army. It is 'Bronze by gold', not 'Bronze et Or' or 'Bronce y hierro' as Morel and Subirat have it, a deliberate placing to convey an order or rank. Against the yeoman captain's wish forcibly expressed in 'The Croppy Boy' 'may all traitors swing!', and against the 'steelyringing' of the stately procession of the Viceregal cavalcade that concludes 'Wandering Rocks' and that begins 'Sirens', 'Bronze by gold' and Ben Dollard's rendering of the song provide a modern, less dramatic reply. It may be only a 'peepofgold' but it's enough to suggest that the Crown doesn't have a monopoly on worth and esteem.

### Sonnez. ... La cloche!

In the Spanish, Italian and Greek translations, 'Sonnez' and 'La cloche' are left as in the original and italicized; in the French only 'sonnez' is italicized. The clock sounds in French but the primary reference is not to a clock – often a word for something else in *Ulysses* – but to Miss Douce's garter smacking against her thigh, the sound Lenehan is anxious to hear again. Appropriately, it is French, the language of the 'beau', which carries the erotic note. In contrast to the more business-like Boylan, who has an instrumental view of his body, Bloom, who's more in tune with his body, knows that 'Time makes the tune' (*U* 11:841). It's a view he shares with the blind piano-tuner, who has left behind his tuning-fork at the Ormond Hotel. With 'prongs buzzing' (*U* 11:316), the tuning-fork is given new life in the Spanish translation where it is rendered as 'cuernos zumbando' (Valverde, 337), and linked with the phrase 'Horn. Hawhorn.' from the Overture where it is translated as 'Cuerno. Cocuerno.' In Valverde's translation, the horn in the Overture suggestively anticipates the prongs of the piano-tuner's tuning-fork. Traditionally, piano-tuners were blind but handy and they feature in English folksongs (and European folktales) playing their part in scenes of seduction. 'Zumbando' is also suggestive – insects 'zumbando', insects buzzing, but the image cannot be sustained. A little later we read that a clock buzzed – 'Zumbó el reloj' (Valverde, 339) – when in the original text the clock 'whirred' (*U* 11:380). Subirat has 'Cuerno. Corneta', horn, bugle. The play on horn as penis is continued with 'Cuerno. ¿Tienes el? Cuer cuer cuerno' (Subirat, 299). Words and sounds, therefore, set up different associations. At times the phonological and semantic fields overlap; at other times they create interesting divergences. De Angelis renders the original 'Corno. Coccocorno' (345), which mixes something that is heard with something that is eaten, a horn with a coconut or an egg (or the berry that lurks in the 'haw' of 'hawhorn'). With 'corno' in Italian close to 'cornuto' or cuckold, Bloom's predicament is never far from the sound. The German translation pulls no punches: 'Ständer, Stistaständer' (Wollschläger, 355), a stand (for an instrument), a stutter, a 'hawhorn', an erection that is.

### Wait while you wait. Hee hee. Wait while you hee.

The meaning of this line becomes clear later in the episode. 'Pat is a waiter who waits while you wait. Hee hee hee hee. He waits while you wait. Hee hee. A waiter is he. Hee hee hee hee.' A possible source for this particular series of puns might be the song that keeps recurring in 'Sirens'. In 'The Croppy Boy', the rebel wants to make a last confession:

> But you must wait till I go and see
> If the holy father alone may be.

The potentially inane, jingling, repetition of 'see' and 'be', together with the heavy obligation to 'wait' and the deception regarding the true identity of 'he' ('the holy father'), point to a potential source. 'But wait' is a phrase also from the song and it is later used by Miss Douce in gossipy conversation with her colleague: 'But wait till I tell you' (*U* 11: 128). A little later in the Overture the song is also recalled along with the stress on 'he': '*Naminedamine*. Preacher is he'. The glee of the yeomen who capture the boy can also be possibly heard in the triumph of 'hee hee'. As for 'wait', Pat is a deaf waiter, is 'bothered' (Irish: 'bodhar', meaning deaf), so hears nothing in an episode devoted to sounds, but he does wait on those who wait. In translation, the play on wait-as-waiter and wait-as-waiting is less straightforward than might be imagined. Morel distinguishes two meanings: 'Pose pendant que vous pausez. Hi hi.' (Morel, 304) He avoids 'servir' (à table) or 'attendre' and can make nothing of 'wait' and 'waiter'. 'Rest or pose while you pause or take a break.' The 'pose' and 'pausez' is a good attempt at phonological insistence. However, it isn't 'Wait while you wait', which is how Subirat renders it 'Espera mientras esperas' (Subirat, 286), but something much more ordinary and transactional, like a management notice on the wall of an office or factory. Valverde makes use of 'sirvir', to wait, sirvir a la mesa, to wait at table, and, instead of the more normal camerero, he deploys 'sirvidor', a waiter, in his translation. 'Sirve a un sirvidor. Ji Ji.' In contrast, Tortosa attends or takes care of: 'Atiende mientras atiendes. Je je.' 'He attends or takes care of while you attend or take care of' is a possible translation, which illustrates something of the problem, whether in Spanish or English, with the use of antanaclasis (a word which is not so much a pun as a word, like 'wait', with different meanings). 'Attento mentre attendi' (de Angelis, 346), careful while you attend, looks a similar construction in Italian but, in the interplay between the letters t and d in 'attento' and attendi', de Angelis manages to capture something more of the original. 'Hee hee' is difficult enough in English. There is clearly a play on the personal pronoun, for what is 'Sirens' but a language exercise in identifying deictic markers? Joyce sets up a constant play in this episode on 'he', and the reader needs to be, like the reader of the *Wake*, wideawake, ever alert as to the identity of 'he' throughout. The phrase also conveys an attitude which is part cynical, part gleeful. 'Hee, hee, serves him right' is a common enough idiomatic phrase in the language. 'Hee-haw' is the sound of a donkey braying, and, not unexpectedly, both 'hee' and 'haw' can be heard in the Overture. 'Hi hi' in French, 'Ji ji' or 'Je je' in Spanish, capture something of the inanity of the original but little or nothing of the identity issue.

## None nought said nothing.

If everything in *Ulysses* speaks in its own way – door hinges creak, noses snort, back passages fart, sometimes with a p, sometimes with a double ff – then so too does nothing. 'None nought said nothing' (*U* 11: 224) is a phrase that might well have appeared in the Overture but in fact it comes later in the episode. The context can be quickly noted. Simon Dedalus has been musing on his name, his drink, the Mourne Mountains, holidays, Miss Douce and now his musing, his music, has come to a stop. 'Musing. Mute' (11:223). The next line is 'None nought said nothing.' In many respects, this is the strangest sentence in 'Sirens', and this is true even if one includes the lines from the Overture, nearly all of which can be on reflection deciphered. It isn't 'There was nothing to be said' but 'None nought said nothing.' Like other interruptions to word order, 'said' is here the problem word – as it is elsewhere in phrases such as the Arranger's 'as said before' (in connection with eating liver) or the delightful cautionary moment in 'Sirens' itself, 'Who said four?'

(in connection with Boylan's rendezvous with Molly). As a verb we assume it is surrounded on either side by a subject and an object. 'None said nothing. Nought.' Or 'Nothing said nought. None.' Or 'Nought said none, nothing.' The muse, that is, runs out of anything to muse on. 'Nothing, nought, none.' But even negatives have a voice, make some sound. As we learn from 'The Croppy Boy', the priest listens to the boy's confession and because he doesn't reply we sense danger for the boy – 'The priest said nought.'

'Ninguno no decía nada' (Valverde, 335) is Valverde's Spanish translation, not dissimilar to de Angelis' Italian translation 'Nessuno non diceva nulla'. No-one said anything / nothing, where a double negative would sometimes produce a positive. Either way, this isn't really what the original is asserting. The alliteration in the initial 'n' in the Spanish has merit, but the original is 'None nought … nothing', which, unlike 'ninguno no decía nada', is not something you'd hear in ordinary conversation. 'Naide cosa nada decía nada' is Tortosa's translation. 'Naide' is a humorous rendering of 'Nadie', not Blake's Old Testament God 'Nobadaddy' but closer to a regional non-standard form of the word, perhaps akin to a word like 'naybody' in English – or 'Noman', the name Odysseus tells the Cyclops is his. 'Naide' conveys something of the oddness of the original but it isn't the sober statement 'None nought said nothing.' Tortosa reminds us of another problem. In English there is an ambiguity at the level of both syntax and meaning: 'none' can be both a person and a thing; 'nadie', on the other hand, is restricted to a person. The process of disentangling a meaning to the original sentence leads us to further entanglements in part because an ambiguity is made unambiguous. 'Pas un mot, personne ne sonne' is the French translation, 'not a word, nobody makes a sound'. Again, this isn't nothing, and, moreover, in the original 'nothing' is governed by something.

The sentence is clearly a problem, as much for native speakers as for translators. What does it mean? With its emphasis on 'nichts' and the philosophical associations that accompany 'nichts', the German translation perhaps gives us a clue: 'Keiner nichtsagte nichts' (Wollschläger, 362), Nobody said nothing. *Ex nihilo nihil fit* was the old Thomist / Aristotelian adage, which, as I mentioned in the Introduction, Joyce would have been familiar with from his schooldays, that out of nothing nothing comes. The sentence we might read as a one-sentence reply or challenge to the philosophical issue of *esse* and *potentia*, of being and potentiality, an issue that occupied the medieval, Jesuit-educated Joyce as well as his character Stephen. The theme of Yeats's medieval play *Where There Is Nothing* (1902) is the individual's search for authenticity away from civilization as embodied in the monastery. This is not Joyce's concern here. For Joyce, nothing is indeed something, nothing can occasion something; nothing also has something to say, for negation is also a positive. In this we might compare it with the opening of 'Proteus' where we catch Stephen responding to the solipsist dilemma about external reality: 'Ineluctable modality of the visible' (*U* 3:1). In 'Sirens', the philosophical moment is disturbed by the sexual encounter in a hotel bar. None of the males make much headway in interesting the barmaids; they might hold their hands but, except for the 'smack', there is little by way of reciprocity. So nothing is in part a rejection. Perhaps, like the three strokes referred to at the beginning of 'The Sisters', there is something decisive about three zeros – none nought nothing. The answer they're looking for is Yes, a Molly O word, the word that completes Simon Dedalus's musing. 'Yes.' But the males get nought at this juncture, only the sonnez of Miss Douce's smack (which might be all they are seeking).

Turning to 'Musing. Mute.', Valverde and Tortosa provide contrasting views of the thinking process. For Valverde, Simon is 'cavilando', thinking deeply, deliberating; for Tortosa he is 'recapacitando', recalling to mind. Neither manage to capture the echo in the vowel sound between musing and mute. Indeed the -ando ending tends to dominate in a way that -ing in 'Musing' does not. Partly because it can also be used as a noun, 'Mudo' is a strong word in Spanish, much stronger than 'mute' in English (whose field today is largely confined to adjectival use), but in this collocation the mudo effect is softened. Simon's musings, not his deliberations or indeed his recalling to mind, have come suddenly to a dead end: this is how 'Musing. Mute.' with the full stop repeated after each word reads in English. Without the two words and just with the punctuation it reads: .. Musing is close to reverie, the mind turning things over, not so much recalling as allowing images and associations and half-formed thoughts to surface and run on. In this episode it is a Sirens word, the male held by the female muse unable in the end to speak. 'Rêveur. En silence.' (401) is the French translation: 'Dreamy. In silence.' But this misses nearly all of the inner drama of 'Musing. Mute.'

## From the rock of Gibraltar ... all the way.

'From the rock of Gibraltar ... all the way' (*U* 11:515). In the Rosenbach manuscript there are no elliptical points but in inserting them Joyce must have realized that these too have a sound or contribution to make. In the same passage we read that Marion was 'a daughter of ...' and the reply is 'Daughter of the regiment'. In the sentence 'From the rock of Gibraltar ... all the way', the elliptical points might suggest one of her exotic advertising puffs as a singer – all the way from Hickville, Tennessee or wherever. On the other hand, in an episode about Boylan going all the way, the phrase might hint at her sexual determination or indeed prowess. Elliptical points are missing points, are cryptic in that they hide something, but nevertheless they also make a sound in writing.

What's left out also has a noise to make, none more so we might add than the wink and nod by males in conversation about women. 'Del peñón de Gibraltar ... nada menos' (Valverde, 343) is Valverde's and Tortosa's Spanish translation. From the rock of Gibraltar ... nothing less. Not quite. De Angelis keeps the meaning slightly ambiguous: 'Dalla roccia di Gibilterra ... tutta quella strada' (de Angelis, 363), from the rock of Gibraltar ... all that road. The French translation seems innocent by comparison. No elliptical points and this: 'Du rocher de Gibraltar, en ligne droite' (Morel, 413). From the rock of Gibraltar in a straight line. Au contraire, as Beckett might say.

## Concluding Remarks

Suggest a connective tissue and, as I indicate in the following chapter on the Berlin Wall, Joyce blocks it. This is partly why I have drawn back from suggesting a strong link between disturbances in language and disturbances in history. After all, Bloom leaves the Ormond Hotel before Dollard finishes 'The Croppy Boy', and, in an episode devoted to music, the Odyssean figure, strapped as it were to the mast, gives voice to the most heretical and double-edged remark in 'Sirens': 'Music. Gets on your nerves' (*U* 11:1182). Equally, not everything fits, for Bloom does not speak Irish, does not, like Haynes, collect Irish sayings, and might only recognize 'buachaill' as boy because of its continuing use in an Ireland no longer bi-lingual. Moreover, Bloom does not love his country above his king, for, as we learn in the following episode, his nation is simply the place where he was born. But, as other scholars have noticed, there is enough in 'Sirens' to suggest a link between Bloom and the events surrounding 1798. My concern in this chapter has been slightly different, not to go over this old ground for the sake of it but to set out a case for drawing a parallel between local disturbances in Ireland with local disturbances in language.

'The Croppy Boy' begins:

Good men and true in this house who dwell,
To a stranger *buachaill* I pray you tell.

Bloom is the stranger, the Ormond Hotel 'this house', 'Good men' the company in the bar (or the reader). Like the croppy boy, Bloom is on the point of being dispossessed of his home, if only temporarily. He is both of this house and a stranger, both Irish and not-Irish. But without the song and the issue of identity it trails, 'Sirens' would be a poorer episode. Bloom's predicament intensifies as the song's tension builds, but it is a predicament that affords no release in confession. Instead, Bloom tries the art of distraction amid his familiar comfort zone as human observer: 'What do they think when they hear music?' (*U* 11:1049), where 'they' refers to women in general. As we see with Maria in 'Clay', lyrics have the capacity to speak to people directly and even reduce them to a catatonic state. They can play, that is, on the nerves. Hence Bloom's attempt to remove himself from the bar, for he knows enough of identity and himself to stop it, to keep his distance from 'good men and true'. In all these moves Joyce reminds us that the representation of identity never fits like a glove, but we would be wrong to conclude there is no lyrical soul behind the 'poisoner of his word' (*FW* 463:13).

A strong reading might want to insist that before the dramatic staging of late-nineteenth-century Irish nationalism in the cave of the 'Cyclops', Joyce furnishes in the episode of the 'Sirens' a tying down, a securing, of Irish nationalism to its eighteenth-century roots in the agitation of hidden Ireland. But I wouldn't go that far. It is curious but the sentences of this episode are easier to read than to describe, as if the reader knows more than can be easily accessed in terms of a linguistic or conceptual vocabulary. On reflection, however, 'Sirens' seems to be about impertinence, corners, avoidance, things not meeting, feelings of betrayal, the struggle for articulation. There is a double movement at work here, where close-up the world presents problems but from a distance there is perspective. After my sceptical, error-strewn reading of 'Wandering Rocks' in Chapter 3, I would want to argue that the sounds in the subsequent episode of 'Sirens', along with their exclamation marks, resemble the local disturbances in rural Ireland in the eighteenth century, disturbances which a commentator such as Lewis in *On Local Disturbances in Ireland* (1836) was anxious to stress were not national in origin or purpose. Lewis's line was more difficult to sustain after the activity of the United Irishmen and the 1798 Rising, for then local disturbances in various parts of Ireland heralded the end of localism. Hence the fusion or telescoping in the Joyce family mind between the Whiteboys in the 1760s, an organization which was not national in character, and the Fenians in the 1860s, who were nothing if not national. Perhaps this is an added reason that sounds and meaning present particular problems for translators, for the local disturbances seem to have a separate life of their own, but they also partake of a wider struggle which because of Joyce's characteristic use of overdetermination has been insufficiently noticed. As I have suggested elsewhere in relation to 'pick, pack, pock, puck' and cricket (Pierce 2005), Joyce is a politically sound writer, but, in the light of 'Sirens', we might also add he shows us how all kinds of sounds are still potentially waiting to be gathered and folded into the political landscape in Ireland.

## Appendix 1

'The Croppy Boy' (1845) by 'Carrol Malone' (James McBurney)

A Ballad of '98

'Good men and true in this house who dwell,
To a stranger *buachaill* I pray you tell
Is the priest at home, or may he be seen?
I would speak a word with Father Green.'

'The Priest's at home, boy, and may be seen,
'Tis easy speaking with Father Green.
But you must wait till I go and see
If the holy father alone may be.'

The youth has entered an empty hall;
What a hollow sound his light footfall!
And the gloomy chamber is chill and bare,
With a vested priest in a lonely chair.

The youth has knelt to tell his sins:
'*Nomine Dei,*' the youth begins;
At '*mea culpa,*' he beats his breast,
And in broken murmurs he speaks the rest.

'At the siege of Ross did my father fall,
And at Gorey my loving brothers all,
I alone am left of my name and race;
I will go to Wexford and take their place.

'I cursed three times since last Easter day;
At mass-time once I went to play;
I passed the churchyard one day in haste,
And forgot to pray for my mother's rest.

'I bear no hate against living thing,
But I love my country above my king;
Now, father, bless me and let me go
To die, if God has ordained it so.'

The priest said nought, but a rustling noise
Made the youth look above in wild surprise;
The robes were off, and in scarlet there
Sat a yeoman captain with fiery glare –

With fiery glare and with fury hoarse,
Instead of blessing, he breathed a curse –
' 'Twas a good thought, boy, to come here and shrive,
For one short hour is your time alive.'

'Upon yon river three tenders float;
The Priest's in one, if he isn't shot—
We hold his house for our Lord the King,
And, amen I say, may all traitors swing!'

At Geneva barrack that young man died,
And at Passage they have his body laid.
Good people who live in peace and joy,
Breathe a prayer and a tear for the Croppy Boy.

# Part IV

# Joyce and the Contemporary World

# 7

# On Reading *Ulysses* After the Fall of the Berlin Wall

## Overture on Walls in *Ulysses* (my paraphrasing)

The protean wall:
Stephen in 'Proteus', ambulating by some big rocks near the south wall, is reminded of prehistoric animal skulls. See *U* 3:205–6.

The wall as protection for others:
In 'Calypso', Bloom's imagination evokes an oriental scene, a high wall and a woman beckoning her children at night. See *U* 4:94–6.

The homely wall:
The homely Bloom imagines a farm with a surrounding wall and cattle grazing. See *U* 4:156–7.

The garden wall:
Going to the outhouse as part of his morning ritual, Bloom notices a sprig of *mentha spicata* germinating by the wall. *U* 4:475.

The wall as cover:
After collecting a letter from Martha Clifford, Bloom finds a place by a station wall to read it in secret. See *U* 5:229–30.

Walls with ears:
Thinking about Catholics and the confessional, Bloom imagines walls having ears. See *U* 5:429.

The wall in a spelling game:
Bloom in the newspaper office recalls a spelling bee on how to distinguish symmetry from cemetery. Isn't it ridiculous, he thinks. See *U* 7:168–9.

Walls are for graffiti:
On his way out of the newspaper office, Bloom notices marks on the walls. See *U* 7:222–3.

Walls for suspending crucifixes:

When Bloom tries to recall an advertisement for luminous crucifixes, he imagines waking up in the dark of his bedroom and seeing a
suspended Jesus. See *U* 8:18–20.

The Chinese wall:

During his walks round the city, Bloom meditates on the cities in the
past, on pyramids built in the sand and on the slaves who built the wall
of China. *U* 8:489–90.

The wall as an American *Well*:

In the library episode, Stephen in his mind mocks an account of an
interview between George Russell and an American interviewer, and
he imagines a phrase similar to 'well, I'll be damned' reproduced in
American English as 'wall, I'll be damned'. See *U* 9:54.

A fixed wall:

At various times throughout the day, Bloom's throwaway is seen
drifting down the Liffey. In Mr Kernan's section in 'Wandering Rocks', it
reaches the North Wall. See *U* 10:752–4.

A wall with a concealed entrance:

In the same section Mr Kernan recalls Robert Emmet's funeral at
Glasnevin and how his body had to be secreted by night through a
concealed entry. See *U* 10:770–1.

A wall as orientation for the blind:

A young blind man is observed traversing the city by hitting his stick
against a wall. See *U* 10:1104–5.

Wall in homage:

The finest homage to the Viceregal cavalcade is paid by the River
Poddle's excrement seen dangling at Wood Quay, it being summer and
the water in the river low. See *U* 10:1196–7.

Wall as accompaniment for the dandy:

Blazes Boylan is observed playing the dandy outside Trinity College
Provost's house. The tune in his head relates to a girl from across the
water. See *U* 10:1240–1.

The wall as puzzle-solver:

In 'Sirens', Bloom recalls the spelling bee and discovers harmony. See
*U* 11:832–3.

The adjectival wall:

In 'Cyclops', the eye of the undertaker Corny Kelleher is compared to
a wall. See *U* 12:1080–3.

The wall as a darling place to relieve oneself:

After masturbating on the beach, Bloom expresses satisfaction that the gas from cider consumed at lunchtime was emitted in a place out of sight and out of earshot. See *U* 13:860–1.

The wall as prologue:

Bloom recalls Molly telling him about her teenage romances on Gibraltar. See *U* 13:888–90.

The wall of death:

In 'Circe', Paddy Dignam, now dead, tells the reader about the condition of the sides of his heart. See *U* 15:1231–2.

The wall as support for the body:

When Bloom returns home late without keys, he begins to negotiate entry into his locked house by placing his feet on the little wall outside and climbing over the railings. See *U* 17:84–9.

The Jewish wall:

In 'Ithaca', a ballad is recited about a ball ending up in the garden of a Jew. See *U* 17:804–5.

The wall as imperfect protection from a neighbour:

In bed, late at night, Molly muses on being disturbed by someone with a throat infection knocking. See *U* 18:352–4.

The wall in memory:

Molly recalls the same incident mentioned by Bloom above about her first romance as a teenager on Gibraltar. See *U* 18:769–70.

The wall as a harbinger of death:

When her son Rudy died, Molly heard a small beetle boring into the wall. See *U* 18:1309.

A promiscuous wall:

In her soliloquy, Molly returns again to her first love on Gibraltar, running it together in her mind with Bloom's proposal on Howth Head. The continuation of this thought is a mixture of realism, cynicism, and not what you'd expect from a young woman contemplating marriage for the first time. See *U* 18:1604–5.

## Exposition

Before the fall of the Berlin Wall it was a privilege to be invited on three separate occasions to speak at conferences in the former German Democratic Republic (GDR).[1] Twice in the 1980s I made the journey to Rostock, to international conferences on modern literature with high-flown titles such as 'Challenge of the Century', titles President

George W. Bush's people might have been proud of. Then in May 1986 at the invitation of Dorothea Siegmund-Schultze I attended one of her bi-annual conferences on Ireland at the Martin Luther University Halle-Wittenberg. I gave papers on Yeats and Joyce, and I also talked to Horst Höhne's undergraduates in Rostock on Dickens, Tony Harrison and contemporary American poetry. I came across academics from all over Eastern Europe, as well as the Soviet Union and the United States, and I learnt something from them all. I was cautioned by my hosts not to refer to Yeats's pro-fascist attitudes since this might jeopardize ever mentioning him again at future conferences. No less telling was a remark made by the African-American poet and critic Michael S. Harper when he reminded his white audience that the American Civil war did not end in 1865, that in fact in a sense it had never ended. I also recall standing in a corridor on a crowded train on the way to Berlin with the fine American poet James Schevill and hearing him express the hope as we passed some huge ugly housing estate that the GDR might be allowed time to create a new society.

The world the GDR tried to construct has almost certainly gone but it remains vivid in my memory, more so in part because it has so rapidly disappeared. The conferences tended to be formal with participants reading papers often, as in the hotel restaurant at Ahrenshoop on the Baltic, with head down and chair facing towards the people at their immediate table. My partner Mary Eagleton caused quite a stir when she insisted on turning her chair to face the audience as a whole and then proceeded to speak about feminism. However, in more informal settings in people's homes or bars, the discussion, interlaced with beautifully seditious Radio Yerevan jokes, opened up and moved freely between literature and politics, East–West relations, the Second World War and the future. Although knowing nothing of their languages, I thought I heard the constant murmuring of dissent among academics across Eastern Europe as if the gulf between the hope and the reality of communist society was tearing them apart. On one occasion I was shown a sword which was given to the Hitler Youth Corps in the last days of the war as they rode on horseback to the Russian front only to encounter the Panzer tanks in retreat. On another occasion at a dinner with high-powered provincial city leaders in Halle, it was candidly admitted that collectivization had been a failure and that it had proved necessary to introduce a degree of private ownership.

The journey to the border was never easy or uneventful. At night, the GDR was covered in darkness only broken by the blaze of light as the plane descended into Tegel airport in West Berlin. It was a little like standing at the top of the Empire State Building in that decade and being struck by the contrast between the lights of mid-town Manhattan and the dark of the Bronx, only now the primary contrast was not race but capitalism. The following day I would take the train to

Friedrichstrasse Station and cross over from one platform in the West to the other in the East. Once through customs and outside, the noise of traffic abated and advertising hoardings gave way to a strange imageless silence. For melancholy and the guilty corridor of history, there was nothing quite like sipping coffee alone in the Unter der Linden, once the hub of Isherwood's Berlin life, but now resembling an empty theatre with the Brandenburg Gate for proscenium arch, with no audience, no razzmatazz, and no young women like Sally Bowles with green finger-nails to wander across the stage and stimulate interest. The re-entry was equally dramatic, especially emerging from the underground, like Fidelio, into Kurfurstendamm and looking up to see the Mercedes Benz logo reassuringly dominating the skyline. It was impossible not to recall cold war films such as *The Ipcress File*, for menace and misunderstanding were never far away, especially when I was once questioned by security forces at the border in broken English about my contacts in the GDR and asked to step inside to be searched and interrogated further.

What I sought on every visit was a line of continuity between East and West. The double-decker trains on both sides of the border helped, as did the perverse way German pedestrians never crossed on red. Whichever system was in control, *Vater Staat* (Father State) ensured signposts were suitably peppered with strong commands, so that the counterpart to polite notices in Britain such as asking people not to walk on the grass would invariably contain the v-word 'verboten'. At that time it was proving almost impossible in Britain to take the pulse of contemporary history. It was common in the period from 1983 until 1987 to hear people say that the Labour Party would never form another government by itself, that the thing called society was a left-wing construction, and that individuals should watch their pockets and look after themselves. But anyone with a dialectical sense of history couldn't hold with such views for long. In Britain, the State was in retreat; in the GDR the State was in the ascendancy.

On the ground of course it was never quite like that. What my student minders clamoured for was the latest album by George Michael not a discussion about Marx's critique of political economy or, following Lenin, where do we go from here. People in the GDR did, however, feel a sense of ownership. Being shown round Rostock by my host in that most democratic of cars the two-stroke Trabant, I felt slightly awkward, especially given my sense of displacement, hearing constant references to 'our hospital', 'our school', 'our ship-building industry', even 'our worker housing development' when in Britain, unless you were part of the machinery of government, few could use such a vocabulary without it sounding like something out of *Brave New World*. That feeling I suspect must have been widely shared by the younger generation in the GDR. Rosa, the protagonist in Monika Maron's savagely ironic, devastating, novel *Silent Close No.6* (1991), recalls her father, a school principal, complaining about the dirt on the metro and how '"our people" simply wouldn't understand that the struggle for Communism begins with candy wrappers' (Maron, 50).

Maron herself was the step-daughter of the Minister of the Interior from 1955 until 1963. In her sights she has the collapse of a distinction between private and Party speech, but in fact, as her novel demonstrates, there was a constant tension between State and community. For some such as Beerenbaum, the old Party official in Maron's novel, the tension could not be admitted. The wall was a 'rampart' (always a possible translation of the English word 'wall') built in 1961 to keep out the imperialist West: 'As you can imagine, those were exciting times just after the construction of our anti-Fascist rampart' (Maron, 88). But in both the GDR and Britain the tension was there, with one enjoying full employment but nothing to buy, the other witnessing the collapse of the coal-mining industry and record levels of unemployment. To borrow Ursula Le Guin's phrase from her 'cold war' novel *The Dispossessed* (1974), the wall was therefore 'ambiguous, two-faced. What was inside it and what was outside it depended on which side of it you were on' (Le Guin, 1). In spite of its showpiece status, West Berlin didn't escape this sense of enclosure for, as Manfred suggests in an unnerving phrase from Christa Wolf's novel *Divided Heaven* (1965), it was 'a city without a hinterland' (Wolf, 189). So the question I kept returning to was what were the historical forces at work promoting and bringing together the individualism of Margaret Thatcher's Britain and the collectivism on show in the GDR, and pairing them in such a way that, within a short space, they would both be abandoned by history?

And where did Joyce fit into any of this? Among left-wing critics, especially in the 1930s, there was a suspicion about Joyce, which was widely shared – until 1934 in the United States and 1936 in the United Kingdom, *Ulysses* was a banned book. In his essay on *Ulysses* in *Crisis and Criticism* (1937), the English Marxist critic Alick West argued that Joyce was 'attached to a social order which is itself doomed, and through that attachment he is unable to decide for any particular activity' (West, 175). Joyce was therefore a symptom of the crisis of capitalism, not someone capable of diagnosing its ills, a symptom as Lukács later claimed in his essay 'Narrate or Describe?' of 'a kaleidoscopic chaos' (Lukács 1970, 133). The 1930s was a decade of Hard Fact, of Storm Jameson's magazine with the one-word, emblematic title *Fact*. It insisted on social action, on doing as opposed to simply feeling or quietly reading, on 'Writing in Revolt' as issue 4 of *Fact* was called, and it tended to turn its back on the movement (or, as Lukács called it, the ideology) of Modernism or recoil from any talk of the Revolution of the Word. In this regard, West was both typical of and yet more generous than others by suggesting that the substance of *Ulysses* was the conflict 'between catholicism, capitalism and the new social forces' (West, 175).

We don't need reminding that for the Left the personal has been a particular problem, both before and after the so-called Marxist Decade. In confronting the forcibly expressed directness of political thought in the GDR, I found myself reflecting on political novelists who have been troubled by the modern predicament of the personal, troubled that is by its politics. In her contact with Russian revolutionaries in London in Dorothy Richardson's insightful novel *Revolving Lights* (1923), Miriam discovers that 'Personal life to them was nothing, could be summed up in a few words, the same for everybody. They lived for an idea.' (Richardson, 3:239). The logic here is at once brutal and attractive. Because everyone is the same, there is nothing personal. At the same time, it is because they live for an idea that, like Yeats's 1916 revolutionaries, they come alive as individuals and can be admired. The restless Miriam, not unlike Carinthia in Kathleen Coyle's *Piccadilly* (1923), allows the Russians space in her life as slightly exotic human beings, but the dilemma would need facing more directly at some point in the future. In many ways it is not surprising that women from left-wing backgrounds or with left-wing sympathies should find the relationship between the individual and the collective troubling and unresolved. A decade and a generation later, the issue surfaces with particular force on a different continent in the fiction of Doris Lessing and Nadine Gordimer, and the same accents, partly because of the influence of Moscow on the South African Communist Party, can be heard as in the 1930s in Europe.

The Martha Quest series of novels as well as *The Golden Notebook* (1962) issue from Lessing's involvement as a young woman in Communist Party activities in the 1940s, and they are edgy novels precisely because her characters want to know if it is possible to live for an idea and what room is left for the personal and the small voice of conscience. For Anna Wulf, the presence of even a third person, let alone a wider collective, changes things. At a writers' group meeting, dated 11 November 1952, five comrades, one of whom has just returned from Moscow, come together to discuss Stalin on linguistics. Anna, invariably out of things, begins to observe that words lose their meaning and thinks of novels like *Finnegans Wake* which focus on the breakdown of language. The talk continues but her mind is elsewhere, and she reflects how 'when two of us meet, our discussions are on a totally different level than when there are three people present' (Lessing, 300). The break with her communist past informs much of Lessing's thinking, but, as these early novels suggest, the recuperation of the self is essentially painful and isolating. Anna also discerns something else in contemporary culture, that fiction as a form 'has become a function of the fragmented society, the fragmented consciousness', a reflection of humanity's 'blind grasping out for their own wholeness' (Lessing, 79).

Gordimer comes up against a similar wall in *Burger's Daughter* (1980), a novel which begins enigmatically with Rosa Burger 'in place, outside the prison' (Gordimer, 15), a schoolgirl at the onset of puberty, waiting to visit her imprisoned father. Written in the aftermath of the Soweto Uprising in 1976, the story is based on Bram Fischer, the South African Communist Party lawyer sentenced to life imprisonment for treason, but Gordimer's focus is the *burgher's* daughter, the citizen's daughter, and her concern is with the relationship between being a daughter and being a citizen, between the female body and a male-dominated society, the private and the public, the demands of the sexualized body and the dormant voice of conscience, the here-and-now and the unknown future, the individual and the collective. Unlike Lessing, however, the story is told with an eye on Rosa's reconnecting with society through a higher form of commitment.

Joyce, who is more often than not held up as a symptom of some general modern crisis or breakdown, is on the fringes of this continuing concern among the Left. But that he had something to say on the individual–collective theme needs little rehearsing here. *A Portrait of the Artist as a Young Man* is about cutting free, about Stephen avoiding the nets arresting the soul's growth in Ireland. *Ulysses* provides a never-ending exploration of limits for, as the examples in my Overture above suggest, Joyce understood walls, walls as barriers, as horizons, as supports. In exploring the relationship between the citizen and the artist, between Bloom and Stephen – and it is always a relationship, a correspondence, on view in *Ulysses*, never simply the isolated individual – he discovered the place of gender and the female body, reserving his most sparkling writing in *Ulysses* for the Molly Bloom soliloquy, the 'clou', the star-turn, of the book (*Letters* I, 170). But, unlike these other novels, *Ulysses* is set on one day and it deliberately exploits not the held moment as in Imagist verse, but the static nature of reality or, what for Joyce amounted to the same thing, the dynamic patterns that encompass a Greek epic written over two and half thousand years ago and the modern world. At the same time, while it is not a *bildungsroman*, *Ulysses* is a journey which takes various forms, at once realistic and spiritual, familial and mythic, outward and inward. Memories and associations never stop flowing, but the growth of the soul is limited. Leaving aside the ending, if there is a climax it takes place around 4.30 in the afternoon, half way through the novel, in Molly's bedroom in 7 Eccles Street, off-stage.

What all this implies is not that Joyce is whimsical but that he handles matters in his own way, investing, as I have already suggested, in a critique that refuses to stop when the point is made. Political commitment in Lessing ends in historical stalemate and personal recoil, in Gordimer in renewal in Europe for Rosa, in Richardson in paths not chosen. But the movement in Joyce is away from writing about something to writing itself, so we never forget the window through which the world is seen and on which, like William Carlos Williams's wheelbarrow, so much depends. Whatever Anna Wulf or the 1930s communist critics might claim, Joyce's use of language is a reminder not of the fragmentation but, as I suggested in Chapter 1, of a compulsion to gather the world on a new material basis, to show how words for example collide to produce new meanings.

The GDR was a product of the 1930s, not only in its anti-Nazi origins but also in its intellectual bearings. British intellectuals such as West, A.L. Morton and Arnold Kettle, who kept faith with a traditional form of pre-War Communism, played a formative role and became like 'father figures' to the first generation of GDR intellectuals (Höhne, 101). It is for this reason that at GDR conferences in the 1980s, the 1930s accent could still be heard loud and clear. Thus, Georg Seehase, in a paper on Joyce's aesthetic system delivered at the Irish conference in Halle in 1984, cites approvingly West's essay as if it were still contemporary. Equally, Seehase revealed a willingness to deal with and not just dismiss Joyce's aesthetic. His paragraph quoting West begins: '*Ulysses* has an arbitrary historical sense. June 16 1904 is not history in the way June 15 1886 is in Galsworthy's *Man of Property*' (Seehase, 216, my translation). Seehase doesn't pursue the matter – perhaps wisely given the unequal achievement of the two novelists in question. As Sean O'Faolain once remarked, June 16 was 'Nobody's Day', 'a day that had no place in history until [Joyce] made it history' (O'Faolain 1954). Seehase quickly moves on to invoke the conflict between different social forces, but the paradox continues to exercise anyone on the Left influenced by the vocabulary of determination.

In *The Ideology of the Aesthetic* (1990), the New Left critic Terry Eagleton, who was no friend of the GDR, characteristically alights on the issue of contingency in *Ulysses*: 'The textual strategies which invest a particular time or place with unwonted centrality, ridding it of its randomness and contingency, do so only to return the whole of that contingency to it' (Eagleton, T., 320). As my Overture implies, what is arbitrary is precisely what makes Joyce's sense of history so central. This was the kind of insight which could never be appreciated by those buffeted by the force of twentieth-century history, the war generation, who used the memory of the camps not only as a badge but also as a weapon, who felt they possessed, in Rosa's phrase, 'a monopoly on misfortune' (Maron, 117). Joyce isn't a committed writer in the sense that Sean O'Casey is, but he is committed to writing and to something other than the present order of things. As Wolfgang Wicht, a leading critic in the GDR, suggests in his post-1989 book about Joyce's anti-utopian stance: 'Joyce implies ... that it is necessary to question the present order by confronting it with what is absent from it' (Wicht, 29).

Ironically, one of the best early editions of *Ulysses* was published in Germany in 1932, the same year the Nazi Party became the largest political party in the Reichstag. This was the Odyssey Press two-volume edition published in Hamburg and printed in Leipzig. In 1997, I was invited to speak at the Haus des Buches in Leipzig and I did so on *Ulysses*. When I held up a copy of the Odyssey Press edition, someone in the audience interrupted me to declare that the original printing press was close by. It was a moment to relish, a point of connection with 1930s Germany in Leipzig, the great city of books, before an audience some of whom had led the night-time candle-lit marches which effectively brought down the Berlin Wall. Fifty years later, in 1984, another edition of *Ulysses*, a synoptical and critical edition, was presented at the James Joyce International Symposium in Frankfurt. Edited by Hans Walter Gabler and a team based in Munich, this edition, which has attracted its fair share of criticism, has become a standard reference text in Joyce studies, which is no mean achievement. So, in one important respect, Germany has twice given Joyce to the English-speaking world, and this in the two crucial decades of the twentieth century – the 1930s and the 1980s. Any history of the reception of Joyce in Germany would need to make something of this outward movement or gesture towards what we might see in cultural or translation terms as both foreignization and domestication.

## Counterpoint

It is only in recent decades that Joyce has come into his own in Ireland, and this in part because he was taken up by others in Europe and the United States. In *So This Is Dublin!* (1927), a breezy take on Dublin and its writers, M.J. MacManus remarked with some venom:

> Mr James Joyce has been paying a visit to Dublin in search of local colour for the new book which he has planned, to be called *An Irish Odyssey*. He spent a considerable time visiting the Corporation Sewage Farm, the Wicklow Manure Factory, and the sloblands at Fairview. Before returning to Paris he stated that he had derived keen satisfaction from his visit to his native city. (MacManus, 63)

The attack did not go unchallenged, and in *Finnegans Wake* Joyce incorporated MacManus's title and turned it into a question about identity: 'So This Is Dyoublong?' (*FW* 13:4). Dublin, the exile's city, was the place where it was legitimate to ask if you belonged to it, where English 'you' contained French 'ou' (where), and where 'oublong' carried within it the French for to forget, the length of time, and a mathematical shape, all elements in the make-up of the world (time, space, location, language, memory, identity). In a little-known essay entitled 'Joyce and the New Irish Writers' (1934), Ernest Boyd, the historian of the Irish Literary Revival, contrasted the European interest in the form of *Ulysses* with the Irish interest in Joyce's 'simple realism', adding somewhat starkly, but at the time with a degree of truth, that 'In Ireland his influence has been nil' (Boyd, 699–700). When John Eglinton (W.K. Magee), who in 1904 as editor of *Dana* had rejected a prose work by Joyce entitled 'A Portrait of the Artist' and who is one of the establishment figures mocked in the Library episode of *Ulysses*, recalled the artist as a young man in an essay published in 1932, what struck him was Joyce's determination to succeed, for at the time 'no one took him at his own valuation' (Eglinton, 404). For Eglinton, Joyce is 'an heroic figure' who 'nursed an ironic detachment from the whole of the English tradition' and who 'succeeded in making logic and rhetoric less sure of themselves among our younger writers' (Eglinton, 407, 410, 411).

Criticism needed a half century and more to mark out the ground of Joyce's achievement. However, in moving back and forth between states and periods, what we observe is movement but not settlement. Some interpretations have fallen by the wayside, but they could as easily be revived. Eglinton believed that at the heart of *Ulysses* was 'an awful inner void' (Eglinton, 411), but, even with the spread of existentialism in France after the Second World War, it is an opinion that has found few adherents. In principle, younger scholars have argued, Joyce is Beckett, Beckett is Joyce. They don't normally want to imply that Joyce shares anything of Beckett's absurd universe, but that might be another tack. More than Joyce, Beckett understood suffering, but it is surprising that so few critics in the GDR or indeed elsewhere devoted to this theme in Joyce the attention it deserves. What is *Dubliners* but a cry against necessity? What is *A Portrait of the Artist as a Young Man* if not a series of farewells and a journey into exile? What is *Exiles* if not a study of the soul on fire? As for Bloom, the Jew hurts. And no-one has commented more forcibly on the hurt in *Finnegans Wake* than John Cowper Powys, writing in 1943:

> I find ... in the chatter of the elm and the stone about Anna Livia, in the ferocious self-humiliations of Shem the Penman, in the comically pathetic blusterings and scandalously touching ribaldries of Shem, and finally in every word about Anna and her daughter ... more of the world-moan and the world-pain, more of feelings hurt and nerves tortured, more of the sick horror which madness imagines to be at the back and *on the back* of the world than in Thackeray and Trollope rolled together! (Powys, 85)

So, reading *Ulysses* after the fall of the Berlin Wall is a reminder of a number of things. Joyce has never sat easily in one historical period; his capital was never used up at any given time; he has always needed not so much coteries as company; and he doesn't recognize walls for he is par excellence an extramural writer. *Ulysses* is set in 1904 but it was published in 1922; it mimes or straddles therefore the emergence of an independent Ireland, and in a single day it crosses two states. Irish history itself in the twentieth century was not quite in sync with European history. If the two world wars dominate most histories of twentieth-century Europe, this is not the case with the Republic of Ireland (prior to 1949 it was called the Irish Free State). The Great War presented Irish nationalists with an opportunity, for England's difficulty was, according to the well-worn adage, Ireland's opportunity. During the Second World War, the Republic of Ireland remained neutral, refusing to side with the colonial power it had engaged in the War of Independence of 1919–21. So, to a large extent the Republic remained outside the formative experience that most Europeans lived through in the twentieth century. In the year that Eliot gave the world *The Waste Land*, an image in its own way of a devastated Europe, Joyce perversely insisted on the centrality of his peripheral vision publishing his Irish Odyssey in Paris with an ex-patriate bookshop run by an American woman which carried the name but not the kudos of the greatest English writer, Shakespeare and Company. If the Great War surfaces in *Ulysses*, it is only by a form of 'retrospective arrangement' on the part of later critics. James Fairhall suggests that the Arranger as a 'suprapersonal consciousness', objectifying and quantifying reality, indifferent to human well-being, belongs to the experience of the trenches (Fairhall, 213), but this potentially valuable insight merely confirms just how out of sync *Ulysses* also is.

## Coda

Put up a wall and Joyce tears it down; suggest a connective tissue and Joyce blocks it. In *Ulysses* he plays fair with the reader, providing enough signposts for the attentive reader to follow from episode to episode. But try and move from context to text, from text to context, and you will never stop playing the game. In the West paralysis has been a traditional prop in classroom discussion of *Dubliners*, but in the GDR paralysis was too close to political reality to be admitted as a theme or entry-point to the stories. Intellectual and political horizons, as Marx and Engels suggested, are closely aligned with social class and the maintenance of power: to think beyond the Wall meant the destruction of the Wall in one's heart (and I think I glimpsed this at the dinner with local politicians in Halle referred to above). Beerenbaum's position as a former high official prevents him from seeing an alienated youth. For Rosa, on the other hand, 'freedom is as much a place as a human being is a place' (Maron, 66). The word in Wicht's *Utopianism in James Joyce's 'Ulysses'* (2000) that resonates the strongest for me is 'containment': 'Joyce calls attention to the fact that the political, messianic, religious and private variations of utopian thought finally serve the purpose of containment, contrary to a Mannheimian or Blochian conjuration of affirmative hope' (Wicht, 236). Only after the fall of the Berlin Wall could such an insight emerge with such force. But the question of hope remains:

> – Are you talking about the new Jerusalem? says the citizen.
> – I'm talking about injustice, says Bloom. (*U* 12:1474–5)

# 8

# Joyce and Contemporary Irish Writing

## The Pen Shop (1997)

In a sequence of poems entitled *The Pen Shop* (1997), Thomas Kinsella, echoing the style of the 'Lotus-Eaters' episode of *Ulysses*, picks his way through the streets of Dublin, passing the sites associated with nationalist and colonial Ireland and ending up in a pen shop for a black refill. This affords a useful starting-point for a consideration of two related topics relevant to a retrospective discussion of Joyce. One concerns cultural belatedness and the afterlife of literature, the other concerns the different ways Joyce features in contemporary writing. The construction of Joyce by the (American) Joyce industry has rarely been held back by the anxiety of influence which a later generation of (Irish) writers have sometimes betrayed. Streets and ink refills, on the other hand, offer a gesture towards Joycean recirculation and another way of conceiving the relationship with the past. Equally, in some texts, such as Jamie O'Neill's novel *At Swim, Two Boys* (2001), the Joycean period can be evoked without the reader thinking this is a pale imitation of the original.

For Kinsella, modern Irish culture is the product of what he defines as the 'gapped tradition'. His exemplar is Yeats, a figure whose isolation is 'the substance of his life', isolation from a people who speak another language and 'whose lives, therefore, he cannot touch' (Yeats / Kinsella, 62–3). 'Nightwalker', a poem from the 1960s which betrays a debt as much to William Carlos Williams and T.S. Eliot as to Joyce, circles round the same issue. It opens with a reference to the Joyce Tower at Sandymount and includes a journey through Irish history in which Kinsella provides a sequence of ironic and ambivalent reflections on the theme of dispossession and the loss of the Irish language in the nineteenth century:

A dying language echoes
Across a century's silence.
It is time,
Lost soul, I turned for home.

Sad music steals
  Over the scene.
Hesitant, cogitating, exit.[1]

Three decades later in *The Pen Shop*, Kinsella, now a 'daywalker', returns
to the same scene, only now his exemplar is Joyce, the figure who stands
for the Irish tradition not as 'broken' – the position Yeats occupies – but as
'continuous' (Yeats / Kinsella, 65). The poem begins with a signature in
fading ink and ends in a pen shop on Nassau Street in Dublin. Before his
Joycean walk commences, Kinsella's mood is established with reference
to a 'final kiss' and an altercation with a woman given to 'fierce forecasts'.
'Another cool acquaintance' is his riposte as he drops the card or letter
into the post box in the GPO. In the cathedral space he thinks of their
souls 'passing among each other' where 'their' has widened to include
all those waiting to be served under the watchful eye of 'the bronze
hero' of Cuchulain, 'the harpy perched on his neck'. Out then through
'the revolving doors' Kinsella proceeds, to be greeted by the statue of
Jim Larkin 'up off our knees' and the other statues on O'Connell Street
– Sir John Gray, Smith O'Brien, where 'Mr Bloom unclasped his hands',
O'Connell himself. At O'Connell Bridge, pausing to observe the river, he
is struck by 'the smell of country' and the movement of Guinness barrels
by barge and boat. In characteristic Kinsella fashion, he is arrested by a
thought which becomes a sentence without a verb: 'Cold absence under
the heart'. Then he crosses to Bewleys, passes the shoppers at the front
of the shop and carries his coffee to the back where 'the black draft /
entered the system direct'. He has difficulty crossing the road from the
Bank of Ireland to Trinity College, and curses a Number 21 bus on its
way past the Castle to Kilmainham (site of execution of the leaders of
the Easter Rising) 'heading Westward' towards 'the pale Western shore
/ where I have seen / the light of cities under the far horizon'. Past the
statues of Burke and Goldsmith, he looks up Grafton Street and thinks
of the shops at the far end and the South beckoning in the shape of
Wicklow, Wexford, 'Finistere'. He continues along Nassau Street, the
side entrance to Trinity on his left, the traffic heading 'Eastward out of
the city' towards 'the thought of voices / beyond Liverpool, rising out
of Europe' and the voices 'rising beyond Jerusalem'. It is at this point he
turns into the tiny pen shop that dates from the 1930s, where he is served
by an attendant 'over alert all my life long / behind the same counter'.

The route is rich in association for Joyceans and non-Joyceans alike,
and Kinsella deliberately deploys the landmarks of the city as a shorthand to history and as a launch-pad for a critique of contemporary
Ireland. If Kinsella still believes Joyce represents tradition as continuous,
we might with some justice conclude, on the basis of reading this poem,
that Joyce does so only because of the discontinuous present. There is a
cold absence about the heart, the city at the axis of north–south–east–

west has lost its centredness and become a dispersal point, its statues strangely directionless, the river full of black currents 'turning among each other', the shoppers 'precise in their needs' with only a 'nod of fellowship' now showing. 'By lorries along sir John Rogerson's quay Mr Bloom walked soberly, past Windmill lane, Leask's the linseed crusher, the postal telegraph office' (*U* 5:1–2). And now Kinsella: 'By Sir John Gray ... By Smith O'Brien ... By Daniel O'Connell.' Kinsella's walk recalls Bloom's but the effect is altogether more sombre and isolating, as if he were closer in sympathy to the dispossessed spirit of Wandering Aengus and Stephen Dedalus. The intense alignment of an interior mood and an external landscape is here accompanied by a commentary on the failures of post-independence Ireland to connect either with itself or with its past. Even as the poet purchases his black refill, the transaction is surrounded by a feeling of cultural belatedness, that he is writing after Joyce, after independence, that newness is no longer purchasable. As he looks to inject a conscience into his race, the poet realizes he is a marginal figure. The fading signature can be put right but nothing can fill the absence under the heart.

### At Swim, Two Boys (2001)

If Heaney's use of Joyce in *Station Island* (1984) is cast in the vocative case – a way of coming to terms with Joyce by formally addressing him as if he were a local saint – then we might well conclude that O'Neill's use of Joyce in *At Swim, Two Boys* is in the genitive case where 'of' can stand for affiliation, possession, debt, influence, derivation. O'Neill's title leads one to expect he will pay homage to Flann O'Brien's *At Swim-Two-Birds* (1939), but in some respects there the comparison ends, for his title represents an unconventional way of freeing himself from debts to the past. Throughout *At Swim, Two Boys* allusions to other writers constantly recur but such allusions enhance rather than detract from O'Neill's achievement. O'Neill's isle is full not of strange but of familiar noises. Dickens hovers over the periphery of the novel especially in the interior shots of Mr Mack's shop and also in a phrase such as 'pal of my heart' which Doyler uses about his friend Jim. Hopkins (as in 'Spelt from Sybil's Leaves') is possibly evoked in 'irrational, irrepressible, irresponsible, iron-brained, irascible, irksome, entirely irresistible' (298), and in the catch-up narrative in chapter 15, when Nancy gives birth to Gordie's daughter, distinct echoes of Lewis Grassic Gibbon's Scottish novel *Sunset Song* (1934) can be discerned. 'God is good, and there wasn't pain but you was blessed for it; and the little blessing lay asleep in her rickety pram' (400). But O'Neill is most taken with Joyce, who himself playfully acknowledged in the phrase 'pelagiarist pen' (*FW* 182:3) that he was both a plagiarist and a follower of the Celtic monk Pelagius, the 'extramural' heretic who denied original sin and the doctrine that salvation could be attained only through the Church.

What *Ulysses* and *At Swim, Two Boys* share is a scrupulous attention to language. The extraordinary word-play, in evidence from the beginning of *At Swim, Two Boys*, immediately recalls the Joycean inheritance. Some words are given a new lease of life. 'Mussitation', a word to describe indistinct sounds or mutterings, is here defined as the 'half-mime half-whisper' (266) deployed by men in prison. Other words such as 'flâneuring' (196) suggest a more recent inflection, as does the repeated knowing play on the word 'straight'. For the inventive O'Neill, language exists for recovery as much as discovery, for relishing and embellishing. Jingles for hoardings or for use by advertisers or newspapermen are rehearsed by Mr Mack, as if he were indeed Bloom (or the man in the macintosh) come into our midst again, ever alert to turning a coin in a world where the printed word signifies money. With a parcel under his arm (not unlike Bloom in 'Lotus-Eaters', his card secure, on his way to the post office), he buys a copy of the *Irish Times* from his old Boer War companion Mr Doyle. '[D]ungman Doyle', as he is known, tells Mack to damn the begrudgers who might accuse him of getting above his station: 'A gent on the up, likes of yourself, isn't it worth it alone for the shocks and stares' (10). 'Shocks and stares', Mack thinks afterwards, 'should send that in the paper. Pay for items catchy like that' (14). O'Neill delights in such malapropisms and pairings – 'gurkhas and gherkins' (248) furnishes another such example. Mack's advice to his teenage son Jim on retiring to bed is: 'Let the word Jesus be the last on your lips. Or Mary. A prayer to the Blessed Virgin would often be the most affectatious' (when he means efficacious) (128).

At times the catchphrase or loaded word is turned to record something more serious, as when 'A Nation Once Again', the anthem of nationalist Ireland in the nineteenth century, is changed to 'A Nation Once for All' (328), a new Ireland therefore for all its citizens, including gays. When the Easter Rising arrives and MacMurrough hears that the Republic has been proclaimed from the GPO, he is overjoyed: 'At last, the Republic of Letters!' (624). Earlier, when the nationalist politician Thomas Kettle, Joyce's much admired friend who was killed in action in the Great War, tackles MacMurrough, he does so in terms that recall Forster's novel *Maurice* (1971) and Wilde's view of fox-hunting: 'Damn it all, MacMurrough, are you telling me you are an unspeakable of the Oscar Wilde sort' (309). Because a certain liberty is established early on in the novel, such conflation works here. Joyce taught all his Irish successors that language belongs to a discourse on freedom. He taught O'Neill something else, for articulation, not confession, is one of the themes of this self-delighting novel of liberation.

What also unites the two novels is voice and character. From the opening pages in which we hear again the interior monologue of

Leopold Bloom to the question-and-answer mode we associate with 'Ithaca' that can be heard in an imaginary conversation between MacMurrough and Scrotes his fellow gay prisoner in Wandsworth (Scrotes' name is equidistant between scrotum and Socrates), the presence of *Ulysses* can be felt throughout *At Swim, Two Boys*. It can also be felt in the parallels between Mr Mack's son Gordie (who died at Gallipoli) and Bloom's son Rudy and in names of characters such as Mrs Conway and Mrs Houlihan and her two daughters. Indeed, when Mack meets Mrs Conway in the street at the beginning of the novel, it is once again John Conmee – as owner of a general stores rather than one-time rector of a Jesuit school – meeting Mrs Sheehy in 'Wandering Rocks': 'Oh hello, Mrs Conway, grand day it is, grand to be sure, tip-top and yourself keeping dandy' (8). And, appropriately, this too comes without any response from Mrs Conway.

The two novels differ in the space they devote to the theme of homosexuality. With lines from Whitman for epigraph and constant references to Wilde, O'Neill's ambitious historical novel about the Easter Rising is from start to finish a gay novel. While *Ulysses* begins at Sandycove with the phallus of the Martello Tower and the Forty Foot – where male nude bathing has been enjoyed for generations and where Buck Mulligan throws out an invitation to a moody Stephen to 'chuck Loyola' – in O'Neill's novel, the male space takes precedence throughout. In O'Neill's novel, swimming is at once an inter-textual marker, a device for narrative cohesion, and scene of seduction between the two boys – lower-middle-class Jim Mack and working-class Danny Doyle ('Doyler') – and the upper-middle-class dilettante Anthony MacMurrough. Set in the year leading up to the Easter Rising, *At Swim, Two Boys* rewrites Irish history, rewrites that is the afterlife of Irish history, and it does so in terms which not only recall the late Victorian and Edwardian era of outdoor pursuits (this was the period when Baden Powell founded the boy scouts, Constance Markievicz the Fianna, and when Standish O'Grady and Yeats celebrated the exploits of the boy hero Cuchulain) but, more importantly, in terms which call attention to the real boys' story which somehow got omitted in the making of modern Ireland. In 'The Statues', Yeats wondered if Cuchulain stalked through the Post Office with Pearse, but O'Neill concentrates on the idea of a rising as ushered in by the boys who were taught by Pearse at his school at Rathfarnham.

Jim joins the struggle for independence not for blood sacrifice or heroic action but because of Doyler: 'It's silly, I know. But that's how I feel' (435). And MacMurrough confirms this view: 'Not courage, but a kind of love, a bonding of disparate souls to the one company' (445). When Doyler admits the rebellion went off 'half-cock' (615), the pun is there to be noticed for this is an extraordinarily physical novel where metaphors act as pointers not to some other world but to this one. As for the sexual theme, this, too, keeps rebounding on the political. At one point in the novel MacMurrough is in discussion with Doyler where he insists that he wasn't watching the two boys at swim 'so much as waiting my turn' (281). We interpret the phrase in sexual terms but the phrase also in a strange way alludes to the mood leading up to Easter 1916. For, as we look back on the events in the novel, it becomes evident that characters such as MacMurrough did indeed move from watching to action, precisely also in some respects the major discourse or trajectory of the novel.[2]

It can also be discerned that a different purpose is at work in *Ulysses* and *At Swim, Two Boys*. It could be argued that O'Neill brings out the homosexual aspect in *A Portrait* and *Ulysses*, as in the incident when Cranly's arm detains Stephen (arms round necks are very important in *At Swim, Two Boys* as a way of inviting intimacy), or in the suggestion of homosexuality at the beginning of *Ulysses*, but this I suspect is not O'Neill's primary intention. Joyce plays with identity in a way that O'Neill doesn't, for O'Neill is deadly serious about creating a nation for all. What, however, I find more intriguing is their fictional reconstruction of an historical period. *At Swim, Two Boys* attends to the period from the summer of 1915 to the events at Easter 1916, with a brief sequel looking to Jim's fate in the Civil War. Joyce, as we know, confined himself to one day in June 1904. But while the movement of the narrative in *At Swim, Two Boys* is forward, in *Ulysses*, although it advances stylistically ever forward, the movement is in certain respects essentially retrospective. Touch any part of *At Swim, Two Boys* and there is a sign pointing to 1916 and to Parnell's future-directed injunction that 'No man has a right to fix the boundary to the march of a nation'. Noticing the cherry trees in blossom in April 1916 is a reminder of authentic local detail to the reader, as indeed is a discussion about turn-ups on men's trousers or MacMurrough wearing Jaeger suits. But such details take us down the road to sepia photographs and historical decoration. It's impossible for O'Neill to still the forward momentum in *At Swim, Two Boys*, so much so that, unfortunately, there are chapters in the second half of the novel detailing the intermediate events leading up to Easter 1916 which have to be got through. This comes at precisely the time when in *Ulysses* there is continuing forward momentum in part because Joyce had abandoned the style of the first half of his book, thus redefining 'momentum' in narrative rather than historical terms.

Nothing in one sense in *Ulysses* points to 1916, and yet in another sense everything does. It is this dual-mode that Joyce somehow manages to exploit whereby history – the history of dispossession for example – moves forward even as the known future is expunged from view. I disagree therefore with Kenner when he claims 'we are always in 1904' (Kenner, 47). Somehow the details that Joyce provides, even when they are wrong or not volitional such as in the reference to Sinn Fein,[3] are more than mere decoration and yet not quite on the way to the new Jerusalem or some Irish post-colonial utopia (though the assumption of Irish independence cannot be missed). Joyce is helped by the limited focus and by an epic reach that studiously avoids the idyll.[4] *At Swim, Two Boys* seems too comfortable by comparison, as if in the rewriting of Irish history something has been gained but something has been not so much lost as missed.[5] Indeed, I would take this further, for *At Swim, Two Boys* has the look of a novel *overtaken by events*.

The contrast with Mark Merlis's gay novel *American Studies* (1996) is most in evidence at this point. Merlis retains a tighter control than O'Neill over the movement back and forth between past and present, and he also has a stronger sense of the balance sheet. At one point Reeve, the protagonist, refers to modern America as 'used up' (Merlis, 245), and what he means is that in the decades between the late 1940s and the 1980s it ceased being a land of discovery. O'Neill wants Ireland to be a land of discovery, but geography and history are against him. There was no more land in Ireland to be discovered and, as *At Swim, Two Boys* serves to illustrate, the gay struggle had been omitted at a crucial moment from the national struggle. Merlis uses settlement as a metaphor for cultural belatedness, and he refers at one point to Thomas Jefferson's belief that it would take a millennium to settle the continent. Jefferson was a little out with his prognosis, but, as Merlis's novel affirms, for gays in the decades after the McCarthy era the country did open up as if the language or march of discovery knew or accepted no boundary.

## Concluding Remarks

O'Neill and Kinsella remind us that contemporary Irish writers continue to find ways of dealing with Harold Bloom's 'anxiety of influence'. A half-century ago, Brian Nolan in his essay 'A Bash in the Tunnel' provided the most fraught case of anxiety in the face of Joyce.[6] In the same period, Brian Moore began his career as a novelist in Joyce's shadow. *The Lonely Passion of Miss Judith Hearne* (1955) is the world of Joyce's Eveline transposed to Belfast. As evening approaches she draws the curtain of her room and says a prayer to a picture of the Sacred Heart which she has just nailed to the wall. The mood is sombre, and, with the memories of the dead and the past all around her, slightly ghostly. The style is at once restrained and overwritten, as if it were being composed by someone trying hard to put into words their new situation, a situation which they will possibly now have to accept: 'With the electric light on and the gas-stove spluttering, warming the white bones of its mantles into a rosy red, the new bed-sitting-room became much more cheerful' (Moore, 17). We are back at the start with 'Eveline', which too is another story about lonely passion and the style in which such passion gets to be written: 'She sat at the window watching the evening invade the avenue' (*D* 36). Equally, with its reference to a man from Belfast buying up the fields where

Eveline used to play and invading her space with new housing, 'Eveline' is also a 'Belfast' story.

Move on fifty years and Joyce's influence has changed both in character and intensity. When Paul Muldoon includes 'Old Gummy Granny' in a translation of Nuala Ní Dhómnhaill's Irish-language poem 'Caitlín', he is deliberately echoing Joyce's phrase in the 'Circe' episode of *Ulysses* (Ní Dhómnhaill, 39). In Joyce, the attack on the image of the Poor Old Woman (Kathleen ni Houlihan) has a certain charge, not least because it connects with Stephen's feelings in 'Telemachus' towards his dead mother. In Muldoon, the phrase resonates against Joyce but, in the way it deliberately takes liberties with nationalist symbols and with the icon that Joyce has become, it can be appreciated for its humour alone. Joyce has contributed to the new Ireland and he has himself become part of the thing that is now being guyed, for, as the poem boldly relays, 'those days are just as truly over'. Ironically, then, Joyce's presence acts as a reminder not of a struggle for the liberation of the Irish soul but of the new world order which knows all the signs and the signposts in the culture but which refuses to follow them.

Joyce spoke of the priesthood of art, that what he was doing in his writing was making sacred everyday life. 'Lipstick on the Host' (1992), an engaging short story by Aidan Mathews, is a down-to-earth, theological response to Joyce's secularized sacramentalism. For the post-Kantian Mathews, the critical question is not only the location of the sacred but also the degree of proximity and the intercourse between the divine and the human. In the character of Meggie, a forty-one-year-old English teacher, Mathews acknowledges throughout his debt to Molly Bloom's soliloquy. As with Joyce's treatment of Molly, there is nothing patronizing in Meggie's portrait, and not a hint of satire. When she receives an invitation to dinner from a gynaecologist, the restaurant he mentions is unfamiliar but she assumes it will be chic and so doesn't ask where. She reminds herself that she's not naive: 'I am not exactly from Oklahoma. I mean, I've read *Ulysses*. In fact, I've read *Finnegans Wake*. Admittedly that was for charity. But, still' (Mathews, 238). 'O Jamesy let me up out of this' (*U* 18:1128–9), pleads Molly to her creator, but there is no such escape for Meggie or from Meggie. Her chattiness – like Molly, her only register – continues and they talk about 'Pope John XXIII and how nice he was, and we talked about the signs in Canada which read: Please walk on the grass' (240).

What Mathews's story serves to illustrate is that Joyce made the whole idea of everything available to everyone and anyone. As Meggie says, 'We talked about everything'. It's sometimes suggested that Joyce, to borrow Reeve's expression in *American Studies*, 'used up' the world, that there was nothing left for writers to write about. But in a sense the opposite is nearer the truth. He wasn't to know it but Joyce also made available Molly's voice for re-use not so much as a monologue but as a 'Mollylogue'.

That Meggie asserts she's read Joyce is a nice touch on Mathews's part, for it confirms her status not so much as a non-reader of Joyce – people who've read *Finnegans Wake* hesitate before claiming they've read it, and, whatever that means, they certainly wouldn't do it for charity – but as a participant in a much larger drama exploring not only the general issue of cultural belatedness but also what happened historically in the culture between 1920s Molly and 1990s Meggie.

In its unusual collocation, Mathews's title 'Lipstick on the Host' calls attention to the history of which Joyce is a part. It was only after the Great War that lipstick became readily available, so it is not surprising that there is no mention of it in *Ulysses*. In the 'Anna Livia Plurabelle' chapter of *Finnegans Wake*, written in the 1920s, mention is made of 'lipstipple', a word that prompts a series of thoughts: lipstick, painting the face and make-up in general, stipple engravings, as well as the tipple which passes the lips. Eyebrows are 'pencilled', lips 'penned' (*FW* 93:25). Mathews's title is more dramatic, for lipstick is not a passive adornment but actively rubs off onto the world as it were. The most poignant reference to lips in the whole of Joyce's work appears in the dying moments of *Finnegans Wake* when there is a final farewell between father and son (between John and James Joyce, between Christ and his disciples, between Christ and the Good Thief on the cross, between Joyce and his readers). Prefaced by 'but softly', the word is rendered without the vowel, just as a sound, lps: 'Bussoftlhee, mememormee! Till thousendsthee. Lps. The keys to. Given! A way a lone a last a loved a long the' (*FW* 628:14–16). In *Ulysses*, the episode which contains more references to lips than any other episode is not, as we might expect, the female-centered episode of 'Penelope' but 'Sirens', the male-centered music episode. Mathews in his title does more than Joyce in this regard, perhaps reminding us again of the discourse on touch and its representation as discussed in Chapter 1.

Over dinner, Meggie imagines being examined by Antony and reading the 'Latin diplomas and degrees that hung from the picture railing on the opposite wall' and wondering 'why his name didn't have a H in it' (240–1). Mathews's literary and suggestive skills are distinctly Joycean. Antony's diplomas and degrees are presumably well-hung, while the H signifies the hymen and, more graphically, the gynaecologist's fingers in her vagina. Picture that! If the story were Sterne's, the title would have served to mock the Church's rituals, perhaps to underline the way Roman Catholicism is riddled with religious scruples. Mathews's concern is to explore the encounter between the sacred and the secular in human sexual terms. Unless the priest had placed the host too far forward on the tip of the tongue, lips rarely came into contact with the sacrament. But Mathews imagines them doing so. As the host enters the mouth, the lipstick leaves a sensuous mark, thereby altering or questioning the view that the sacred and the secular exist in wholly separate spheres. Canon lawyers tended to ignore this issue, for they were more concerned about

teeth. It used to be thought a sin to chew or allow the teeth to touch
the host; the Godhead had to be consumed without any suggestion
of cannibalism or impropriety on the part of the communicant, and
preferably consumed by allowing the host to melt on the tongue. The
Jesuit-educated Mathews knows his canon law, avoids teeth (and, at
one level, any suggestion of vagina dentata), and does something more
interesting or at any rate something different. In many respects, all this
is reminiscent of Sterne's satire on Catholic theologians at the Sorbonne
resorting to an injection, a squirt, to baptize an infant in danger in the
womb or of the medieval discourse on the number of angels who could
dance on the head of a pin. But in Mathews's hands the title constitutes
a witty intervention in a serious debate which can be interpreted in
theological or secular terms.

From all that has been said, it can be appreciated that Joyce allows
room for different kinds of relationship. Kinsella's walk provides him
with scope to discover the material for his own signature, to step into
and out of Bloom's shoes without being either saved or damaged by
the contact. O'Neill displays the kind of familiarity with Joyce that is
entertaining rather than instructive. There is an argument at work in
Mathews, which isn't always apparent in 'Penelope'. William Trevor has
the superb audacity to call one of his stories in *The News from Ireland*
(1986) 'Two More Gallants', as if he was adding to the series that Joyce
had begun in *Dubliners*. The Cork writer includes a skit on 'The Society
of the Friends of James Joyce' and doesn't stop there, for in his fanciful
story Corley's skivvy reappears in later life to disclose that Joyce got the
story of 'Two Gallants' from her when she worked at a dentist's in North
Frederick Street in Dublin. In an attempt to come to terms with Joyce
the master, the penitential Heaney in *Station Island* (1984) addresses
him directly. That Joyce is neither a saint nor a confessor in an odd way
restores literature to its pre-eminence over religion – precisely what
Joyce sought. At the same time it reminds us that piety, a word with both
religious and literary connotations, can itself be liberating – something
which Joyce would perhaps not have understood or countenanced. In
the early 1950s, Patrick Kavanagh, in an intemperate attack on the Joyce
industry, composed a famous poem with the memorable title 'Who
Killed James Joyce?' Looking at today's Irish writers suggests Kavanagh
was a little hasty in his judgement, for it is now evident that the death
of this particular author has given birth not to anxiety but to new and
varied forms of writing, forms which in turn continue to interest scholars
in their quest to make sense of Joyce and company.

# Notes

## Introduction

1   These were titles of extracts that appeared in *Tit-Bits* from October 1883 to April 1884. I could have taken any six-month period in the 1880s or 1890s for similar titles.

## Chapter 1: Joyce, Sterne and the Eighteenth Century

1   From his sermon 'Inquiry After Happiness'. Sterne is describing humanity as a whole.
2   David Hayman (1970) was the first critic to identify this figure as the Arranger.
3   From 'The House of Feasting and the House of Mourning Described'.
4   See Ian Campbell Ross (2001).
5   Michael S. Harper (1971).
6   For further discussion, see 'The Birth of Sensibility' in Paul Langford (1989).

## Chapter 2: Joyce, Erudition and the Late Nineteenth Century

1   For more on Arnold's character and personality, see Jesuits (Ireland) (1930), 89–93. One student recalled that Arnold's published work was 'scarcely an index to his real temper. He was rather quixotic, liked to tilt at the vane', and possessed a 'radical and fiery imagination' (242).

## Chapter 3: Reading Dublin 1904

1   It's impossible to know how many Dublin expressions lie outside of Joyce's scope. He certainly seems to have got the measure of his city, but on reading Allan Pred (1990), a study of late nineteenth-century Stockholm which contains an extraordinary array of words and expressions in common use (including a fascinating series of

collective nicknames for policemen and prostitutes for example), there must be the suspicion that much of the quarry remained.

2   See DVD *The Lost World of Mitchell and Kenyon* (BBC, 2005).

3   Whether or not Joyce had read all the books mentioned in this episode is a matter for speculation. The contents of some of the books, such as the lives of the Curé of Ars or Maria Monk, would have been known to him from his Catholic schooldays – without his having to have read a line. Sir Jonah Barrington's memoirs – as, for example, in *Personal Sketches of His Own Times*, published in three volumes between 1827 and 1832 – were widely available in the nineteenth century and could be quickly dipped into. He had only to pick up a copy of an eighteenth-century edition of *Aristotle's Masterpiece* (Joyce plays along with the view that Aristotle was the author, but in fact it should be italicized as here to indicate it is a title) to see the plates of infants 'cuddled in a ball in bloodred wombs like livers of slaughtered cows' (U 10:587). *The Woman in White* Joyce must have read – or, at least, as far as Miss Dunne does, before she decides that there is 'Too much mystery business in it' (*U* 10: 371).

4   The Vaughan family were sufficiently distinguished for the papers of one of its members to be lodged in the Herbert Cardinal Vaughan Collection in Special Collections, Lauinger Library at Georgetown University in Washington D.C.

5   For more examples of his sermons, see Vaughan (1887, 1908 and 1928). Vaughan preached loyalty to the Queen, hostility to socialism and care for the poor, claiming that 'the noble poor are God's aristocracy'.

6   Interestingly, there must have been some discussion among the Jesuits and others at the time about Vaughan's zeal and whether or not he possessed an 'interior life', for this is specifically raised by Martindale (72). Martindale defends Vaughan and refers to his preaching on Prayer, his devotion to the Blessed Sacrament and his daily visits to confession:

> Surely in an age such as this when the sacred character of private life seems to have been imperilled where it has not even lost its meaning, when children are few, and have almost ceased to be regarded as the golden links uniting in closer love the hearts of husband and wife, it is a comfort to turn our eyes to the pictures given us of that royal family life that for so many years was lived in peace, and joy, and gladness by the children of our Queen. (Vaughan 1887, 12–13)

7   Again, Conmee is not being entirely fair. Vaughan spent part of his childhood in Achill in the west of Ireland and the family also owned property in County Mayo. See Martindale, 22.

8   Cited by W.R. Rodgers in his review of Richard Ellmann's *James Joyce*, *The Listener*, 26 November 1959.

## Chapter 4: Joyce, Woolf and the Metropolitan Imagination

1   See *England Plans of the Barracks in the London District* (1861).
2   Other militia barracks were located in City Road, E.C., City Road, Finsbury, Globe Street, Bethnal Green and Hampstead.
3   For more details on London and Dublin, see Roy Porter (2000), 331–2, Jonathan Schneer (1999), *passim* and Joseph V. O'Brien (1982), 179ff.
4   Compare the consciously inflated use of 'metropolis' (and 'impression') in a letter from 'Dubliner' to *Tit-Bits* on 31 July 1886: 'Apropos of the article in your impression of July 17 entitled "Sunday on the Continent", perhaps you will allow me to make a few remarks concerning the metropolis of this "disthressful country" – Ireland.'
5   Forster also composed a pageant entitled *England's Pleasant Land: A Pageant Play*, which was published by the Woolfs' Hogarth Press in 1940.

## Chapter 5: The Issue of Translation

1   See 'The problems facing the would-be translator of "Wakese"', panel chaired by Leo Knuth (1971), 146.

## Chapter 7: On Reading *Ulysses* After the Fall of the Berlin Wall

1   I would like to thank Wolfgang Wicht for commenting on this chapter. His scholarly and authoritative account of Joyce's reception in the German Democratic Republic (2004) provides the necessary insider's background to my own remarks here.

## Chapter 8: Joyce and Contemporary Irish Writers

1   Thomas Kinsella (1968), 67. The initial letters of the three words of the last line – HCE – recall the Humphrey Chimpden Earwicker figure in *Finnegans Wake*.
2   O'Neill might have developed the gay theme by making more of Casement, whose afterlife continues to intrigue scholars. See for example W.J. McCormack (2002) and Jeff Dudgeon (2002).
3   As has often been commented on, Sinn Fein was a term that wasn't used before 1905. It seems to have been coined by Mary Ellen Butler. The first Convention of the National Council of Sinn Fein was held on 28 November 1905. For historical details, I am relying on William

G. Fitzgerald (1924), 106. The reference to Sinn Fein in *Ulysses* constitutes one of the few inaccuracies in Joyce's scheme of things.

4   For an extended discussion germane to my comments here, see Andras Ungar (2002).

5   For an insightful discussion of the novel's strengths and weaknesses in the light of gay theory, see David Halperin (2003).

6   Brian Nolan (1951).

# Select Bibliography

Alter, Robert (2005), *Imagined Cities: Urban Experience and the Language of the Novel*. New Haven, CT and London: Yale University Press.

Arnold, Thomas (1897), *A Manual of English Literature: Historical and Critical*. London, New York and Bombay: Longman, Green.

Atherton, James S. (1959; 1974a), *The Books at the Wake: A Study of Literary Allusions in James Joyce's 'Finnegans Wake'*. Carbondale and Edwardsville: Southern Illinois University Press.

— (1974b), 'The Oxen of the Sun' in Clive Hart and David Hayman (eds) *James Joyce's 'Ulysses': Critical Essays*. Berkeley, Los Angeles, London: University of California Press.

Bakhtin, Mikhail (1983), *The Dialogic Imagination: Four Essays* (ed. M. Holquist, trans. C. Emerson and M. Holquist). Austin and London: University of Texas Press.

Barry, Sebastian (1995), *The Steward of Christendom*. London: Methuen.

— (1998), *Our Lady of Sligo*. London: Methuen.

Bartholomew, J.G., (ed.) (1904), *The Survey Gazetteer of the British Isles*. London: George Newnes.

Beckett, Samuel (1929; 1972), 'Dante ... Bruno. Vico ... Joyce' in *A Symposium: Our Exagmination Round His Factification for Incamination of Work in Progress*. New York: New Directions.

Behan, Brendan (1956), *The Quare Fellow*. London: Methuen.

Benstock, Bernard (1972), '*Ulysses* without Dublin', *James Joyce Quarterly* 10:1.

— (1994), 'Middle-Class values in *Ulysses* and the value of the middle class', *James Joyce Quarterly*, 31:4.

Bergonzi, Bernard (2003), *A Victorian Wanderer: The Life of Thomas Arnold the Younger*. Oxford: Oxford University Press.

Bergson, Henri (1896; 1911), *Matter and Memory* (trans. Nancy Margaret Paul and W. Scott Palmer). London: Swan Sonnenschein.

Bertram, James (ed.) (1980), *The Letters of Thomas Arnold the Younger (1850–1900)*. Auckland: Auckland University Press/Oxford University Press.

Bosinelli, Rosa Maria (1980), Review of Gianfranco Corsini and Giorgio Melchiori (eds), *Scritti Italiani / James Joyce*. *James Joyce Quarterly* 17:3.

Boyd, Ernest (1934), 'Joyce and the new Irish writers', *Current History* 39:6.

Briggs, Julia (2005), *Virginia Woolf: An Inner Life*. London: Allen Lane.

Budgen, Frank (1972), *James Joyce and the Making of 'Ulysses'*. Oxford and New York: Oxford University Press.

Butcher, S.H. and A. Lang (1897), *The Odyssey of Homer: Done into English Prose*. London: Macmillan.

Corsini, Gianfranco and Giorgio Melchiori, eds (with Louis Berrone, Nino Frank and Jacqueline Risset) (1979), *Scritti Italiani / James Joyce*. Milan: Mondadori.

Coyle, Kathleen (1923), *Piccadilly*. London: Jonathan Cape.

Crackanthorpe, Hubert (1896), *Vignettes: A Miniature Journal of Whim and Sentiment*. London and New York: John Lane The Bodley Head.

Daiches, David (1969), *A Critical History of English Literature* 4 Volumes, 2nd edn. London: Secker and Warburg.

Deutscher, Isaac (1959), *The Prophet Unarmed: Trotsky 1921–1929*. London: Oxford University Press.

Döblin, Alfred (1929; 1930), *Berlin Alexanderplatz: Die Geschichte vom Franz Biberkopf*. Berlin: S. Fischer.

— (1929; 1978), *Berlin Alexanderplatz: The Story of Franz Biberkopf* (trans. Eugene Jolas). Harmondsworth: Penguin.

Douet, James (1998), *British Barracks 1600–1914: Their Architecture, Use and Role in Society*. London: Stationery Office.

Drinkwater, John (1934), *A Pageant of England's Life: Presented by Her Poets*. London: Thornton Butterworth.

Dudgeon, Jeff (2002), *Roger Casement: The Black Diaries*. Belfast: Belfast Press.

Eagleton, Mary (2000), 'Adrienne Rich, location and the body', *Journal of Gender Studies* 9:3.

Eagleton, Terry (1990), *The Ideology of the Aesthetic*. Oxford: Blackwell.

Eco, Umberto (1989), *The Middle Ages of James Joyce: The Aesthetics of Chaosmos* (trans. E. Esrock). London: Hutchinson Radius.

Eglinton, John (1932), 'The beginnings of Joyce', *Life and Letters* 8:47.

Eliot, George (1859; 1961), *Adam Bede*. New York: New American Library.

Ellmann, Richard (1982), *James Joyce*, revised edn. Oxford and New York: Oxford University Press.

— (1984), *'Ulysses' on the Liffey*, corrected edn. London: Faber and Faber.

*England Plans of the Barracks in the London District* (1861).

Faerber, Thomas and Markus Luchsinger (1988), *Joyce in Zürich*. Zürich: Unionsverlag.

Fairhall, James (1993), *James Joyce and the Question of History*. Cambridge: Cambridge University Press.

Fitzgerald, William G. (ed.) (1924), *The Voice of Ireland: A Survey of the Race and Nation from All Angles*. Dublin and London: Virtue.

Ford, Ford Madox (1905; 1995), *The Soul of London* (ed. Alan G. Hill). London: Everyman.

Fordyce, James (1766), *Sermons to Young Women, In Two Volumes.* London: A. Millar and T. Cadell, J. Dodsley, J. Payne.

Forster, E.M. (1910; 1968), *Howards End.* Harmondsworth: Penguin.

— (1924; 1967), *A Passage to India.* Harmondsworth: Penguin.

Fritzsche, Peter (1996), *Reading Berlin 1900.* Cambridge, MA and London: Harvard University Press.

Gass, William H. (1975), *On Being Blue: A Philosophical Inquiry.* Boston, MA: D.R. Godine.

Gideon-Welcker, Carola (1948), 'James Joyce in Zürich', *Horizon* 18:105. Reprinted in Willard Potts (ed.) (1979), *Portraits of the Artist in Exile: Recollectioins of James Joyce by Europeans.* Seattle: University of Washington Press.

Gifford, Don, with Robert J. Seidman (1989), *'Ulysses' Annotated: Notes for James Joyce's* Ulysses, 2nd edn. Berkeley, Los Angeles and London: University of California Press.

Gordimer, Nadine (1980), *Burger's Daughter.* Harmondsworth: Penguin.

Gordon, John (2004), *Joyce and Reality: The Empirical Strikes Back.* Syracuse, NY: Syracuse University Press.

Grierson, Herbert J.C., (ed.) (1912), *The Poems of John Donne* 2 Volumes. Oxford: Clarendon Press.

Groden, Michael, (ed.) (1978a), *The James Joyce Archive:* Ulysses *Notes & 'Telemachus'–'Scylla and Charybdis'.* New York: Garland.

— (1978b), *The James Joyce Archive:* Ulysses *Page Proofs 'Telemachus'–'Hades'.* New York: Garland.

*Guide to London* (1904). London, New York, Melbourne: Ward Lock.

Halperin, David (2003), 'Pal o' Me Heart', *London Reivew of Books* 22 May.

Harper Michael S. (1971), *History Is Your Own Heartbeat Poems.* Urbana: University of Illinois Press.

Hart, Clive (1974), 'Wandering Rocks', in Clive Hart and David Hayman (eds), *James Joyce's 'Ulysses' Critical Essays.* Berkeley, Los Angeles and London: University of California Press.

— (1993), 'Gaps and cracks in *Ulysses*', *James Joyce Quarterly* 30:3.

Hayman, David (1970), *'Ulysses': The Mechanics of Meaning.* Englewood Cliffs, NJ: Prentice-Hall.

Heaney, Seamus (1984), *Station Island.* London: Faber and Faber.

Höhne, Horst (1989), 'Literature as liberation', *Zeitschrift fur Anglistik und Amerikanistik* 37:2.

Hughes, Robert (1981), *The Shock of the New: Art and the Century of Change.* New York: Alfred A. Knopf.

Hyde, Douglas (1892; 1894), 'The Necessity for De-Anglicising Ireland', reprinted in Charles Gavan Duffy, George Sigerson and Douglas Hyde, *The Revival of Irish Literature.* London: T. Fisher Unwin.

Ibsen, Henrik (1900), *When We Dead Awaken* (trans. William Archer). London: Heinemann.

Jameson, Storm (1937), 'Documents', *Fact* 4.

Jesuits (Ireland) (1930), *A Page of History: Story of University College, Dublin 1883–1909. Compiled by Fathers of the Society of Jesus.* Dublin and Cork: Talbot Press.

Jolas, Eugene (1948), 'My friend James Joyce' in Sean Givens (ed.), *James Joyce: Two Decades of Criticism*. New York: Vanguard Press.

Joyce, James (1914; 1979), *'Dubliners': Text, Criticism, and Notes*, (eds Robert Scholes and A. Walton Litz). New York: Viking.

— (1916; 1968), *'A Portrait of the Artist as a Young Man': Text, Criticism, and Notes* (ed. Chester Anderson). New York: Viking.

— (1939; 1964), *Finnegans Wake*. London: Faber and Faber.

— (2002), *Finnegans Wake* (trans. Erik Bindervoet and Robbert-Jan Henkes). Amsterdam: Athenaeum-Polak and Van Gennep.

— (1959; 1966), *The Critical Writings of James Joyce* (eds Ellsworth Mason and Richard Ellmann). New York: Viking.

— (1957), *Letters of James Joyce* Vol. I (ed. Stuart Gilbert). London: Faber and Faber.

— (1966), *Letters of James Joyce* Vol. II (ed. Richard Ellmann). New York: Viking.

— (1975), *'Ulysses' A Facsimile of the Manuscript* (intro. Harry Levin, preface Clive Driver). London: Faber for the Philip H & A.S.W. Rosenbach Foundation.

— (1922; 1986), *Ulysses: The Corrected Text* (ed. Hans Walter Gabler with Wolfhard Steppe and Claus Melchior). London: The Bodley Head.

— (1929; 1957), *Ulysse* (trans. Auguste Morel with the assistance of Stuart Gilbert). Paris: Gallimard.

— (1952), *Ulises* (trans. J. Salas Subirat) (2nd edn). Buenos Aires: Santiago Rueda.

— (1960; 1967), *Ulisse* (trans. Giulio de Angelis). Milan: Arnoldo Mondadori Editore.

— (1975; 1996), *Ulises* (trans. José María Valverde). Barcelona: Editorial Lumen.

— (1975; 1981), *Ulysses* (trans. Hans Wollschläger). Frankfurt am Main: Suhrkamp.

— (1990), Οδυσσέας (trans. Socrates Kapsaskis). Athens: Kedros.

— (1993), *Ulysses* (ed. Jeri Johnson). Oxford: Oxford University Press.

— (2003), *Ulises* (trans. Francisco García Tortosa) (revised edn). Madrid: Cátedra.

Joyce, Stanislaus (1958), *My Brother's Keeper* (ed. Richard Ellmann). London: Faber and Faber.

Kenner, Hugh (1978), *Joyce's Voices*. London: Faber and Faber.

Kiberd, Declan (1995), *Inventing Ireland*. London: Jonathan Cape.

Kinsella, Thomas (1968), *Nightwalker and Other Poems*. Dublin: Dolmen.

— (1997), *The Pen Shop*. Dublin: Dedalus; Manchester: Carcanet.

Knuth, Leo (1971), 'The problems facing the would-be translator of "Wakese",' Atti del 3rd *International James Joyce Symposium. Trieste 14–16 guigno.*

Langford, Paul (1989), *A Polite and Commercial People: England 1727–1783.* Oxford: Oxford University Press.

Le Corbusier (1924; 1971), *The City of Tomorrow and Its Planning* (trans. Frederick Etchells). London: The Architectural Press.

Le Guin, Ursula (1974; 1994), *The Dispossessed.* New York: HarperPrism.

Lessing, Doris (1962; 1974), *The Golden Notebook.* St Albans: Panther.

Lewis, George Cornewall (1836), *On Local Disturbances in Ireland and On the Irish Church Question.* London: B. Fellowes.

Lukács, Georg (1964), *Essays on Thomas Mann* (trans. Stanley Mitchell). London: Merlin Press.

— (1970), *Writer and Critic* (trans. Arthur Kahn). London: Merlin Press.

MacKillop, James (1986), *Fionn mac Cumhaill: Celtic Myth in English Literature.* Syracuse, NY: Syracuse University Press.

Maron, Monika (1991; 1993), *Silent Close No.6* (trans. David Newton Marinelli). London: Readers International.

Martindale, C.C. S.J. (1923), *Bernard Vaughan, S.J.* London: Longman, Green & Co.

Mathews, Aidan (1992), *Lipstick on the Host.* London: Secker and Warburg.

McCormack, W.J. (2002), *Roger Casement in Death; or, Haunting the Free State.* Dublin: University College Dublin Press.

McCormick, Kathleen (1987), 'Just a flash like that': the pleasure of 'cruising' the interpolations in "Wandering Rocks"', *James Joyce Quarterly,* 24:3.

McCourt, John (2000), *The Years of Bloom: James Joyce in Trieste 1904–1920.* Dublin: Lilliput.

MacManus, M.J. (1927), *So This Is Dublin!* Dublin and Cork: Talbot Press.

McMichael, James (1991), *'Ulysses' and Justice.* Princeton, NJ: Princeton University Press.

Melchiori, Giorgio, (ed.) (1984), *Joyce in Rome: The Genesis of* 'Ulysses'. Rome: Bulzoni.

Merlis, Mark (1996), *American Studies.* London: Fourth Estate.

Minto, Edward (1886), *A Manual of English Prose Literature: Biographical and Critical.* Edinburgh and London.

Montague, John (1982), *Selected Poems.* Oxford: Oxford University Press.

Moore, Brian (1955; 1959), *The Lonely Passion of Miss Judith Hearne.* Harmondsworth: Penguin.

Murray, Lindley (1819), *An English Grammar Comprehending the Principles and Rules of the Language* 2 Vols, 4th edn. York.

Ní Dhómnhaill, Nuala (1992), *The Astrakhan Cloak.* Oldcastle, Co Meath: Gallery Press.

Nolan, Brian (1951), 'A Bash in the Tunnel', *Envoy*, 5:17 (April).

Norburn, Roger (2004), *A James Joyce Chronology*. Basingstoke: Palgrave Macmillan.

O'Brien, Joseph V. (1982), *'Dear Dirty Dublin': A City in Distress, 1899–1916*. Berkeley and Los Angeles: University of California Press.

O'Faolain, Sean (1954), '50 years after Bloomsday', *The New York Times* June 13.

— (1956), Review of Hugh Kenner, *Dublin's Joyce*, *The Listener* 14 June.

O'Neill, Jamie (2001), *At Swim, Two Boys*. London: Scribner.

Parrinder, Patrick (1984), *James Joyce*. Cambridge: Cambridge University Press.

Peake, Charles (1977), *James Joyce: The Citizen and the Artist*. London: Edward Arnold.

Petre, M.D. (1912), *Autobiography and Life of George Tyrrell* 2 Volumes. London: Edward Arnold.

Pierce, David (1992), *James Joyce's Ireland*. London and New Haven, CT: Yale University Press.

— (2005), *Light, Freedom and Song: A Cultural History of Modern Irish Writing*. London and New Haven, CT: Yale University Press.

Pordage, Samuel (1681; 1965), *Thomas Willis The Anatomy of the Brain and Nerves* (facsmile of 1681 edition) (ed. William Feindel). Montreal: McGill University Press.

Porter, Roy (2000), *London: A Social History*. London: Penguin.

— (2003), *Flesh in the Age of Reason*. London: Penguin.

Powys, John Cowper (1943), *'Finnegan's Wake'*, *Modern Readings* 7 (ed. Reginald Moore). London: Wells Gardner, Darton.

Pred, Allan (1990), *Lost Words and Lost Worlds: Modernity and the Language of Everyday Life in Late Nineteenth-Century Stockholm*. Cambridge: Cambridge University Press.

Pugliatti, Paola (1996), Review of Giorgio Melchiori, *Joyce: Il Mestiere Dello Scrittore*. *James Joyce Quarterly* 33:1.

Rabb, Melinda Alliker (1984), 'Engendering accounts in Sterne's *A Sentimental Journey*' in James Engell, (ed.), *Johnson and His Age*. Cambridge, MA and London: Harvard University Press.

Richardson, Dorothy (1979), *Pilgrimage* 4 Vols. London: Virago.

Rodgers, W.R. (1959), review of Richard Ellmann's *James Joyce*, *The Listener*, 29 November.

Rose, Jonathan (2002), *The Intellectual Life of the British Working Classes*. New Haven, CT and London: Yale University Press.

Ross, Ian Campbell (2001), *Laurence Sterne: A Life*. Oxford: Oxford University Press.

Rousseau, G.S. (2004), *Nervous Acts: Essays on Literature, Culture and Sensibility*. Basingstoke: Palgrave.

Saintsbury, George (1912), *A History of English Prose Rhythm*. London: Macmillan.

Schlauch, Margaret (1943), *The Gift of Tongues*. London: George Allen and Unwin.

Schneer, Jonathan (1999), *London 1900: The Imperial Metropolis*. New Haven, CT and London: Yale University Press.

Seehase, Georg (1985), 'James Joyces ästhetisches System im Roman "Ulysses"' in Dorothea Siegmund-Schulze (ed.), *Irland: Gesellschaft Und Kultur* IV. Halle: Martin-Luther-Universität Halle-Wittenberg.

Senn, Fritz (1966), 'He was too scrupulous always: Joyce's "The Sisters"', *James Joyce Quarterly*, 2:2.

— (1972), 'Book of many turns', *James Joyce Quarterly*, 10:1.

— (1995), *Inductive Scrutinies: Focus on Joyce* (ed. Christine O'Neill). Dublin: Lilliput.

Sennett, Richard (1994), *Flesh and Stone: The Body and the City in Western Civilization*. London: Faber and Faber.

Seremetakis, C. Nadia (ed.) (1994), *The Senses Still: Perception and Memory as Material Culture*. Boulder, CO, San Francisco, CA, Oxford: Westview Press.

Shklovsky, Viktor (1965), 'Sterne's Tristram Shandy: a stylistic commentary' in L.T. Lemon and M.J. Reis (eds), *Russian Formalist Criticism*. Lincoln: University of Nebraska Press.

Simmel, Georg (1964), *The Sociology of Georg Simmel* (trans. Kurt H. Wolff). New York: The Free Press.

Squier, Susan M. (1985), *Virginia Woolf and London: The Sexual Politics of the City*. Chapel Hill and London: University of North Carolina Press.

Sterne, Laurence (1760), *The Sermons of Mr Yorick* Vol. 1. London: R. and J. Dodsley.

— ([1759–68]; 1978), *The Life and Opinions of Tristram Shandy, Gentleman* (eds Melvyn New and Joan New). Gainesville: The University Press of Florida.

— (1989), *A Sentimental Journey Through France and Italy by Mr Yorick* with *The Journal to Eliza* and *A Political Romance* (ed. Ian Jack). Oxford: Oxford University Press.

Symonds, John Addington (1893), *In the Key of Blue And Other Prose Essays*. London: Elkin Mathews.

*Tit-Bits* (1881–1904).

*Tit-Bits Monster English Dictionary* (1899). London: George Newnes.

*Tit-Bits Monster Table Book* (1902). London: George Newnes.

*Fifty Prize Stories from Tit-Bits* (1902). London: George Newnes.

Trevor, William (1986), *The News From Ireland and Other Stories*. London: The Bodley Head.

Ungar, Andras (2002), *Joyce's 'Ulysses' as National Epic: Epic Mimesis and the Political History of the Nation State*. Gainesville: University Presses of Florida.

Vaughan, Bernard, S.J. (1887), *Her Golden Reign: a Sermon Preached in the Church of the Holy Name, Manchester*. London: Burns & Gates.

— (1908), *Society, Sin and The Saviour: Addresses on the Passion of Our Lord Given in the Church of the Immaculate Conception, Mayfair 1907*. London: Kegan Paul, Trench, Trubner & Co.

— (1928), *Notes of Retreats Given by Father Bernard Vaughan*. London: Burns & Gates.

Warner, John M. (1993), *Joyce's Grandfathers: Myth and History in Defoe, Smollett, Sterne and Joyce*. Athens, GA and London: University of Georgia Press.

West, Alick (1937), *Crisis and Criticism*. London: Lawrence and Wishart.

Wicht, Wolfgang (2000), *Utopianism in James Joyce's 'Ulysses'*. Heidelberg: Winter.

Wicht, Wolfgang (2004), 'The Disintegration of Stalinist Cultural Dogmatism: James Joyce in East Germany, 1945 to the Present', in Geert Lernout and Wim Van Mierlo (eds), *The Reception of James Joyce in Europe Volume 1: Germany, Northern and East Central Europe*. London and New York: Thoemmes Continuum.

Wicke, Jennifer (1993), 'Modernity must advertise: aura, desire, and decolonization in Joyce', *James Joyce Quarterly* 30:4–31:1.

Wilde, Oscar (1998), *The Importance of Being Earnest and Other Plays* (ed. Peter Raby). Oxford: Oxford University Press.

Williams, Raymond (1975), *The Country and the City*. St Albans: Paladin.

Willis, Thomas (1664; 1666), *Cerebri Anatome Cui Accessit Nervorum Descriptio Et Usus Studio*. Amsterdam: Gerbrandum Schagen.

Wolf, Christa (1965; 1983), *Divided Heaven* (trans. Joan Becker, intro. Jack Zipes). Evanston, IL: Adler's Foreign Books.

Woolf, Leonard (1969), *The Journey Not the Arrival Matters: An Autobiography of the Years 1939–1969*. London: Hogarth Press.

Woolf, Virginia (1919; 1969), *Night and Day*. Harmondsworth: Penguin.

— (1925; 1938), *The Common Reader*. Harmondsworth: Penguin.

— (1925; 1992), *Mrs Dalloway*. Oxford: World's Classics.

— (1928; 1999), *To the Lighthouse*. Oxford: World's Classics.

— ([1929; 1938]; 1993) *A Room of One's Own and Three Guineas* (ed. Michèle Barrett). Harmondsworth: Penguin.

— (1931; 1975), *The Waves*. Harmondsworth: Penguin.

— (1932; 1972), *The Common Reader: Second Series*. London: The Hogarth Press.

— (1933; 1998), *Flush*. Oxford: World's Classics.

— (1941; 1992), *Between the Acts*. Oxford: World's Classics.

— (1943), *The Death of the Moth and Other Essays*. London: Readers Union/ Hogarth Press.

— (1953; 1981), *A Writer's Diary* (ed. Leonard Woolf). London: Triad/Granada.

— (1980), *The Letters of Virginia Woolf* Vol. VI (eds Nigel Nicolson and Joanne Trautmann). New York: Harcourt Brace Jovanovich.

— (1982), *The London Scene: Five Essays*. New York: Random House.

Yeats, William Butler (1954), *The Letters of W.B. Yeats* (ed. Allan Wade). London: Rupert Hart-Davis.

— (1955), *Autobiographies*. London: Macmillan.

Yeats, William Butler and Thomas Kinsella (1970), *Davis, Mangan, Ferguson?: Tradition and the Irish Writer*. Dublin: Dolmen.

# INDEX